SOCIETY
AND THE
ADOLESCENT
SELF-IMAGE

———◆———

BY MORRIS ROSENBERG

PRINCETON UNIVERSITY PRESS

PRINCETON, NEW JERSEY

136
.7354
R813s
1972

Published by Princeton University Press, 1965

L.C. Card: 67-30454

ISBN 0-691-02805-2 (paperback edn.)

ISBN 0-691-09335-0 (hardcover edn.)

First PRINCETON PAPERBACK Edition, 1968

Second Printing, 1970

Third Printing, 1972

This book, in manuscript, was co-winner of the American Association for the Advancement of Science Socio-Psychological Prize for 1963.

Printed in the United States of America
by Princeton University Press, Princeton, New Jersey

To Irving, Bill, and Sylvia

PREFACE

THERE are few topics so fascinating both to the research investigator and the research subject as the self-image. It is distinctively characteristic of the human animal that he is able to stand outside himself and to describe, judge, and evaluate the person he is. He is at once the observer and the observed, the judge and the judged, the evaluator and the evaluated. Since the self is probably the most important thing in the world to him, the question of what he is like and how he feels about himself engrosses him deeply. This is especially true during the adolescent stage of development.

This study takes as its point of departure the assumption that the self-image is central to the subjective life of the individual, largely determining his thoughts, feelings, and behavior. At first glance this topic would appear to be a purely private, personal, and idiosyncratic phenomenon. And yet it is equally plain that the individual's self-picture is not purely non-objective art, reflecting the impulses and inspiration of the creator, but is rather a more or less clear portrait based upon the information provided by his social experience.

It is the nature and influence of this social experience that I have been especially interested in understanding. The child is raised in a family, whether broken or intact; he may have brothers or sisters, in varying combinations; he has parents who have certain feelings toward him. From this ferment of social interaction a self-picture begins to emerge. This family lives in a neighborhood, belongs to a social class, usually identifies with a religious group, derives from a national background. These social groupings impose on the child a characteristic style of life, set of values, and system of beliefs and ideals which covertly, imperceptibly, unintentionally, but no less powerfully, provide the bases for self-judgment. With a different background the child would *be* different and would see himself differently.

While clinical and experimental studies have taught us a great deal about the nature of the self-image, less information has been available regarding the broader social experiences which contribute to its formation. Convinced of the importance of these experiences, I undertook a survey of over 5,000 adolescents, attempting to understand how they saw themselves, how they felt about themselves, and what criteria for self-evaluation they employed. The outcome of this undertaking is reported in the following pages.

In a study of this scope, the investigator must call upon the aid and cooperation of many people, and this aid was given most generously. My chief debt of gratitude is owed to Erma Jean Surman, secretary and assistant, whose intelligence, loyalty, and diligence were unstintingly granted to this study from beginning to end. I am also grateful to Joan Prentice Collings, who succeeded in maintaining order in a research project permanently on the brink of chaos during her two years' service as assistant.

My major professional debt is owed to my friends and colleagues, Melvin Kohn, Leonard I. Pearlin and Carmi Schooler. I hope they know how deeply I appreciate their generous expenditure of time and effort; they did not blunt the sharpness of their critical acuity on the grounds of warm friendship. I am also grateful to the following people who read and criticized a late draft of the manuscript: Edward A. Suchman, Paul F. Lazarsfeld, Sheldon Korchin, Stanley Coopersmith, Earle Silber, and Joan Snyder. To absolve these people of any responsibility for the flaws in this report is more a reflection of truth than an expression of courtesy.

Since I pledged to maintain the anonymity of the high schools, I cannot acknowledge by name the various school superintendents, principals, and research directors who granted permission to conduct this study and who cooperated so generously in the collection of the data. To them, to the teachers who administered the questionnaires, and to the students who completed them, my thanks are due.

Margaret Browell Renfors was responsible for most of the machine tabulations, a task she handled with impressive care, accuracy, and intelligence.

Several of the chapters are slightly modified versions of papers that have appeared elsewhere. Chapter 4 appeared in the *American Journal of Sociology*, Vol. 68, July 1962, pp. 1–10 (copyright 1962 by the University of Chicago); Chapter 7 in *Sociometry*, Vol. 26, March 1963, pp. 35–49; Chapter 8 in the *Journal of Psychiatric Research*, Vol. 1, 1962, pp. 135–152; and Chapter 10 in the *Public Opinion Quarterly*, Vol. 26, 1962, pp. 201–211. I am grateful to the University of Chicago Press, the American Sociological Association, the Pergamon Press, and the Princeton University Press, respectively, for permission to reprint this material. My thanks are also due to Harper and Row for permission to quote material from Robert R. Sears, Eleanor E. Maccoby, and Harry Levin, *Patterns of Child Rearing*, 1957; to the *Journal of Personality* for permission to quote from Andras Angyal, "A Theoretical Model for Personality Studies," Vol. 29, 1951; and to the American Sociological Association for permission to quote from Melvin L. Kohn and Eleanor E. Carroll, "Social Class and the Allocation of Parental Responsibilities," *Sociometry*, Vol. 23, 1960.

MORRIS ROSENBERG

Bethesda, Maryland
September 1964

CONTENTS

CONTENTS

PART I
DEFINITION AND MEASUREMENT

CHAPTER 1

SELF-ATTITUDES AND OTHER ATTITUDES

IN RECENT years the fields of psychiatry, psychology, and sociology have all experienced an upsurge of interest in the nature of the self-image. The fact that these three fields should come to share an interest in this aspect of personality bespeaks, perhaps, the power of this concept to intrude itself upon established ways of thought and procedure. Though each field bears with it the inert weight of its distinctive tradition, all have found the idea of the self-image relevant to their concerns.

Clinical and experimental studies have provided valuable insights into the nature of the self-image (particularly its pathological manifestations), but we still know very little about the nature and distribution of self-esteem, self-values, and self-perceptions in the broader society. The present report sets forth the results of a study of self-attitudes in the stage of later adolescence, i.e., among a sample of 5,024 high school juniors and seniors from ten high schools in New York State.

At this stage of development—between about 15 and 18 years of age—the individual tends to be keenly concerned with his self-image. What am I like? How good am I? What should I, or might I, become? On what basis shall I judge myself? Many adolescents are consumed with questions of this sort. There are several reasons for this heightened awareness of the self-image during this period of development.

For one thing, late adolescence is a time of major decision. For example, the individual must give serious thought to his occupational choice. But does he have the intellectual ability and assiduity to become a doctor? Does he have the logical and oratorical talents required for the law? Does

3

he have the seriousness of purpose required for the ministry? The individual must urgently think about what he is like if he is not to make a disastrous choice. The adolescent must also start thinking about marriage. Is he "ready" for marriage? Does he have the qualities which will enable him to acquire the kind of mate he wants, and, if not, is it possible to acquire these qualities? When an individual is faced with a serious and urgent decision, and when a major basis for this decision is his view of what he is like, then the self-image is likely to move to the forefront of attention.

A second reason for a heightened awareness of the self-image is that adolescence is a period of unusual change. Gross and rapid physical changes abound. A boy grows several inches or gains 20 pounds in a matter of months; the adolescent looking in the mirror suddenly sees a face covered with pimples; the flat-chested girl becomes a well-developed young lady. Internal physiological changes proceed apace. Sexual drives achieve an intensity which was unimaginable in the period of latency; new desires surge through the youth. Finally, psychological changes are taking place. New interests, attitudes, and values come to the fore. Whether it is now a concern with automobiles or dates, an awakened interest in philosophy or religion, a new concern for aesthetic experience or world affairs, the effect is to *shake up* the adolescent's picture of what he is like and to intensify his interest in this picture.

Third, late adolescence is a period of unusual status ambiguity. Society does not have a clear set of expectations for the adolescent. In some ways he is treated as a child, in other ways as an adult. He is thus unclear about his social duties and responsibilities just as he is unclear about his social rights and privileges. This ambiguity is accentuated by the fact that both remnants of the past and portents of the future influence the self-image. A girl who was stout as a child but has slimmed down in adolescence may still, in her mind's eye, continue to see herself as fat.

4

A boy who intends to become an artist begins to rehearse his future occupational role in the present. Tentatively and awkwardly, perhaps, he begins to adopt the dress, speech, attitudes, manners, mores, etc., of his concept of an artist. The same is probably true of other occupational choices. We would suggest that where such sources of ambiguity exist, the concern with the self-image is likely to be heightened.

These observations highlight the point that the adolescent is pregnant with potentialities but is largely lacking in fulfillment. Compared to the young child, whose interest is chiefly in the present, the adolescent's vision extends more into the future. He may go in many directions, become many possible things; but this vision of the future takes as its springboard the picture of what the individual actually or potentially is.

Because this is a time of life when the individual actually is changing visibly; because it is a period when an awareness of, and concern with, the self-image tends to be high, and because the self-image at this time is so vitally implicated in such important life decisions, late adolescence is a particularly interesting time of life for studying the self-image.

But what is a self-image? Often it is treated as a rather mysterious and indefinable entity. In the present study, we conceive of the self-image as an attitude toward an object. (The term "attitude" is used broadly to include facts, opinions, and values with regard to the self, as well as a favorable or unfavorable orientation toward the self.) In other words, this study takes as its point of departure the view that people have attitudes toward objects, and that the self is one of the objects toward which one has attitudes.

Intuitively, however, we feel that there is something different about our attitudes toward ourselves and our attitudes toward other objects in the world. One way to clarify the nature of the self-image, then, is to ask: In what way are self-attitudes similar to attitudes toward other objects (whether people, groups, organizations, nations, ideas, etc.) and in what ways are they different?

Self-Attitudes and Attitudes toward Other Objects

Social psychology has shown that attitudes vary in terms of certain common characteristics. These characteristics, relevant to attitudes toward all objects, appear to be completely applicable to attitudes toward the self. Putting it baldly, there is no qualitative difference in the characteristics of attitudes toward the self and attitudes toward soup, soap, cereal, or suburbia.

On the basis of thousands of attitude studies conducted in recent decades, a number of dimensions by which attitudes toward any object in the world can be classified have evolved. Attitudes may differ in content, in direction, in intensity, in importance, in salience, in consistency, in stability, and in clarity.[1]

Let us compare attitudes toward the self and toward the Soviet Union in terms of these dimensions. (1) Content—We may ask: What is the individual's picture of the Soviet Union (his picture of its political structure, economic structure, scientific capabilities, educational system), just as we may study the content of the self-picture (whether one sees oneself as intelligent or kind and considerate or good at painting, etc.). (2) Direction—We may ask whether attitudes toward the Soviet Union are favorable or unfavorable, just as we may ask whether our self-attitudes are positive or negative. (3) Intensity—We may feel very strongly about the Soviet political system as very bad, just as we may feel strongly about our self-estimate as "very likeable." (4) Importance—We would want to con-

[1] These dimensions are drawn or adapted from David Krech and Richard S. Crutchfield, *Theory and Problems of Social Psychology*, New York: McGraw-Hill, 1948, Chap. 5, and Theodore Newcomb, *Social Psychology*, New York: Dryden, 1950, Chap. 5.

sider whether the Soviet Union is an important subject to the individual, and the self may also be located along this dimension. (5) Salience—Some people think a great deal about the Soviet Union—it is often in the forefront of consciousness—whereas others give the matter less thought; the same is true of attitudes toward the self. (6) Consistency—We may alternately think of the Soviet Union as very strong and very weak; contradictory self-attitudes are also common. (7) Stability—Some people have firm, stable, relatively unchanging opinions of the Soviet Union whereas other people's attitudes are more shifting and unstable; similarly, there are those who have stable self-attitudes and others who have shifting self-attitudes. (8) Clarity—Some people have a clear, sharp, unambiguous picture of the Soviet Union, whereas others have more vague, hazy, and blurred pictures; self-pictures also vary in clarity.

We suggest that the structure of the self-image is largely revealed by the classification of individuals in terms of these universal dimensions. Thus, if we can learn *what* the individual sees when he looks at himself (his social statuses, roles, physical characteristics, skills, traits, and other facets of content); whether he has a favorable or unfavorable opinion of himself (direction); how strongly he feels about his self-attitudes (intensity); how important the self is, relative to other objects (importance); whether he spends a great deal of time thinking of what he is like—whether he is constantly conscious of what he is saying or doing—or whether he is more involved in tasks or other objects (salience); whether the elements of his self-picture are consistent or contradictory (consistency); whether he has a self-attitude which varies or shifts from day to day or moment to moment, or whether, on the contrary, he has a firm, stable, rock-like self-attitude (stability); and whether he has a firm, definite picture of what he is like or a vague, hazy, blurred picture (clarity)—if we can characterize the individual's self-picture in terms of each of these dimensions, then we would have a good, if still incomplete, description of the structure of the self-image. And the same would be true of any other object in the world.

But the nature of self-attitudes is also clarified by pointing to certain properties of self-attitudes which are different from most other attitudes. For contrast, let us consider the kinds of attitudes usually examined in public opinion studies—attitudes toward the Soviet Union, toward Cuba, toward the Republican Party, toward the President, toward minority groups, toward X brand of tomato soup. We will call these "public opinion attitudes."

One difference is that the public opinion investigator attempts to examine different attitudes toward the same object whereas the self-image investigator studies different attitudes toward different objects. (It may be argued, of course, that there are as many Cubas as there are people who think about Cuba, but at least the attempt is made to get people to think about the same thing.) In a self-image study, there are exactly as many different objects of study as there are respondents. Thus, to compare upper-class and lower-class attitudes toward the self is not the same as comparing upper- and lower-class attitudes toward the Democratic Party. Of course, self-attitudes are not absolutely unique in this regard; we might ask children how they feel about their parents, or parents how they behave toward their children, and compare social groups in these terms. Self-attitudes do, however, differ from most public opinion studies in focusing upon completely different objects.

A second difference between self-attitudes and public opinion attitudes resides in the area of motivation. Motivation, to be sure, is an important determinant of most, if not all, attitudes. For example, a Russian who wishes to be accepted by his peers and to be integrated into his society is motivated to adopt a positive attitude toward Brezhnev; an American who wishes to be accepted by his peers is likely to hold a negative attitude toward Brezhnev. Group

8

differences in attitudes are often inspired by identical motivations.

The distinctive characteristic of self-attitudes, however, is that everyone is motivated to hold the same attitude toward the object, namely, a positive attitude. This may, indeed, be a universal motivation. As Murphy notes: "The main self-attitudes, those involving the fear of losing the self-esteem, are horrified [at violating one's standards] and struggle to keep the self-picture good." [2] It can hardly be disputed that, as a rule, people would prefer to have a favorable opinion of themselves rather than an unfavorable opinion.

A third difference between self-attitudes and public opinion attitudes lies in the dimension of importance. Objects of public opinion vary widely in importance, whereas this is not true of the self. To a Republican National Committeeman, the Republican Party is an important object, whereas X brand of whitewall tires may be extremely unimportant. The self, on the other hand, is probably an important object to everyone. Fundamentally, it may be the most important object in the world. "Whatever the self is, it becomes a center, an anchorage point, a standard of comparison, an ultimate real. Inevitably, it takes its place as a supreme value." [3] The self may vary in salience, but it is hard to imagine someone to whom the self is unimportant.

In conducting research on the self, then, one can be reasonably certain that this is a subject in which nearly everyone will be interested. This point was strikingly demonstrated in intensive interviews with adolescents. It was amazing how eager they were to talk about themselves; this was a subject they found interesting and important to them. Almost invariably they thanked me for the interview, saying they had found it very enlightening. And yet

[2] Gardner Murphy, *Personality*, New York: Harper, 1947, p. 536.
[3] *Ibid.*, p. 498.

I had only asked questions; they had provided all the answers.

Another distinctive quality of self-attitudes, brought sharply to the fore by George Herbert Mead, is that the self is reflexive.[4] The person holding the attitude and the object toward whom the attitude is held are encased within the same skin. Mead distinguished between the "I," i.e., the functioning, spontaneous part of the self, and the "me," i.e., the part of the self that reflects upon, judges, and evaluates the person. It is thus characteristic of the human being that he may be both subject and object. Statements such as "I hit myself," "I hurt myself," "I hate myself" express this duality. Among all the attitudes which might be studied, then, self-attitudes are unique in this regard—the person holding the attitude and the object toward whom the attitude is held are the same.[5]

As a result, the bases of self-attitudes differ in certain ways from public opinion attitudes. There is, first, the element of immediate experience. We alone can be certain whether we feel angry or happy, whereas we can never be sure that another person manifesting such emotions really feels them. Second, there is the matter of unexpressed thoughts. We may feel ashamed of some base thought or wild fantasy which enters our consciousness, whereas this information is completely inaccessible to anyone else. Third, there is the matter of unique perspective. Most people hearing their voices played back on a recorder for the first time feel that they sound strange. Inevitably, we cannot perceive ourselves exactly as we see other objects; from the viewpoint of the outside observer, our

[4] *Mind, Self and Society,* Chicago: University of Chicago, 1934.

[5] Indeed, one way in which man differs from the lower animals is this—while all animals have consciousness, man alone has self-consciousness. The lion may be king of the jungle, but it is hardly likely that he reflects upon the fact, feels pride in it, and experiences contented feelings of self-satisfaction at contemplating his exalted status.

perceptions of ourselves often appear somewhat distorted. Fourth, there is the factor of permanence. Unlike any other object in the world, the self is inescapable. Our attention to other objects may shift and change, but the self is always there, even if it is at the remote periphery of attention. And it enters into each situation with a frequency shared by no other object. In sum, the fact that the self is reflexive brings to bear certain influences upon self-attitudes which differ in degree or kind from public opinion attitudes.

A fifth difference between attitudes toward the self and attitudes toward public opinion objects is the characteristic set of emotions associated with self-attitudes. Cooley's discussion of the "looking-glass self" is relevant in this regard: "A self-idea of this sort seems to have three principal elements: the imagination of our appearance to the other person; the imagination of his judgment of that appearance, and some sort of self-feeling, such as pride or mortification." [6]

The point is that these emotions—pride and mortification—are aroused only with regard to the self or ego-involved [7] objects. This is not to say that the emotions associated with self-attitudes and public opinion attitudes are entirely different. If we hold strongly negative attitudes toward Castro or toward ourselves, the feelings toward each may well be the same—hatred and contempt. If we hold strongly positive attitudes toward Eisenhower and toward ourselves, similar emotions are likely to come into play, e.g., respect and liking. But there are certain emotional responses which are aroused only with reference to the self (or to ego-involved objects). William James, discussing the issue of self-feeling, distinguished different

[6] Charles Horton Cooley, *Human Nature and the Social Order*, New York: Charles Scribner's Sons, 1912, p. 152.

[7] Muzafer Sherif and Hadley Cantril, *The Psychology of Ego-Involvements*, New York: John Wiley and Sons, 1947.

types of emotional reactions: "Thus, pride, conceit, vanity, self-esteem, arrogance, vainglory, on the one hand; and on the other modesty, humility, confusion, diffidence, shame, mortification, contrition, the sense of obloquy and personal despair. These two opposite classes of affection seem to be direct and elementary endowments of our nature." [8]

In sum, while certain emotions are common to both self-attitudes and public opinion attitudes, other emotions—shame, guilt, mortification, pride, self-complacency, etc.—are characteristic *only* of attitudes toward the self or toward ego-involved objects. This is one reason why the study of self-attitudes has greater significance for mental health than does the study of most other attitudes.

Finally, there are certain differences in the socially significant sources of influence. For example, the mass media of communication—press, radio, television, etc.—may influence our attitudes toward the Democratic Party but rarely toward ourselves. In addition, public opinion attitudes are importantly influenced by group consensus; i.e., partly through communicative interaction, members of various social classes, religious groups, nationality groups, geographical groups, etc., come to share roughly similar attitudes toward the Democratic Party. There are no such widely shared and broadly based group opinions about most of us as individual objects.

This does not imply, however, that social factors are unimportant for the formation of the self-image; on the contrary, they may be exceedingly important.

On a general level, the work of Cooley, Mead, and James makes clear that the individual's self-appraisal is to an important extent derived from reflected appraisals—his interpretation of others' reactions to him. In the process of communication, as Mead notes, the individual must "take the role of the other"; to some extent he must attempt to

[8] William James, *The Principles of Psychology*, Dover Publications, 1950 (originally published in 1890), p. 306.

see himself as others see him. Whether or not one wishes to accept the Meadian thesis in its entirety, one point is incontestable: our attitudes toward ourselves are very importantly influenced by the responses of others toward us.

To say, with Mead, that the self arises from reflected appraisals based on taking the role of the other is important and true, but it fails to communicate the specific nature of social influences on self-attitudes. Let us consider how the reactions of others toward us become organized. For one thing, the hypothesis has been advanced that if groups are differentially esteemed in the broader society, then group members who internalize this value system may judge themselves accordingly. This is fundamentally the phenomenon which Kurt Lewin has described as "self-hatred among Jews" [9] and which is at the root of Kardiner and Ovesey's [10] description of Negro psychopathology as characterized by socially induced feelings of inferiority. A related point is that membership in a minority group in one's neighborhood—especially among children—may produce exclusion and rejection, and, through the medium of reflected appraisals, feelings of inadequacy. Third, social groups may differ in their norms regarding family structure, authority in the family, child-rearing values, practices, etc. As a result, children in different social groups are likely to be exposed to characteristic reactions from others which may be decisive in the formation of self-esteem.

Group norms aside, however, interactional influences may have a powerful bearing upon self-evaluation. The child's prestige in his peer group or the adult's position in the occupational world almost inevitably has a bearing upon the individual's self-feelings. For example, in a society which so strongly emphasizes occupational success, what is the effect of occupational failure upon self-esteem?

[9] Kurt Lewin, *Resolving Social Conflicts*, New York: Harper, 1948, Chap. 12.

[10] Abram Kardiner and Lionel Ovesey, *The Mark of Oppression: A Psychosocial Study of the American Negro*, New York: Norton, 1951.

What is the effect of widespread competitiveness in social life—in school, in sports, in business? When a massive economic depression strikes the land, can self-attitudes remain entirely unaffected?

Finally, social factors importantly determine the individual's self-values; these self-values, as we shall indicate, have an important bearing upon self-esteem. No one evaluates himself in the abstract; evaluation is always with reference to certain criteria. But the criteria of excellence will derive from the particular historical conditions of the society and the characteristic emphases of the group. In medieval Europe, military prowess and valor were highly important criteria for self-evaluation; today, business acumen or organizational skill are more likely to be applauded. Every society or group has its standards of excellence, and it is within the framework of these particular standards that self-evaluation occurs.

To summarize, we have suggested that there are certain factors especially characteristic of, or completely unique to, self-attitudes. In studying self-attitudes, in contrast to public opinion attitudes, respondents are describing different objects; they are all motivated to hold the same (positive) attitudes toward these objects; unlike other objects, the self is important to everyone; the person holding the attitude and the object toward whom it is held are the same; there are certain kinds of emotional reactions which are unique to the self and ego-involved objects; and certain social forces which influence public opinion attitudes are largely irrelevant to self-attitudes.

At the same time, all the fundamental dimensions of attitudes—content, direction, intensity, importance, salience, consistency, clarity, stability—are completely relevant and significant aspects of the self-image. Thus, the study of attitudes legitimately encompasses the study of self-attitudes. It is an obvious extension of this point to suggest that the social psychology of attitudes—the study of the social factors determining opinions, attitudes, and beliefs—should include the social psychology of self-attitudes: the study of the social factors determining opinions, attitudes, and beliefs about the self. The fact that there may be some quantitative differences between self-attitudes and attitudes toward other objects does not in any way undermine the point that the fundamental dimensions are equally applicable to all attitudes.

If this is so, then certain methods which have been developed for collecting and analyzing information about opinions and attitudes—the sample survey, scaling, multivariate analysis, typological analysis, panel analysis, etc.—might profitably be employed in the study of self-attitudes. Several of these techniques are used in the present study.

In the following chapters we shall deal with several dimensions of the self. We shall also devote considerable attention to self-values—the conceptions of the desirable which represent the individual's criteria for self-judgment. But our main concern, or, to use Lazarsfeld's phrase, our "pivotal variable," will be self-esteem. In other words, what is the direction of the self-attitude? Does the individual have a favorable or unfavorable opinion of himself? Does he consider himself worthy or unworthy? The main aim of the present study is the following: to specify the bearing of certain social factors on self-esteem and to indicate the influence of self-esteem on socially significant attitudes and behavior.

It is an unfortunate fact that, although hundreds of self-concept studies have been conducted in recent years, no generally accepted measure of self-esteem is available in the literature. Since this variable is of decisive importance in this study, it is necessary to examine in some detail precisely how self-esteem was measured and to discuss the degree of confidence which can be placed in the measuring instrument.

CHAPTER 2

THE MEASUREMENT OF SELF-ESTEEM

THE measure of self-esteem employed in this study is a ten-item Guttman scale which has satisfactory reproducibility and scalability. In constructing this measure, we were guided by the following practical and theoretical considerations:

(1) *Ease of administration*—Since a large sample is required for multivariate analysis, it was not practicable to use a technique which required apparatus—such as blocks, ink blots, direct measures of physiological response—or which required individual administration—such as interviews, clinical appraisal, etc. Our instrument simply required the respondent to check his answers to ten items.

(2) *Economy of time*—In order to obtain the cooperation of school authorities, it was necessary to use anonymous questionnaires which could be filled out within a single class period. At the same time, we wished to obtain a great deal of other information about the respondent—his social statuses, group memberships, neighborhood environment, high school activities, occupational aspirations and values, etc. Complex and time-consuming measuring instruments, such as the MMPI or the Q-sort, were ruled out. It was thus necessary to employ a measure of self-esteem which would be completed in two or three minutes.

(3) *Unidimensionality*—An instrument was required which would enable us to rank people along a single continuum ranging from those who had very high to those who had very low self-esteem. The Guttman scale insures a unidimensional continuum by establishing a pattern which must be satisfied before the scale can be accepted. The adequacy of each item is not determined primarily by its relationship to a total score but by its patterned relation-

16

ship with all other items on the scale. The reproducibility of this scale is 92 percent and its scalability is 72 percent; these coefficients are satisfactory in terms of the criteria established by Guttman and Menzel.[1]

(4) *Face validity*—While the Guttman model can usually insure that the items on a scale belong to the same dimension, they cannot define the dimension. As Suchman notes: ". . . even if an item is reproducible perfectly from scale scores, this is not proof that the item is part of the definition of the universe. . . . Only a judgment of content can determine what belongs to a universe, and not correlations or reproducibility."[2]

For this reason we explicitly attempted to select items which openly and directly dealt with the dimension under consideration. Respondents were asked to strongly agree, agree, disagree, or strongly disagree with the following items:

1) On the whole, I am satisfied with myself.
2) At times I think I am no good at all.
3) I feel that I have a number of good qualities.
4) I am able to do things as well as most other people.
5) I feel I do not have much to be proud of.

[1] The concept of reproducibility is discussed by Louis Guttman in S. A. Stouffer, *et al.*, *Measurement and Prediction*, Princeton: Princeton University Press, 1950, Chap. 3. The measure of scalability appears in Herbert Menzel, "A New Coefficient for Scalogram Analysis," *Public Opinion Quarterly*, Vol. 17, 1953, pp. 268–280. The measure of self-esteem employed is a 10-item scale (described in the next section) which, through the use of "contrived" items, yields a seven-point scale. The use of contrived items is discussed in S. A. Stouffer, *et al.*, "A Technique for Improving Cumulative Scales," *Pub. Opin. Qtrly.*, Vol. 16, 1953, pp. 273–291. The ordering of the scale items, the cutting points, and the components of the contrived items appear in Appendix D-1.

[2] Edward A. Suchman, in S. A. Stouffer, *et al.*, *Measurement and Prediction*, p. 129.

6) I certainly feel useless at times.
7) I feel that I am a person of worth, at least on an equal plane with others.
8) I wish I could have more respect for myself.
9) All in all, I am inclined to feel that I am a failure.
10) I take a positive attitude toward myself.

"Positive" and "negative" items were presented alternately in order to reduce the effect of respondent set. While the reader may question one or another item, there is little doubt that the items generally deal with a favorable or unfavorable attitude toward oneself.

Such "logical validation" or "face validity," while important, is not sufficient to establish the adequacy of the scale. Unfortunately, there are no "known groups" or "criterion groups" which can be used to validate the scale. The adequacy of this measure must thus be defended on the following grounds: if this scale actually did measure self-esteem, then we would expect the scores on this scale to be associated with other data in a theoretically meaningful way. Let us consider some of these relationships.

Depression. It is a familiar clinical observation that depression often accompanies low self-esteem. If such depressed feelings rise to the surface, and if the scale measures self-esteem, then people with low self-esteem should appear more depressed to outside observers. This hypothesis was examined among a special group of subjects.

In pursuance of its research objectives, the National Institutes of Health retain a group of "normal volunteers" who serve as research subjects for a variety of scientific investigations. Technically, a normal volunteer is defined as "a healthy person—that is, one with no scientifically contraindicatory abnormalities—who has been admitted as a patient of the Clinical Center in order to serve as a volunteer subject for approved research projects." Most of these volunteers are young adults who are housed on the wards of the Clinical Center.

In the course of pretesting our research instruments, 50 normal volunteers were asked to fill out various questionnaires, all of which contained the self-esteem scale. Independently of these results, nursing personnel on the wards on which the volunteers were located were asked to fill out Leary scales [3] on these subjects. Of special interest were the following facts: the normal volunteers did not know that the nurses would fill out the Leary scales; the nurses did not know what answers the subjects gave to the questionnaires, did not see the questionnaires, and in most cases, we believe, did not even know that the subjects had filled out self-esteem scales; and in most cases the research investigator did not know who the nurses were who filled out the questionnaires, and most of them did not know him. We may thus have reasonable confidence in the independence of the data.

The Leary scale consists of a series of "interpersonal" items designed to characterize an individual. The rater is simply asked to say whether the subject is or is not like the word or phrase presented. We amended this form to allow the nurse to say that she was undecided. For about half the subjects, one nurse filled out a Leary scale for each normal volunteer; a large number of different nurses participated, depending upon where the volunteer was housed. For the other half, two nurses filled out the scales for each subject independently of one another. In the latter case their joint appraisals were used. If they disagreed, the response was placed in the "undecided" category.

We find a significant [4] association between the individ-

---

[3] An elaborate discussion of this scale appears in Timothy Leary, *Interpersonal Diagnosis of Personality*, New York: Ronald, 1957.

[4] The .05 level of significance is employed throughout this report. When three or more groups are compared, the significance of difference

ual's self-esteem and the likelihood that he will appear depressed to nurses. Table 1 shows that nurses were far more likely to deny that those with high self-esteem scores were "often gloomy" or "frequently disappointed" than those with low self-esteem scores. (Table 1) [5]

Not only are people with low self-esteem scores more likely to appear depressed to others but they are, as we would expect, more likely to express feelings of unhappiness, gloom, discouragement, etc. Indeed, if they did not, we would have strong reason to question the validity of the scale. Table 2 shows a very strong and consistent relationship between the self-esteem scale and a Guttman scale of "depressive affect." [6] For example, only 4 percent of those with the highest self-esteem scores, but 80 percent

---

is based on the chi-square test. If the chi-square is computed for the entire table, an asterisk before the table title indicates that the chi-square for the entire table is significant. Where it is appropriate to compute a chi-square for a subgroup in a table, an asterisk before the title of the group indicates that the chi-square is significant for the subgroup.

When two groups are compared, the significance of difference between percentages is employed. An asterisk between two percentages indicates that this difference is significant. Where certain groups are combined in order to permit comparison of significance of difference between percentages, the basis of the combination is indicated at the foot of the table. (For example, in Chap. 3, Table 9 shows that Jews differ significantly from Protestants and Catholics combined in terms of proportions with high self-esteem.)

"Control tables" (i.e., tables designed to show that a relationship is maintained when certain variables are held constant) and standardized tables are indicated by ‡ before the table title. Significance levels are not computed for these tables.

The bases of the significance computations in Chap. 13, Tables 5–8, are indicated in footnote 5 of that chapter.

[5] The calculation of significance levels for all tables in this report dealing with normal volunteers is based upon the chi-square test. In each case, the "undecided" response has been combined with the minority category (i.e., the response less frequently given for the entire sample); hence, each of these tables has 2 d.f.

[6] This scale is described in Appendix D-5.

TABLE 1

Guttman Scale of Self-Esteem and Leary Scale
Descriptions as Gloomy and Disappointed

Described by nurses as . . .	Self-Esteem score		
	High	Medium	Low
* "often gloomy"			
Yes	—	20%	33%
Undecided	9	—	42
No	91	80	25
Total percent	100	100	100
(Number)	(23)	(15)	(12)
* "frequently disappointed"			
Yes	4%	13%	50%
Undecided	9	13	25
No	87	73	25
Total percent	100	100	100
(Number)	(23)	(15)	(12)

TABLE 2

* Self-Esteem and Depressive Affect

"Depressive affect" scale	Self-Esteem						
	High 0	1	2	3	4	5	Low 6
Not depressed	88%	77%	60%	44%	30%	13%	3%
Intermediate	7	15	24	29	30	22	18
Highly depressed	4	8	15	27	40	65	80
Total percent	100	100	100	100	100	100	100
(Number)	(456)	(775)	(683)	(425)	(214)	(108)	(34)

* See footnote 4, pages 19–20.

of those with the lowest self-esteem scores, were "highly depressed" according to this measure.

Psychophysiological indicators. The presence of low self-esteem among neurotics is commonly observed in clinical practice. Indeed, some clinicians go so far as to characterize low self-esteem as one of the basic elements of neurosis. Horney[7] and Fromm[8] stress that an underlying feeling of worthlessness is characteristic of the sick personality. Angyal states: "In the neurotic development there are always a number of unfortunate circumstances which instill in the child a self-derogatory feeling. This involves on the one hand a feeling of weakness which discourages him from the free expression of his wish for mastery, and on the other a feeling that there is something fundamentally wrong with him and that, therefore, he cannot be loved. The whole complicated structure of neurosis appears to be founded on this secret feeling of worthlessness, that is, on the belief that one is inadequate to master the situations that confront him and that he is undeserving of love . . ."[9]

The measure of "neuroticism" employed in this study was developed by the Research Branch of the U.S. Army in World War II.[10] It is based on a list of "psychosomatic symptoms" which proved extremely effective in differentiating between large samples of normal and neurotic soldiers. (The "neurotics" were a criterion group of soldiers

[7] Karen Horney, *Neurosis and Human Growth,* New York: Norton, 1950, especially Chap. 5.

[8] Erich Fromm, *Escape From Freedom,* New York: Rinehart, 1941. See also his "Selfishness, Self-Love, and Self-Interest" in *Man For Himself,* New York: Rinehart, 1947, pp. 119–141.

[9] Andras Angyal, "A Theoretical Model for Personality Studies," *Journal of Personality,* Vol. 20, No. 1, 1951, p. 137.

[10] The development and validation of this measure appears in Shirley A. Star, "The Screening of Psychoneurotics in the Army: Technical Development of Tests," in S. A. Stouffer, *et al., Measurement and Prediction,* Chap. 13. One of the 15 symptoms, viz., "Do you have any particular physical or health problem?" was omitted from our score.

whose psychological malfunctioning was so serious that they could no longer carry on their duties and were hospitalized as a result.) The symptoms utilized are typical secondary physiological manifestations of anxiety: trouble in getting to sleep and staying asleep; hand trembling; nervousness; heart beating hard; pressures or pains in the head; fingernail biting; shortness of breath when not exercising or working hard; hands sweating; sick headaches; nightmares; "cold sweats"; fainting spells; dizziness; and upset stomach.

Table 3 shows that, without exception, each step down

TABLE 3

* Self-Esteem and Physiological Indicators of "Neurosis" Used by the Research Branch

Number of psychosomatic symptoms	Self-Esteem						
	High 0	1	2	3	4	5	Low 6
1 or less	60%	50%	41%	37%	28%	19%	16%
2–4	35	39	43	46	44	50	42
5 or more	5	10	16	18	28	31	42
Total percent	100	100	100	100	100	100	100
(Number)	(516)	(866)	(784)	(506)	(265)	(126)	(38)

the self-esteem scale finds a larger proportion of respondents with many psychosomatic symptoms. At the extremes the differences are particularly great. Whereas 60 percent of the highest self-esteem group had few symptoms, this was true of only 16 percent of those with the least self-esteem.

This already strong relationship can be made even sharper if we select 10 out of these 14 symptoms for consideration. [11] Table 4 shows that fully 69 percent of those highest in self-esteem, but only 13 percent of those lowest

TABLE 4

* Self-Esteem and Frequency of Report
of Psychosomatic Symptoms

Number of psychosomatic symptoms	Self-Esteem						
	High 0	1	2	3	4	5	Low 6
2 or less	69%	57%	45%	40%	31%	22%	13%
3	12	15	15	17	14	18	18
4 or more	19	28	40	43	55	61	69
Total percent	100	100	100	100	100	100	100
(Number)	(518)	(872)	(786)	(509)	(268)	(126)	(38)

in self-esteem, experienced two or fewer symptoms. Conversely, 69 percent of the latter, compared with 19 percent of the former, reported four or more symptoms.

In order to bring additional evidence to bear on this question, we presented to our respondents a list of "ailments" which are often thought to have psychogenic components and asked them to indicate how much they had been bothered by such ailments during the past five years. People with high and low self-esteem differed in reporting

[11] The 4 omitted are fainting, dizziness, "cold sweats," and upset stomach. Probably the reason fainting and dizziness discriminate less well in this sample than in the army study is that half of our sample are female, in contrast to the all-male army sample. Because of cultural factors, it may be a less serious sign of psychological malfunction for a female to report having experienced fainting and dizziness than a male; this might account for the weakening of the relationship. The other two items were reported so rarely in the total sample that they could not powerfully differentiate groups in terms of neurosis. The items included in this score, as well as the cutting points, appear in Appendix D-7.

"nervousness," "loss of appetite," "insomnia," and "headache"—items which, it may be noted, were similar to some appearing in the psychosomatic symptom score. The results indicate that as self-esteem scores declined, the proportions reporting being bothered by three or more of these ailments were 15 percent, 18 percent, 24 percent, 22 percent, 33 percent, 37 percent, and 64 percent. There is thus a clear, though imperfect, relationship between self-esteem and psychosomatic symptoms of anxiety. Since anxiety may be considered a central component of neurosis, we shall have frequent occasion in this report to present data dealing with anxiety.

Peer-group reputation. Cooley, Mead, James and others agree that the individual's self-opinion is largely determined by what others think of him. Two items of evidence bear on this question. The first is based on a sociometric study conducted among 272 seniors from two high schools in the vicinity of Washington, D.C.

Since all students take English, sociometric ratings were confined to this class. Our respondents were given the following directions: "Think of the people in your English class. If you were asked to vote for a leader in your English class today, which person would you be most likely to choose? Second most likely? Third most likely?" Table 5 shows that among those with high self-esteem scores, 47 percent received two or more choices as a leader; among those with medium self-esteem scores, the proportion was 32 percent; and among those with low self-esteem scores, the proportion was 15 percent. Otherwise expressed, low self-esteem people were half as likely as medium self-esteem people and one-third as likely as high self-esteem respondents to be selected as leaders *by others*. When we asked these students who they felt would actually be chosen as a class leader if an election were held, similar results appeared.

Leadership in a classroom is determined by a variety of factors, one of which undoubtedly is participation in that

DEFINITION AND MEASUREMENT
TABLE 5
Self-Esteem and Number of Choices as Class Leader

	Self-Esteem		
	High	Medium	Low
* Selected as leader by two or more classmates	47%	32%	15%
(Number)	(88)	(144)	(33)
Judged likely to be elected by two or more classmates	44%	35%	12%
(Number)	(88)	(144)	(33)

class. One question used to examine the degree of participation was the following: "When people in your English class discuss topics of interest, which people are most likely to participate actively in such discussions? Name five people (in any order) in your English class who usually talk up, express their views, and participate actively. (Put down whichever names come to mind first.)" We find that the lower the individual's self-esteem, the less likely is he to be described as an active class participant. Eighteen percent of those with lowest self-esteem received four or more choices, compared with 26 percent of those with medium self-esteem and 31 percent of the high self-esteem group.

In addition, we attempted to select out those students who are conspicuous by their inconspicuousness—the people who are inordinately subdued, inactive, apathetic. We therefore asked: "Now name five people (in any order) who rarely talk up, rarely express their views, and do not tend to participate actively. (Put down whichever names come to mind first.)" Unfortunately, it was possible to ask this question in only one of the two high schools studied. In this school we find that people with low self-esteem scores tend to be outstanding in their social invisi-

TABLE 6

Guttman Scale of Self-Esteem and Leary Scale Descriptions of Reputation

Described by nurses as . . .	Self-Esteem score		
	High	Medium	Low
* "well thought of"			
Yes	78%	67%	25%
Undecided	4	20	25
No	17	13	50
Total percent	100	100	100
(Number)	(23)	(15)	(12)
"makes good impression"			
Yes	61%	53%	33%
Undecided	22	20	25
No	17	27	42
Total percent	100	100	100
(Number)	(23)	(15)	(12)
"often admired"			
Yes	39%	20%	8%
Undecided	17	27	17
No	43	53	75
Total percent	100	100	100
(Number)	(23)	(15)	(12)
"respected by others"			
Yes	39%	53%	25%
Undecided	39	20	25
No	22	27	50
Total percent	100	100	100
(Number)	(23)	(15)	(12)

bility. Sixty-seven percent of this group were so designated by two or more of their peers, compared with 55
percent of the medium self-esteem group, and 43 percent
of those with the highest self-esteem.

The second body of evidence is drawn from the normal
volunteer data described above. As Table 6 indicates, nurses
were less likely to say that those with low self-esteem
scores were "often admired," "respected by others," "well
thought of," and "makes good impression."

Parenthetically, we may note a point made by Cooley:
the individual imagines his appearance to other people
and feels pride or mortification on the basis of their *assumed* feelings. It is thus consistent, though hardly surprising, to note the responses to the question, "What do
you think most people think of you?" Thirty-eight percent
of those with high self-esteem scores, but only 8 percent
of those with low self-esteem scores, said "very well." (Table
7) While this finding is undoubtedly accounted for in
large measure by the mechanism of projection, it is also

TABLE 7

* Self-Esteem Score and Respondent's Opinion
of What Others Think of Him

	Self-Esteem score						
"What do you think most people think of you?"	High 0	1	2	3	4	5	Low 6
Think very well of me	38%	28%	23%	16%	9%	6%	8%
Think fairly well of me	61	71	76	80	84	78	68
Think fairly poorly or very poorly of me	1	1	2	5	7	16	24
Total percent	100	100	100	100	100	100	100
(Number)	(512)	(867)	(785)	(496)	(261)	(112)	(38)

clearly in agreement with the hypothesis advanced by Cooley.

Other evidence. In Chapters 8–12, we shall discuss the relationship of self-esteem to various other aspects of psychological functioning, interpersonal attitudes, peer group participation and leadership, concern with broader social affairs, and occupational values and aspirations. To the extent that the relationships reported there appear to be theoretically meaningful and consistent with expectations, they would suggest that the scale actually is measuring self-esteem.

There is one further item of evidence which may provide some sense of what is meant by self-esteem. Is the person with a low self-esteem score someone who is constantly beating his breast, berating himself, telling everyone within earshot how worthless he is? Does he habitually use expressions of self-reproach without conviction for the purpose of gaining comfort or advantage from others?

Consider the Leary scale item "able to criticize self." It is interesting to note (Table 8) that, according to the

TABLE 8

Self-Esteem Score and Description as "Able to Criticize Self"

Described by nurses as "able to criticize self"	Self-Esteem score		
	High	Medium	Low
Yes	43%	33%	25%
Undecided	30	40	33
No	26	27	42
Total percent	100	100	100
(Number)	(23)	(15)	(12)

nurses, those normal volunteers with low self-esteem scores were actually somewhat less "able to criticize self" than those with high self-esteem scores. Clearly, these results lend no support to the assumption that a low self-esteem score simply reflects a tendency to berate oneself publicly.

In sum, practical considerations required the utilization of a measure which was easy and economical to administer. This scale is internally reliable [12] and unidimensional and appears to have face validity. If the scale actually measures low self-esteem, then we would expect those with low scores to appear depressed to others and to express feelings of discouragement and unhappiness; to manifest symptoms of "neuroticism" or anxiety; to hold a low sociometric status in the group; to be described as commanding less respect than others and to feel that others have little respect for them. The evidence supports these expectations.

The Meaning of Self-Esteem

Thus far we have used the term "self-esteem" rather loosely, implying that its meaning was self-evident. Self-esteem, as noted, is a positive or negative attitude toward a particular object, namely, the self. But self-esteem has two quite different connotations. One connotation of high self-esteem is that the person thinks he is "very good"; a very different connotation is that he thinks he is "good enough." It is thus possible for a person to consider himself superior to most others but to feel inadequate in terms

[12] "From general considerations of scale theory, it should be clear that if a set of items has high reproducibility, then the items must necessarily have high test-retest reliability. If there were a substantial unreliability factor operating in the responses to the items, this would create appreciable scale error; there would be more than a single factor present. Hence, if scalogram analysis shows that essentially only a single factor is operating in the responses, this must mean that there cannot be many additional factors, including unreliability." Louis Guttman, in Stouffer, *Measurement and Prediction,* p. 305. A study by Earle Silber and Jean S. Tippett showed a test-retest reliability of .85.

of certain standards he has set for himself. Conversely, an adolescent may consider himself an average person but be quite contented with the self he observes. In one sense a person's self-esteem may be high whereas in the other sense it may be medium or low.

High self-esteem, as reflected in our scale items, expresses the feeling that one is "good enough." The individual simply feels that he is a person of worth; he respects himself for what he is, but he does not stand in awe of himself nor does he expect others to stand in awe of him. He does *not* necessarily consider himself superior to others.

One might consider using the term "self-acceptance" to describe these people, since this term implies that the individual knows what he is, is aware of his virtues and deficiencies, and accepts what he sees without regret. But our high self-esteem students do not simply accept themselves for what they are; they also want to grow, to improve, to overcome their deficiencies. They respect the self they observe, but they note imperfections and inadequacies, and hope, usually with confident anticipation of success, that they will overcome these deficiencies.

One might also consider applying the term self-satisfaction to describe these people, were this term not too loaded with the connotation of smugness.

When we speak of high self-esteem, then, we shall simply mean that the individual respects himself, considers himself worthy; he does not necessarily consider himself better than others, but he definitely does not consider himself worse; he does not feel that he is the ultimate in perfection but, on the contrary, recognizes his limitations and expects to grow and improve.

Low self-esteem, on the other hand, implies self-rejection, self-dissatisfaction, self-contempt. The individual lacks respect for the self he observes. The self-picture is disagreeable, and he wishes it were otherwise.

The Sample

A major purpose of this study was to learn how different social experiences, stemming from membership in groups characterized by different values, perspectives, or conditions of existence, would bear upon levels of self-esteem and upon self-values. Two approaches may be used in attempting to maximize the range of social experiences, statuses, or group affiliations in a sample. The first approach is to select groups which are known to differ in their social characteristics: one might choose a predominantly upper-class school, a predominantly middle-class school, a predominantly working-class school; one might choose a school in a farming community, a middle-sized town, a metropolitan center. The other approach is to select a population which is known to be socially heterogeneous and to sample randomly from this population. This is the method we have chosen. The population selected for study was the student body attending public high schools in New York State. Various social classes, races, religious groups, rural and urban communities, and nationality groups are all well represented in this state. Broad geographical range was sacrificed by the selection of a single state, but a wide range of other social characteristics did appear in our sample.

The sample consists of ten high schools selected by random procedures from the roster of public high schools in New York State. High schools were stratified by size of community, and the ultimate selection was made by means of a Table of Random Numbers. Since the sampling unit was the high school rather than the individual, the adequacy with which the sample represents the population of students cannot be determined. A further limitation of the sample lies in the fact that it omits students in parochial or private secular schools, adolescents who have dropped out of school before reaching their junior or senior years, and students absent from school on the day the questionnaires were administered. The sample, then, consists of 5,024 high school juniors and seniors from ten randomly selected public high schools present on the day of administration.[13]

Within the classrooms, teachers distributed three questionnaire forms alternately to their students and read instructions to them. Each student completed one questionnaire form. The questionnaires were anonymous. In response to two questions added at the end of the questionnaires, the great majority of students said that they found the questionnaires interesting to fill out and that they had little difficulty answering the questions.

Standardization

One of the main purposes of selecting a large sample is to permit the use of multivariate analysis. For example, the introduction of a third (or higher order) variable may refine or explain [14] the relationship between two variables. In survey research, a third variable is often introduced for the purpose of "controlling on" or "holding constant" certain factors when examining the relationship between two variables. Fundamentally, there are three methods for controlling on these factors: partial correlation, subclassification, and standardization.[15] The first is applicable to variable data whereas the other two can be applied to attribute data. Although subgroup classification is the usual control procedure in survey analysis, we have found that the use of standardization often yields a clearer picture

[13] A more detailed discussion of the selection of the sample appears in Appendix A.

[14] Hans Zeisel, *Say It With Figures*, New York: Harper and Bros., 1947, Chaps. VIII and IX.

[15] A clear discussion of subclassification and standardization appears in John H. Mueller and Karl F. Schuessler, *Statistical Reasoning in Sociology*, Boston: Houghton Mifflin, 1961, pp. 189–202.

of the effect of the control factor.[16] Since we shall have frequent occasion to use this technique in the present study, it may be useful to indicate what is involved in this procedure.

Standardization has long been used in demographic and public health research for the purpose of controlling on certain population characteristics when comparing group rates. The demographer, for example, may find that the death rates in Florida are higher than those in New York State. This finding might lead to the erroneous supposition that the conditions of life in Florida are somehow more unhealthy than those in New York State. It is known, however, that many older people migrate to Florida for reasons of health; the differences in death rates may thus be due to the fact that a larger proportion of people living in Florida are old people. The demographer thus determines "age-specific" death rates, i.e., the death rates which appear within each age group. He then selects some "standard population," e.g., the total population of the United States, and determines what the death rate in Florida and New York would be if the age distribution in these states were exactly the same as that in the entire country. These are "theoretic rates." He might find that the death rates in New York and Florida would actually be the same, or that the death rate in New York would be higher, if there were no differences in the age distributions of their populations.

In the present report we shall frequently use standardization to observe the relevance of a "test factor" for an observed relationship. For certain purposes, e.g., the specification of conditional relationships, subgroup classification will be employed. Standardization, on the other hand, will usually be employed to determine what the relationship between two variables would be when controlled on

[16] Morris Rosenberg, "Test Factor Standardization as a Method of Interpretation," *Social Forces,* Vol. 41, No. 1 (1962), pp. 53–61.

one or more test factors. The usefulness of this procedure will, we hope, become apparent as the report proceeds.

Organization

The present report is divided into six parts. Part II, Chapter 3, begins by considering the distribution of self-esteem among several broad social groupings—social class, religious groups, races, and nationality groups. In Chapter 4, the focus is narrowed to the neighborhood. Here we attempt to indicate how the relevance of broad social group memberships may be influenced by the neighborhood contexts in which they are imbedded. The next three chapters (Part III—Chapters 5–7) focus upon a still narrower interpersonal environment—the family. The following kinds of questions are considered: What is the self-concept of the child whose family has been broken by divorce, separation, or death? What happens when the parent marries again? What is the effect of birth order in the family? Does it make a difference whether the child has mostly brothers or mostly sisters, whether he is one of the younger children or one of the older children? What bearing does the parents' interest in the child have upon his self-esteem?

In Part IV we turn to a consideration of some of the inner states associated with self-esteem. Chapter 8 discusses certain psychological conditions associated with self-esteem which may lead to feelings of anxiety. Chapter 9 considers the interpersonal attitudes and behavior of the person afflicted with feelings of self-contempt.

In Part V (Chapters 10–12), attention is again turned outward toward the social realm. How is self-esteem associated with certain socially significant attitudes and behavior in the adolescent—his participation and leadership in the high school community, his concern with public affairs which may influence his role as a citizen, and his occupational values and aspirations?

Part VI (Chapter 13) deals with the adolescent's self-values, the conceptions of the desirable which he uses as a basis for self-evaluation. What is the relationship between these self-values and global self-esteem? How are self-values modified in the interest of maintaining a satisfactory level of self-esteem? How do social groups vary in the qualities they care about in themselves?

Part VII (Chapter 14) suggests a number of directions which future research might take.

In general, then, the main focus of the present report is on the broader social, and narrower interpersonal, factors associated with the self-concept and upon certain psychological responses and social behavior in which the self-concept appears to be significantly implicated.

PART II
THE BROADER SOCIAL
ENVIRONMENT

CHAPTER 3

THE SOCIAL FABRIC

THE student of society, embarking upon a study of the relationship of social structure and the self-image, is most likely to begin with the question: How do broad social groups differ in their self-esteem levels? Do upper-class students have higher self-esteem than lower-class students? Are the self-esteem levels of Protestants, Catholics, and Jews different? Do whites differ from Negroes? Are there differences in terms of nationality background, e.g., English or Welsh, Irish, Italian, Russian, Polish, German, etc.? Such differences would point to the significance of social experiences for personality development.

Socio-Economic Status

If a person's self-esteem is influenced by what others think of him, then there is reason to expect those with the highest prestige in the society—the upper classes—to be more likely than others to accept themselves. At the same time it must be recognized that we are dealing with adolescents. Their location in the stratification system is not based upon their personal achievements but upon the prestige of their parents. It is thus possible that, within this age group, the neighborhood, family, or peer group, rather than prestige in the broader society, may predominantly influence the individual's feelings of self-worth.

The index of socio-economic status employed in this study consists of a weighted score of the median income of the father's occupation, father's education, and source of income. Children in the highest class have fathers who generally have gone to college, whose occupations provide incomes which are well above average, and who, in many cases, are in independent professions. Children in the lowest class have fathers who are chiefly service workers or manual laborers, have not gone beyond grade school, and who almost all work for someone else. Table 1 indicates

TABLE 1

* Social Class and Self-Esteem

Self-Esteem	Social class		
	Upper	Middle	Lower
High	51%	46%	38%
Medium	23	25	26
Low	26	29	35
Total percent	100	100	100
(Number)	(195)	(2686)	(340)

that children from higher social classes are somewhat more likely to accept themselves—to consider themselves worthy —than those from the lower social strata. Whereas 51 percent of the members of the highest class ranked high on our scale of self-esteem, this was true of 38 percent of those in the lowest class.[1]

[1] It was not possible to use either the Hollingshead or Warner indices of socio-economic status. (See August Hollingshead and Frederick Redlich, *Social Class and Mental Illness,* New York: Wiley, 1958, pp. 389–397, and W. Lloyd Warner, Marcia Meeker, *et al., Social Class in America,* Chicago: Science Research Associates, 1949.) It may be that the use of other status indicators would have shown greater differences in self-esteem. Alternative indices of SES derived from our data showed even smaller differences in self-esteem among classes than those reported above. It should be emphasized once more that these data apply to students attending school. We do not know the self-esteem of drop-outs, most of whom are likely to come from the lower class. It may be that lower-class children who continue on to the 11th grade differ in self-esteem from those who have left school and are thus not adequately representative of their class group.

For a more detailed discussion of the computation of social class scores and assignment to class categories, see Appendix B.

It is interesting, however, to note the following fact: that class differences in self-esteem are considerably greater among boys than among girls. Whereas the highest-class boys are substantially (19 percent) more likely than the lowest-class boys to have high self-esteem, the highest-class girls are only slightly (6 percent) more likely than the lowest-class girls to have high self-esteem. (Table 2)

TABLE 2

Social Class and Self-Esteem, by Sex

Self-Esteem	* Boys			Girls		
	Social class					
	Upper	Middle	Lower	Upper	Middle	Lower
High	55%	47%	36%	47%	46%	41%
Medium	17	25	26	28	25	27
Low	28	28	39	24	29	32
Total percent	100	100	100	100	100	100
(Number)	(89)	(1383)	(168)	(106)	(1311)	(172)

Why should this be? Obviously, social prestige is not sufficient to explain the relationship of social class to self-esteem, since such an interpretation would apply equally to boys and girls. Perhaps, then, the answer may be sought in differential group norms—specifically, in certain characteristic child-rearing attitudes and values in the several social classes. If we were to use this level of explanation, however, we would have to show that upper-class parents differed considerably from lower-class parents in their values and behavior toward their sons, but differed very little in their values and behavior toward their daughters —and that these values and behavior were relevant for the youngster's self-esteem. Although this hypothesis may appear to be highly complex, there are data from this and other studies which bear upon it.

Recent studies of social class and parental values have clearly shown that middle-class and working-class parents tend to differ in their child-rearing values and practices. Let us here consider one particular facet of parent-child relationships, viz., the father's relationship to the son and to the daughter. A study conducted by Kohn and Carroll [2] is extremely interesting in this regard.

In their study of social class and parent-child relationships, these authors developed a Guttman scale of "supportiveness," indicating whether the parent tended to support, encourage, or praise the child. Since the father was very rarely more supportive than the mother, this scale ranged from those families in which the father was as supportive as the mother to those in which the father was considerably less supportive.

In general, Kohn and Carroll found, middle-class children were more likely than working-class children to have supportive fathers. The main point, however, is this: middle-class fathers were *considerably* more likely than working-class fathers to be supportive of their sons, but middle-class fathers were only *somewhat* (if at all) more likely than working-class fathers to be supportive of their daughters. Mothers, fathers, and children, all interviewed independently, were in agreement on this matter. (Table 3)

Our own data show very similar results.[3] We constructed a score of "closeness of father-child relationships." In general, this score was designed to reflect whether the child

[2] Melvin L. Kohn and Eleanor E. Carroll, "Social Class and the Allocation of Parental Responsibilities," *Sociometry,* Vol. 23, No. 4 (1960), pp. 372–392.

[3] Unfortunately, these data were obtained from a random one-third of the total sample, i.e., those who filled out one of the three questionnaire forms. In the discussion which follows, we shall deal with this group which, of course, is an inexact reflection of the results derived from the total sample.

TABLE 3 [4]

Social Class and Paternal Supportiveness

| | Reports by mothers—Fathers highly supportive of . . . | | | |
| | Sons | | Daughters | |
	Middle class	Working class	Middle class	Working class
Father supportive	51% *	29%	37%	28%
(Number)	(82)	(73)	(81)	(73)

| | Reports by fathers—Fathers highly supportive of . . . | | | |
| | Sons | | Daughters | |
	Middle class	Working class	Middle class	Working class
Father supportive	64% *	36%	19%	9%
(Number)	(25)	(25)	(21)	(11)

| | Reports by children—Fathers highly supportive of . . . | | | |
| | Sons | | Daughters | |
	Middle class	Working class	Middle class	Working class
Father supportive	68% *	24%	15%	18%
(Number)	(25)	(25)	(23)	(11)

[4] Table 3 is adapted from Kohn and Carroll, *op. cit.*, p. 378.

felt as close, or closer, to his father as to his mother; [5] several of the items and cutting points were similar to those used by Kohn and Carroll. Table 4 shows that upper-

TABLE 4

Social Class and Closeness of Father-Child Relationships among Girls and Boys

Relationship with father	* Male			Female		
	Social class					
	Upper	Middle	Lower	Upper	Middle	Lower
Close	65%	40%	28%	52%	39%	41%
Intermediate	19	37	40	30	39	41
Not close	15	24	32	19	23	18
Total percent	100	100	100	100	100	100
(Number)	(26)	(365)	(50)	(27)	(365)	(61)

class boys were 37 percent more likely than lower-class boys to report close relationships with their fathers, but that upper-class girls were only 11 percent more likely than lower-class girls to report close relationships with their fathers.

But what is the relevance of all this for self-esteem? Table 5 indicates that adolescents who report close relationships with fathers are considerably more likely to have high self-esteem and stable self-images than those who describe these relationships as more distant.

These results suggest that one reason upper-class boys

[5] The decision concerning which items reflected a "close relationship with the father" is based upon the combined judgment of three colleagues. The items and cutting points employed in constructing this score appear in Appendix D-11.

TABLE 5

* Father-Child Relationships and Self-Esteem

Self-Esteem	Father-child relationships		
	Close	Intermediate	Not close
High	52%	48%	37%
Medium	23	26	21
Low	25	26	41
Total percent	100	100	100
(Number)	(339)	(325)	(193)

have an advantage in self-esteem is that they tend to have closer relationships with their fathers. In order to test this hypothesis, we have examined the relationship between social class and self-esteem controlling (by means of standardization) on closeness of father-son relationships. Table 6-A shows the original relationship of social class to self-esteem and Table 6-B shows what this relationship would be if class groups were equal in terms of closeness of father-son relationships. Let us first consider those with high self-esteem. Table 6 shows that, for this subgroup of the sample, upper-class boys are 13.4 percent more likely than lower-class boys to have high self-esteem; if, however, both groups were equal in terms of father-son closeness, this difference would be reduced to 8.0 percent. Now let us consider the proportions with low self-esteem. Originally, in this table, upper-class boys are 7.5 percent less likely than lower-class boys to have low self-esteem; if, however, father-son relationships are standardized, then upper-class boys are actually 3.9 percent *more* likely than lower-class boys to have low self-esteem. It seems likely that differential father-son relationships are importantly involved in the general self-esteem advantage of upper-class over lower-class boys. Among girls, the effect of stand-

45

TABLE 6

† Social Class and Self-Esteem: (A) Original Relationship
and (B) Relationship Standardized on Closeness of
Relationship with Father (Boys)

A. Original relationship

| Self-Esteem | Social class | | |
	Upper	Middle	Lower
High	54.2%	50.1%	40.8%
Medium	12.5	22.0	18.4
Low	33.3	27.8	40.8
Total percent	100.0	100.0	100.0
(Number)	(24)	(345)	(49)

B. Standardized relationship

| Self-Esteem | Social class | | |
	Upper	Middle	Lower
High	52.3%	50.1%	44.3%
Medium	7.5	21.9	19.5
Low	40.2	27.9	36.3
Total percent	100.0	100.0	100.0
(Number)	(24)	(345)	(49)

ardization is to eliminate the already small class differences
in high self-esteem, although class differences in low self-
esteem are maintained.

We suggest, then, that social classes are cultural sub-
groups sharing certain norms; that among these norms is
a somewhat complex system of family relationships involving the closeness of the father to sons and to daugh-

TABLE 7

Father's Present Occupation and Self-Esteem of Child

Self-esteem of child	Father's occupation (Census categories)								
	Professional, technical and kindred workers	Farmers, farm managers, farm laborers	Managers, officials, proprietors (except farm)	Clerical and kindred workers	Sales workers	Craftsmen, foremen, kindred workers	Operatives and kindred workers	Service workers	Laborers, except farm or mine
High	45%	38%	46%	43%	48%	45%	44%	44%	44%
Medium	28	25	24	25	21	24	25	27	22
Low	26	38	29	32	31	31	30	28	34
Total percent	100	100	100	100	100	100	100	100	100
(Number)	(617)	(32)	(955)	(258)	(273)	(863)	(578)	(204)	(80)

ters; and that these norms may have a bearing upon the child's self-esteem. But these results, it should be emphasized, are not a direct consequence of the general prestige of the social class in the broader society. (The "general prestige" interpretation has already been cast in doubt by the finding that class differences in self-esteem are not the same for boys and for girls.) Upper-class children do tend to have somewhat higher self-esteem, but this is not simply because the broader society evaluates them highly. Factors internal to the family also appear to be involved.

Authoritarian occupations. In general, it is difficult to detect a clear and consistent association between the father's occupation and the adolescent's self-esteem. Actually, if we simply consider the prestige ranks of occupations classified according to the ten major occupational groupings employed by the Census Bureau, only minor differences in the self-esteem of children appear.[6] (Table 7) One group, however, merits special attention because the type of occupation may reflect something about the attitudes and personality of the father. This is the small group of students whose fathers are in highly "authoritarian" and "violent" occupations—so violent, in fact, that the incumbents carry guns. Specifically, respondents whose fathers were members of the armed forces, policemen or detectives, or sheriffs and bailiffs had unusually low self-esteem. Naturally, only small numbers of cases appeared in each occupational group, but if we consider all of them combined, the total comes to 39 cases. Among these 39 respondents, only 26 percent had high self-esteem compared with 45 percent of the remainder. Conversely, 54 percent of the former, but only 29 percent of the latter, had low self-esteem.[7] (Table 8)

[6] Children of farmers have slightly lower self-esteem, but the number of cases is small.

[7] We considered including with this group those students whose fathers appeared in the Census category "guards, watchmen, door-

TABLE 8

Self-Esteem of Children Whose Fathers Are in "Coercive" and Other Occupations

Child's self-esteem	Father's occupation	
	"Coercive" occupation	Other occupation
High	26% ✱	45%
Medium	21	25
Low	54	29
Total percent	100	100
(Number)	(39)	(3821)

Fathers in these occupations may well possess an affinity for an authoritarian occupational structure as well as a willingness to face and to utilize violence. Perhaps the occupational imperatives influence the individual's personality; more likely, the personality helps draw the individual to the occupation. Of course, even if these fathers do have authoritarian personalities, we do not know how such personalities influence the self-conceptions of the children. Nevertheless, it is an interesting finding, and one worth further investigation, that lower self-esteem is found among children whose fathers are in authoritarian occupations and whose stock in trade is the use of physical violence for the control of physical violence.

keepers." While the work of guards and watchmen is to some extent similar to the occupations cited above, the work of doorkeepers is clearly different; the inclusion of this group would thus introduce unknown contamination into the results. If this group is included, the number of cases increases to 63 and the proportion with high self-esteem becomes 30 percent.

Religion

That religious groups are differentially evaluated in the broader society is a matter of common observation as well as a finding of systematic research.[8] If the prestige of a religious group were closely associated with self-attitudes in adolescence, then we would expect Protestants to have the highest self-esteem, Catholics to be somewhat lower, and Jews to be lowest.

The data, however, do not support this expectation. Although Jews rank lowest in terms of religious prestige, they have somewhat *higher* self-esteem than Protestants and Catholics. (Table 9) The distribution in self-esteem of

TABLE 9

Religion and Self-Esteem

| | Religion | | |
Self-Esteem	Catholics	Protestants	Jews
High	43%	43%	53%
Medium	26	25	23
Low	31	32	23
Total percent	100	100	100
(Number)	(1727)	(1913)	(592)

* Jews vs. Catholics and Protestants: Proportion "High."

the two Christian groups, on the other hand, is the same. Fifty-three percent of the Jewish students, but 43 percent of the Catholic students and 43 percent of the Protestant

[8] For example, Eugene L. Hartley and Ruth E. Hartley, *Fundamentals of Social Psychology*, New York: Knopf, 1952, point out that ". . . whenever studies have been made, 'Jews' have consistently rated low in the hierarchy of preference. In other words, they are a group against whom there is much feeling." (p. 694)

students had high self-esteem. These differences are not very large, although they are statistically significant.

In view of the burden of discrimination borne by Jews in American society, this relatively high level of self-acceptance may appear surprising.[9] As a first thought one might be inclined to attribute these results in part to social class, although, as we have seen, social class is not very strongly related to self-esteem. In our sample, Jewish students do tend to come from higher social classes, but this turns out to be a very minor factor in accounting for their higher self-esteem levels. Even if all religious groups came from equal class backgrounds, Jewish students would still have higher self-esteem than others.

Another possibility that one might consider would be academic performance. Our data show that school grades are clearly related to self-esteem, and the Jewish children in our sample tend to do better in school. But this does not account for their higher self-esteem levels. Even if there were no difference in school grades among the three religious groups, the differences in self-esteem would remain almost the same.

The answer apparently must be sought elsewhere, and our data suggest that one of the more profitable lines of inquiry leads once again into the area of child-rearing practices and norms. Our evidence is admittedly scanty in this regard, but there is one aspect of parental attitudes on which some interesting evidence is available, viz., the degree of parental interest in the child.

On the basis of students' reports of their parents' be-

[9] It is interesting to note, however, that a study of college students, using very different instruments, yielded similar results. See Moshe Anisfeld, Norman Bogo, and Wallace E. Lambert, "Evaluational Reactions to Accented English Speech," *J. Abnor. Soc. Psychol.*, Vol. 65, No. 4 (1962), pp. 223–231. They note: "The unexpected finding that Jewish students have decidedly more favorable self-images than gentile students warrants further study." (p. 230)

havior in several fairly concrete situations, we developed an index of "parental interest in the child." [10] We divided our sample into those parents who, in these situations, manifested some indifference to their children and those who did not. In all three groups, we find, very few parents gave any indication of indifference toward their children; but where such evidence did appear, it was least likely to be found among Jewish parents. (Table 10)

TABLE 10

* Religious Affiliation and Parental Interest

	Religion		
Parental interest	Catholics	Jews	Protestants
Some sign of indifference	23%	12%	19%
No sign of indifference	77	88	81
Total percent	100	100	100
(Number)	(475)	(152)	(430)

Parental interest is, we find, closely related to the child's self-esteem. We would thus expect that if Jews did not differ from others in terms of parental interest, then their advantage in self-esteem would be reduced. And this, in fact, is the case. In the subsample under consideration,[11]

[10] Most of the items in the "parental interest" index consider reports of relatively objective parental behavior, but one of the items represents a subjective interpretation of parental attitudes.

[11] The questions on parental interest were asked on one of the three questionnaire forms, i.e., to one-third of the sample. Because of sampling variation, we find that in this subsample the differences in high self-esteem between Jews and Christians are somewhat less than for the entire sample and that the differences in low self-esteem are somewhat greater than in the entire sample. For this reason we shall ask how much the larger difference, i.e., the difference in low self-esteem, is reduced.

we find that if Jews and Catholics did not differ with regard to parental interest, then the difference in low self-esteem between them would be reduced from 9 percent to 6 percent. If Jews and Protestants did not differ in this regard, the difference would be reduced from 10 to 8 percent. (Table 11) These data thus suggest that level of parental interest may play a part in the observed self-esteem differences, although other factors, still unknown, are apparently also implicated in the result.

Joint Effect

Although social class and religious affiliation independently do not show very strong relationships to self-esteem, their cumulative impact is substantial. To illustrate this, let us compare upper-class Jews with lower-class Catholics and Protestants. Table 12 indicates that 60 percent of the upper-class Jews, but 39 percent of the lower-class Catholics and Protestants, had high self-esteem—a difference of 21 percent; conversely, 35 percent of the latter group, compared with 15 percent of the former group, had low self-esteem.

Since social class is more clearly related to self-esteem among boys than among girls, we would expect these differences to be more conspicuous among the boys. And Table 12 indicates that this is so. Sixty-one percent of the upper-class Jewish boys, but only 36 percent of the lower-class Catholic and Protestant boys had high self-esteem; conversely, the latter were nearly three times as likely as the former to have low self-esteem (38 percent to 13 percent). We thus see that certain specific combinations of sex, social class, and religion are clearly associated with differences in levels of self-acceptance.

Ethnic and Racial Group Characteristics

The oft-quoted description of American society as a "melting pot" is intended to convey the idea that a variety

TABLE 11

† Religion by Self-Esteem: (A) Original Relationship and
(B) Relationship Standardized on Parental Interest

A. Original relationship

| | Religion | | |
Self-Esteem	Catholics	Jews	Protestants
High	43.7%	50.7%	43.7%
Medium	25.3	27.6	25.1
Low	30.9	21.7	31.2
Total percent	100.0	100.0	100.0
(Number)	(475)	(152)	(430)

B. Standardized relationship

| | Religion | | |
Self-Esteem	Catholics	Jews	Protestants
High	44.5%	48.6%	43.4%
Medium	25.3	27.5	25.2
Low	30.1	23.8	31.4
Total percent	100.0	100.0	100.0
(Number)	(475)	(152)	(430)

of national groupings, characterized by distinctively different subcultures, in the course of time come to lose their distinctive cultural characteristics and increasingly come to assume cultural elements in common. And yet nationality may be the major basis of cultural differentiation, and national groupings in American society may represent the most distinctive subcultures in the broader society.

Today, however, it is less easy to distinguish such na-

TABLE 12

Self-Esteem of Upper-Class Jews and Lower-Class Protestants and Catholics

Self-Esteem	Total sample		Boys		Girls	
	Upper class Jews	Lower class Protestants and Catholics	Upper class Jews	Lower class Protestants and Catholics	Upper class Jews	Lower class Protestants and Catholics
High	60%	* 39%	61%	* 36%	60%	43%
Medium	24	26	26	26	23	26
Low	15	35	13	38	17	31
Total percent	100	100	100	100	100	100
(Number)	(53)	(294)	(23)	(146)	(30)	(148)

tional groupings than it was in the early decades of this century. Almost all our respondents are American-born, and most of their parents are as well. In many cases the father is of one national origin, the mother of another. Or either parent may be of mixed national origin. In the present analysis we have identified the ethnic or racial origins of those students whose parents had the same single national, religious or racial background.

Table 13 presents the distribution of self-esteem among 14 ethnic and racial groups (including mixed categories of "others"). The question may immediately be raised whether the ethnic differences in self-esteem are not simply reflections of social class differences. In order to check this possibility, we have computed standardized self-esteem distributions for each of these groups, i.e., the self-esteem which would appear if the social class positions of all groups were equal.

Our procedure was as follows: We first placed our 14 ethnic groups in a rank order based upon the proportion in each group with high self-esteem. After standardizing each group on social class, we rank-ordered these groups on the basis of the standardized figures. The Spearman Rank Correlation Coefficient between the original and the standardized groups is .97. This would suggest that if the social class distributions of these groups were the same, the general pattern appearing in Table 13 would remain virtually unchanged.

Since the observed results do not appear to be a reflection of social class, it is worth calling attention to several points in Table 13:

1) First, it may be noted that there is no indication that the distribution of self-acceptance in a group is related to the social prestige of that group in American society. In Table 13, we see that Negroes, who are exposed to the most intense, humiliating, and crippling forms of

TABLE 13

* Ethnic or Racial Group and Self-Esteem

	Self-Esteem			Total percent	(Number)
Catholics	High	Medium	Low		
German Catholics	48%	27	25	100	(64)
Italian Catholics	45%	25	30	100	(643)
Irish Catholics	39%	25	36	100	(120)
Spanish-Portuguese Catholics	28%	32	40	100	(25)
Polish Catholics	28%	28	45	100	(65)
‡ All other Catholics	44%	26	30	100	(998)
Jews					
German Jews	62%	19	19	100	(21)
Russian Jews	59%	21	21	100	(63)
Polish Jews	51%	20	29	100	(35)
‡ All other Jews	52%	24	24	100	(474)
Protestants					
German Protestants	53%	21	26	100	(150)
English-Welsh Protestants	39%	24	37	100	(122)
Negro Protestants	39%	28	34	100	(80)
‡ All other Protestants	43%	25	32	100	(1375)

‡ Includes those of mixed national origin, i.e., either (1) father and mother are of different national origins, or (2) father or mother is of mixed national origin.

discrimination in virtually every institutional area, do not have particularly low self-esteem. They are, indeed, below average, but not by a conspicuous margin (only 6 percent). At the same time, adolescents of English or Welsh descent, who are certainly the heart of the Old Yankee stock and whose pride is buttressed by a long tradition and an historical location in an established position, are also slightly lower in self-esteem than other groups. (Appendix C suggests that the Negro and English-Welsh results are not simply due to sampling accident.) For the other groups, the distribution of self-esteem within the group shows no striking similarity to the prestige rank accorded them in the broader society. For example, we have compared the Bogardus attitudes toward ethnic groups,[12] based on data collected in 1956, with the proportion of corresponding ethnic groups (represented by 25 or more cases) with high self-esteem. The Spearman Rank Correlation coefficient is .04, indicating virtually no correlation.

Having said this, a number of qualifications must immediately be introduced. (1) First, there are a large number of ethnic groups—e.g., Scandinavians, French, Yugoslavians—which are not sufficiently represented in our sample. It may be that if the full range of ethnic groups were adequately represented, the results would lead to a different over-all conclusion. (2) Even among those ethnic groups which are represented, the number of cases is often considerably less than would be desired. (3) Although the high schools in our study were selected on the basis of strictly random procedures, the small number of high schools studied introduces the possibility of sampling error. We may, then, repeat the statement that our data provide no indication of a linear relationship between an ethnic group's prestige rank and the distribution of self-esteem in the group, but view this generalization in the light of the above mentioned statistical considerations.

2) The second point is that various ethnic groups do differ substantially in their distribution of self-esteem.[13]

---

[12] Emory S. Bogardus, "Race Reactions by Sexes," *Sociology and Soc. Res.*, 43 (July–Aug. 1959), p. 441.

[13] We have restricted our comparisons to those groups represented by 25 or more cases (with the exception of the German Jews).

The most conspicuous groups in our study are the Germans and the Poles. It may be noted that, within each religious group, Germans are more likely to have high self-esteem than others. German Catholics are more likely to have high self-esteem than other Catholics, German Jews than other Jews, and German Protestants than other Protestants. On the other hand, in the two religious groups in which adolescents of Polish origin are represented, the group self-esteem is lowest. Polish Catholics are more likely to have low self-esteem than other Catholics, and Polish Jews are more likely to have low self-esteem than other Jews.

We thus see that national origin is associated with self-esteem. The most striking differences, for which an adequate number of cases are available, appear between the Russian Jews and the Polish Catholics. Fifty-nine percent of the former, but only 27 percent of the latter, had high self-esteem; conversely, the Polish Catholics were over twice as likely as the Russian Jews to have low self-esteem (45 percent to 21 percent).

These two groups, it may be noted, also differ in terms of other indicators of mental health. Consider the psychosomatic symptoms measure discussed in Chapter 2. Fifty-four percent of the Polish Catholics but 29 percent of the Russian Jews reported four or more of these symptoms. (Table 14) With regard to psychosomatic symptoms, Russian Jews have only a slight advantage over the remainder of the sample, but Polish Catholics have a clear disadvantage compared to all others.

Given the limited number of cases at our disposal, we cannot determine why Russian Jews and Polish Catholics differ to this extent. Whether these results stem from differences in family structures, child-rearing attitudes and practices, parental values, family solidarity, objective achievement, or social stresses of other kinds can only be determined by further research.

TABLE 14

Psychosomatic Symptoms of Students of Russian Jewish
Origin and of Polish Catholic Origin

Number of psychosomatic symptoms	Russian Jews	Polish Catholics	All others
Two or fewer	50%	30%	51%
Three	21	16	15
Four or more	29 ✱	54	34
Total percent	100	100	100
(Number)	(38)	(43)	(3101)

Discussion

In considering the relationship of broad social group memberships to self-esteem, one is likely to be guided in a general way by one of two hypotheses:

The stratification hypothesis. Many studies have shown that, in American society, religious groups, races, nationality groups, and, of course, social classes differ in social prestige. If the respect accorded the individual by others is influenced by the prestige rank of the group, then we might expect an association between group social esteem and individual self-esteem. As Cartwright expresses the point: "The groups to which a person belongs serve as primary determiners of his self-esteem. To a considerable extent, *personal* feelings of worth depend on the social evaluation of the *groups* with which a person is identified. Self-hatred and feelings of worthlessness tend to arise from membership in underprivileged or outcast groups." [14]

The subcultural hypothesis. According to this approach, members of broad social groups—classes, religions, nation-

[14] Dorwin Cartwright, "Emotional Dimensions of Group Life," in Martin L. Reymert, ed., *Feelings and Emotions,* New York: McGraw-Hill, 1950, p. 440.

alities, races—are seen as sharing certain interests, attitudes, values, or other aspects of styles of life. These groups, for example, might differ in the way they raised their children. If child-rearing practices had a bearing upon self-esteem, then this differential treatment might create differences in levels of self-acceptance.

Of course, differences in prestige may have an influence on styles of life and group styles of life may influence social prestige. Nevertheless, at a given point in time, one may ask: Do group differences in self-esteem appear to be closely associated with social prestige in the broader society or do they appear to stem from differences in group thoughts, customs, practices or characteristic life experiences?

As an over-all pattern, our data do not lend strong support to the stratification hypothesis. We have seen that the social prestige of a nationality or religious group is generally unrelated to the self-acceptance of its members. As far as social class is concerned, students from higher social classes are more likely than those from lower social classes to have high self-esteem, but the differences are not large, they are not the same for boys and girls, and they appear to be due in part to certain kinds of parent-child relationships. It seems likely that, among adolescents, subcultural norms, or other characteristic aspects of experience deriving from cultural factors, are more important than general social prestige as determinants of self-esteem.

It is important, however, to emphasize that the members of our sample are adolescents, not adults, and that their class, nationality, and religious statuses are ascribed, not achieved. In other words, in the adult world, differential occupational achievement, dominance or submission, power or impotence, prestige or disesteem, may influence one's self-esteem, whereas in the adolescent world, the reflected glory deriving from the occupational achievement of one's father may be less important. Nor does this mean that achievement is unimportant for the adolescent. On the contrary, a successful school record or successful interpersonal relationships are, as we shall see, definitely related to self-esteem. But these reflect the adolescent's own achievements, whereas his class, religion, and nationality are assigned to him by society; he has nothing to do with it.

The second point is that the individual need not necessarily accept the social evaluation of his worth as his personal definition of his worth; on the contrary, there is a wide variety of "coping mechanisms" that may be adopted in order to save one's self-esteem in the face of social disprivilege. For one thing, members of an ethnic group will often rank their own group higher than others rank it. Secondly, group members may tend to react to the disesteem in which they are held by interpreting this as an expression of the selfishness or pathology of the discriminator rather than as inadequacy in themselves. Third, a group member may compare himself with the nationals of his country of origin (or even of his parents), over whom he has considerable material superiority, rather than the still more highly prestigious groups in his present country of residence. Fourth, group members living in socially homogeneous neighborhoods are likely to confine their other associations to people of the same class or ethnic background; hence, their feelings of self-esteem may be based upon relative prestige within a class or ethnic group than between groups.

The third point is the following: When we deal with self-esteem, we are asking whether the individual considers himself adequate—a person of worth—not whether he considers himself superior to others. Implicated in such a feeling of adequacy is the relationship between one's standards and one's accomplishments; or, to quote the felicitous formula of William James, Self-Esteem $= \dfrac{\text{Success}}{\text{Pretensions}}$.[15] Thus,

[15] William James, *op. cit.*, p. 310.

a person who has modest goals and fulfills these may consider himself a perfectly worthwhile person. He will not deem himself superior to others, but he will be relatively satisfied with himself; such self-satisfaction would, in our study, be reflected in a high self-esteem score. Differential occupational goals might have similar consequences for self-esteem. It is reasonable to assume that a middle-class youth will be at least as uncertain about his ability to become a doctor as a working-class youth is about his ability to become a plumber.[16] Group-determined goals and standards, as well as accomplishments, must be considered in attempting to account for feelings of self-worth.

The most striking differences in self-esteem appear, then, not when we consider the factor of prestige rank in the broader society, but when we consider specific groups which probably represent distinctive subcultures. Such groups tend to be characterized by distinctive styles of life; they possess characteristic conceptions of right or wrong; they share certain patterns of values and systems of aspirations; very likely they show distinctive kinds of family life; they may well share characteristic child-rearing values and practices; their degree of group acceptance and integration may vary; their perspectives of human nature and of the nature of the world may differ; and so on. Such groups might be upper-class Jews, lower-class Catholics, German Protestants, Italian Catholics, Russian Jews, Polish Catholics, etc. It is in the comparisons among such groups that the most distinctive differences in self-esteem appear.

[16] This point is highlighted by some data brought to my attention by my colleague, Dr. Melvin Ember. In his study of nursing personnel in a mental hospital, he found that among attendants, who are the lowest ranking nursing personnel, Negroes had *higher* self-esteem than whites, according to our scale. In this Middle Atlantic city, the job of attendant is a relatively good position for a Negro but a very poor position for a white. Self-esteem may be more a matter of one's position within one group than the rank of the group in relation to other groups.

CHAPTER 4

THE DISSONANT RELIGIOUS CONTEXT

W E HAVE suggested that the prestige of a group in the broader society is not clearly related to the self-acceptance level of its adolescent members. Does this mean that minority group membership, with its notorious interpersonal consequences—prejudice, discrimination, social rejection, exclusion, and isolation—leaves no psychic scars on the adolescent? By no means. The effects of being socially defined and treated as a minority group member may be profound.

The apparent contradiction arises from the failure to specify the effective interpersonal environment of the individual. Particularly in childhood, when the fundamental structure of personality is being formed, a more important interpersonal environment than the total society is a tiny segment of it, namely, the neighborhood. For example, in the broader society a Protestant is considered a majority group member, whereas Catholics and Jews are considered minority group members. But take a Protestant family that moves into a neighborhood which is 90 percent Catholic. Who is then the minority group member? Can the Protestant child "discriminate against," "exclude," or "isolate" the Catholic children who outnumber him 9 to 1? In other words, it may be less important to ask: What is the prestige rank of the adolescent's membership group in the broader society? than to ask: Is there a discrepancy between, or concordance of, the individual's social characteristics and those of the population by which he is immediately surrounded? For example, it may be a very different experience for a white child to be raised in a Negro neighborhood than for a Negro child to be raised in the same neighborhood; for a Catholic child to be raised in a Protestant

64

neighborhood than for a Protestant child to be raised in the same neighborhood; for a middle-class child to be raised in a working-class neighborhood than for a working-class child to be reared in this social context. It is not simply the individual's social characteristics nor the social characteristics of those in the neighborhood in which he lives which are crucial, but the relationship between the two—their concordance or discordance—which is of central significance.[1]

In this chapter we will consider the religious composition of the neighborhood in which the child was reared. In order to examine this question, we gave our respondents the following instructions:

> This section deals with the neighborhood in which you grew up. If you lived in more than one neighborhood, think of the neighborhood in which you lived *longest.*
>
> Think back to the time when you were in grammar school. Generally speaking, what was the religious affiliation of most of the people in the neighborhood in which you lived?

[1] The influence of the individual's social context upon his attitudes and behavior has been pointed up in a number of recent sociological studies, e.g., Alan B. Wilson, "Residential Segregation of Social Classes and Aspirations of High School Boys," *American Sociological Review,* XXIV (1959), 836–845; Robert K. Merton and Alice S. Kitt, "Reference Group Behavior," in R. K. Merton and P. F. Lazarsfeld, eds., *Continuities in Social Research: Studies in the Scope and Method of "The American Soldier"* (Glencoe, Ill.: The Free Press, 1950), pp. 71ff.; Paul F. Lazarsfeld and Wagner Thielens, *The Academic Mind* (Glencoe, Ill.: The Free Press, 1958), *passim;* Leonard Pearlin and Morris Rosenberg, "Nurse-Patient Social Distance and the Structural Context of a Mental Hospital," *American Sociological Review,* XXVII, No. 1 (1962), 56–65. A methodological discussion of contextual analysis appears in Paul F. Lazarsfeld, "Problems in Methodology," in R. K. Merton, L. Broom, and L. S. Cottrell, Jr., eds., *Sociology Today* (New York: Basic Books, 1959), pp. 69–73.

Respondents were then asked to indicate, within broad categories, the approximate proportions of each religious group in these neighborhoods.[2] It was thus possible to compare those who were predominantly surrounded by co-religionists in childhood, those whose neighborhoods were about evenly divided between members of their own and another religion, and those who were in a distinct religious minority.

Table 1 suggests that the experience of living in a dissonant religious context has certain psychic consequences for the individual exposed to it. In every case, we see, students who have been raised in a dissonant social context are more likely than those who have been reared in a consonant or mixed [3] religious environment to manifest symptoms of psychic or emotional disturbance. For example, Catholics raised in non-Catholic neighborhoods are more likely than Catholics raised in predominantly Catholic or half-Catholic neighborhoods to have low self-esteem and to report many psychosomatic symptoms. Similarly, Protestants or Jews raised in dissonant social contexts are more

[2] Since it was assumed that respondents could only offer very general approximations of the religious compositions of their neighborhoods, they were asked to reply in terms of the following broad categories:

1. Almost all were _____.
   (religion)
2. About half were _____ and half were _____.
   (religion)   (religion)
3. About three-quarters were _____ and one-quarter were
                              (religion)

_____.
   (religion)

4. Other (Specify _____).

[3] "Consonant" means that almost all or about three-quarters of the people in the neighborhood were of the same religion as the respondent; "mixed" means that about one-half were of the same religion; and "dissonant" means that one-quarter or almost none were of the same religion.

TABLE 1

Contextual Dissonance and (a) Self-Esteem, (b) Psychosomatic Symptoms, by Religious Affiliation

	Catholics		Protestants		Jews	
Self-Esteem	In non-Catholic neighborhoods	In Catholic or mixed neighborhoods	In non-Protestant neighborhoods	In Protestant or mixed neighborhoods	In non-Jewish neighborhoods	In Jewish or mixed neighborhoods
Low	41%	29%	31%	25%	29%	18%
Medium	30	25	27	30	10	23
High	30	46	42	45	61	60
Total percent	100	100	100	100	100	100
(Number) ‡	(37)	(458)	(164)	(241)	(41)	(80)
Number of psychosomatic symptoms						
Many	65%	55%	54%	48%	55%	51%
Few	35	45	46	52	45	49
Total percent	100	100	100	100	100	100
(Number) ‡	(37)	(467)	(164)	(245)	(42)	(77)

‡ The differences in number of cases in the table are due to the fact that "no answers" have been omitted from the calculations. Most of the "no answers" have been so classified because they did not complete all the items in each scale or score because of lack of time.

67

likely than those reared in neighborhoods inhabited chiefly or equally by their co-religionists to manifest these signs of emotional disturbance.

The effect of the dissonant context does not appear to be a powerful one; many of the differences are quite small. While some of these differences are not statistically significant and some others are barely so, it is interesting to note that the results are all perfectly consistent. For all six comparisons made, those in the dissonant context are without exception more likely than others to manifest these symptoms of psychological disturbance.

It is important to note that there is no clear difference in emotional distress between those raised in neighborhoods inhabited almost exclusively by co-religionists and those reared in areas in which only about half the members are co-religionists. This result would suggest that whether everyone in the neighborhood is of one's group is less important than whether there are enough of them to give one social support, a feeling of belonging, a sense of acceptance. Thus, two groups may well look down upon one another, but each group may take pride in itself. Even if members of each group challenge and attack the other, every individual still has a large group with which he can identify. It is only when the individual is in the distinct minority, when it is impossible for him to restrict his associations to members of his own group, that the deleterious psychological consequences of the dissonant religious context become evident.

The Effect of Discrimination

The child who is isolated from his religious group thus tends to face his immediate environment without the sustenance of group support. It is not difficult to envision the experiences he might undergo. The nature of ethnocentrism is such that the majority group tends to define the minority outgroup member as different and inferior. Specifically, this may take the form of excluding the minority group member from participation in activities, taunting him, hurling derogatory epithets at him, or using the abundant variety of instruments of cruelty of which children are capable.

To examine this question, we asked our respondents: "When you were a child, were you ever teased, left out of things, or called names by other children because of . . . your religion?" Table 2 shows that within every religious group, students reared in the dissonant context are much more likely than those raised in a consonant or mixed context to say that they have experienced such taunting or exclusion on the basis of religious affiliation.

Such discrimination, we would expect, can hardly fail to have some effect upon the psychic state of the individual. And Table 3 shows that this is so. Within each religious group, those who report experiences of discrimination are more likely to have low self-esteem and many psychosomatic symptoms. This is true for all six comparisons made. The most conspicuous relationship is found between the experience of prejudice and the report of psychosomatic symptoms. This would suggest that the child who experiences prejudice is more likely to develop feelings of fear, anxiety, insecurity, and tension—a striking testimony to the penalty in human happiness and psychic well-being paid by the innocent and unwitting victims of prejudice.

We have seen that students raised in dissonant social contexts experience greater psychic disturbance than others, that such students are more likely to have experienced prejudice, and that those who have experienced prejudice are more likely to manifest such disturbance. This would suggest that one reason students in the dissonant context are more disturbed is that they have experienced such prejudice. In order to see whether this is so, we have examined the relationship of contextual dissonance to

TABLE 2

Dissonant Context and Subjection to Religious Discrimination, by Religious Affiliation

"When you were a child, were you ever teased, left out of things, or called names by other children because of your . . . religion?"	Catholics		Protestants		Jews	
	In non-Catholic neighbor-hoods	In Catholic or mixed neighbor-hoods	In non-Protestant neighbor-hoods	In Protestant or mixed neighbor-hoods	In non-Jewish neighbor-hoods	In Jewish or mixed neighbor-hoods
Ever ‡	22% *	5%	22% *	6% *	48% *	26%
Never	78	95	78	94	52	74
Total percent	100	100	100	100	100	100
(Number)	(37)	(454)	(162)	(238)	(42)	(78)

‡ "Ever" refers to those who answered "often," "sometimes," or "rarely."

TABLE 3

Experience of Prejudice and Self-Esteem and Psychosomatic Symptoms, by Religious Affiliation

	Catholics		Protestants		Jews	
	Experienced prejudice in childhood . . .					
Self-Esteem	Ever	Never	Ever	Never	Ever	Never
Low	35%	31%	37%	29%	24%	23%
Medium	40	26	26	26	20	18
High	25	43	37	45	55	59
Total percent	100	100	100	100	100	100
(Number)	(40)	(601)	(62)	(494)	(61)	(112)

Number of psychosomatic symptoms

	Catholics		Protestants		Jews	
Many	75% *	55%	64% *	48%	56%	45%
Few	25	45	36	52	44	55
Total percent	100	100	100	100	100	100
(Number)	(40)	(616)	(62)	(496)	(59)	(113)

psychic disturbance, controlling (i.e., standardizing) on experiences of prejudice. The results show that in five out of six cases, the relationship between contextual dissonance and emotional disturbance is reduced when prejudice experiences are controlled. The relationships do not, however, completely disappear.

The experience of discrimination thus appears to contribute to the psychological consequences of contextual dissonance but does not account for them completely. To be reared in a dissonant context thus reflects more than the experience of being taunted, ridiculed, attacked, or excluded on the basis of one's group affiliation. What is also probably involved is the insecurity which stems from lack of integration in a group, issuing from a feeling of social isolation, a sense of being "different," an absence of "belongingness." It is apparent why such experiences may be associated with an individual's level of self-acceptance as well as his feelings of anxiety.

Differential responsiveness to discrimination. While the data in Table 3 suggest that all the religious groups are emotionally responsive to the effects of prejudice, attention is drawn to the fact that they are not equally responsive to it. Specifically, it appears that Catholics and Protestants are more affected by the experience than Jews. Why the Jewish children, who, as Table 2 indicates, have experienced by far the most prejudice, should be least affected by it is not certain. Perhaps the prejudice against Jews in the society is so pervasive that its expression is taken for granted; perhaps Jewish children are taught early to expect such slights and to harden themselves against them; perhaps, since discrimination plays such a relatively large role in the lives of Jewish children, they may tend to react to it by attributing the fault to the discriminator rather than to themselves. Whatever the reason, our results suggest that the group which experiences the most prejudice is, in terms of our indicators of emotional disturbance, least affected by it, whereas the group which, in our sample, experiences the least prejudice is most affected by it. Many of the most serious victims of prejudice, then, are those in the majority group.

Contextual Specification

Given the fact that children reared in a dissonant religious context are more likely to suffer the pangs of self-contempt and to experience various psychosomatic manifestations of anxiety, the question arises: Are certain dissonant contexts more prejudicial to the individual's psychic well-being than others? Perhaps Catholics living in

Protestant neighborhoods are less affected by their minority group position than Catholics in Jewish neighborhoods. Perhaps Jews in Protestant neighborhoods are less affected than Jews in Catholic neighborhoods. In other words, while we have seen that the dissonant religious context appears to have a bearing upon one's psychic and emotional state, it may be that certain contexts are "more dissonant" than others.

Considering only those students who have been reared in a dissonant religious context, we have compared the levels of self-esteem and anxiety of members of each religious group reared in neighborhoods occupied chiefly by members of the other two religious groups. Table 4 suggests the following: (1) that Catholics in Jewish areas have lower self-esteem than Catholics in Protestant areas; (2) that Protestants in Jewish areas have lower self-esteem

TABLE 4

Psychic States of Students in Different Religious Contexts

	Catholics in predominantly ...		Protestants in predominantly ...		Jews in predominantly ...	
Self-Esteem	Protestant areas	Jewish areas	Catholic areas	Jewish areas	Protestant areas	Catholic areas
Low or medium	68%	75%	58%	78%	20%	45%
High	32	25	42	22	80	55
Total percent	100	100	100	100	100	100
(Number)	(28)	(8)	(149)	(9)	(10)	(20)
Number of psychosomatic symptoms						
Many	68%	62%	56%	62%	55%	60%
Few	32	38	44	38	45	40
Total percent	100	100	100	100	100	100
(Number)	(28)	(8)	(150)	(8)	(11)	(20)

than Protestants in Catholic areas; and (3) that Jews in Catholic areas have lower self-esteem than Jews in Protestant areas. With one exception, the same holds true for psychosomatic symptoms. Since we are dealing only with those in dissonant contexts, the number of cases is small and the results therefore cannot be considered reliable.[4] Further studies utilizing a larger number of cases would be required to strengthen these conclusions. In light of the general consistency of the data, however, these results appear to warrant further analysis.

Though we lack sufficient cases for statistical adequacy, there is another way of approaching the problem. If some principle can be enunciated which is consistent with these findings, it would increase our confidence that the observed differences are real and meaningful. The principle we propose to account for these findings is the concept of cultural similarity or dissimilarity. We will suggest that if an individual lives in a culturally dissimilar neighborhood, then this context is "more dissonant" than if he lives in a culturally similar neighborhood.

Cultural Similarity

The question of cultural similarity is complex. In gross terms, of course, it is obvious that American and British

[4] It may be noted that there are discrepancies in the total number of cases classified as "dissonant" in Table 1 and Table 4, particularly among the Jewish respondents. One reason is that a number of respondents reported that they grew up in "Christian" neighborhoods. Jewish students who gave this reply were classified in Table 1 as growing up in non-Jewish neighborhoods, but it was not possible to determine whether these neighborhoods were Catholic or Protestant. Hence, these cases have been omitted from Table 4. Another reason is that in Table 4 we are dealing with those who grew up in *predominantly* (all or three-quarters) Catholic, Protestant, or Jewish neighborhoods. We have thus omitted, for example, Catholics reared in approximately half Protestant-half Jewish neighborhoods; Protestants reared in half Catholic-half Jewish neighborhoods; and Jews reared in half Catholic-half Protestant neighborhoods.

societies have more cultural elements in common than, say, American and Chinese societies. If one were to make a more detailed comparison of two cultures, however, one would have to compare their traditions, customs, mores, values, perspectives, philosophies, art, technology, goals, ideals, etc. Given our limited data, such comparisons are manifestly impossible. We have, however, selected one area which would generally be considered culturally relevant—the area of values.

If we consider a value to be "a conception of the desirable which influences the selection from available modes, means, and ends of action," [5] then there are four areas in our study which appear to fit this description: (1) Self-values—which traits, qualities, or characteristics does the individual consider important in judging himself? (2) Maternal values—for what types of behavior was the individual most likely to gain the approval of his mother? (3) Paternal values—for what types of behavior was the individual most likely to gain the approval of his father? (4) Occupational values—what satisfactions, gratifications, or rewards is the individual most concerned with obtaining from his life's work? [6]

A simple procedure for comparing the similarity of religious groups was employed. With regard to each item, we

[5] Clyde Kluckhohn, et al., "Values and Value-Orientations in the Theory of Action," in T. Parsons and E. A. Shils, eds., *Toward A General Theory of Action*, Cambridge, Mass.: Harvard Univ. Press, 1954, p. 395.

[6] Self-values included such items as: ambitious; clear-thinking or clever; hard-working or conscientious; dependable and reliable. Parental values were measured by asking whether mothers and fathers were most likely to approve of the child for being strong and aggressive; for doing well in school; for getting along with other children; etc. Occupational values dealt with whether the individual was most concerned with using his abilities at his work; gaining status and prestige; having the opportunity to be creative and original; etc. The list of occupational values is drawn from Morris Rosenberg, *Occupations and Values*, Glencoe, Ill.: The Free Press, 1957, pp. 141–142.

asked whether the proportion of Catholics choosing the item was closer to the proportion of Protestants choosing it or to the proportion of Jews; whether the proportion of Protestants choosing it was more similar to the proportion of Catholics or of Jews; and whether the proportion of Jews choosing it was more similar to the proportion of Protestants or of Catholics. This involved 44 comparisons of self-values, 5 comparisons of maternal values, 6 comparisons of paternal values, and 6 comparisons of occupational values.

Table 5 indicates that in each of the four value areas under consideration, Catholics were more often similar to Protestants than they were to Jews; Protestants were more often similar to Catholics than they were to Jews; and Jews were more often similar to Protestants than they were to Catholics.

Of course we cannot be certain that similar results would appear if other areas of culture were considered. Assuming, however, that these are reasonable indicators of cultural similarity, this would mean that some contexts are "more dissonant" than others in the manner specified.

Given these results, we can now return to our earlier discussion of varying dissonant contexts. As we noted in Table 4, Catholics in Protestant areas generally showed less disturbance than Catholics in Jewish areas; Protestants in Catholic areas showed less disturbance than Protestants in Jewish areas; and Jews in Protestant areas showed less disturbance than Jews in Catholic areas. In each of these three comparisons, those who were reared in a "more dissonant" religious context appeared to experience greater disturbance than those reared in a "less dissonant" context. These results would suggest that it may not only be a question of whether the context is dissonant, but how dissonant it is, which has implications for mental health.

It is obvious, of course, that, given the small number of cases in this section of the report and the breadth of the concepts involved, one can only advance such a generaliza-

TABLE 5

Comparisons of Cultural Similarity or Dissimilarity

| | Number of comparisons | | | |
	Forty-four self-values	Five maternal values	Six paternal values	Six occupational values
Catholics more similar to Protestants	27	5	6	4
Catholics more similar to Jews	11	—	—	2
Equal	6	—	—	—
Number of comparisons	44	5	6	6
Protestants more similar to Catholics	29	3	4	4
Protestants more similar to Jews	12	1	1	2
Equal	3	1	1	—
Number of comparisons	44	5	6	6
Jews more similar to Protestants	22	4	2	4
Jews more similar to Catholics	15	1	1	2
Equal	7	—	3	—
Number of comparisons	44	5	6	6

tion with the utmost tentativeness. It can only be stated that the results are consistent with such a conclusion. Further studies utilizing more adequate samples and other indicators of cultural similarity would be required to support or falsify this conclusion.

Discussion

We have seen that children raised in dissonant religious contexts are in subsequent years more likely to manifest disturbances in self-esteem and to report psychophysiological symptoms. Our data do not suggest that the dissonant social context is a powerful factor in producing these signs of emotional disturbance, but the consistency of the results suggests that it may be a real factor. We doubt whether the dissonant context often produces these psychological consequences independently of other factors. Rather, we would be inclined to assume that its main influence is exercised upon those already predisposed to psychological disturbance; those standing near the cliff are pushed ever closer to it or actually over it. The child who is uncertain about his worth becomes all the more doubtful when others define him as different and inferior; the child who is tense becomes all the more tense when threatened by others. But if these predispositions did not exist, it is doubtful whether the dissonant religious context per se would be powerful enough to generate such consequences.

Let us, however, attempt to spell out in greater detail how the dissonant social context might exercise its influence on self-esteem. Our data have suggested that children raised in a dissonant religious context have lower self-esteem than those raised in a consonant context, and that the more dissonant the context, the smaller the proportion who accept themselves. One factor which undoubtedly plays a role is prejudice in its direct and unabashed form. Thus, children who have been raised in a dissonant context are far more likely than others to report that they have been teased, called names, or left out of things because of their religion, and those who have had such experiences are less likely to accept themselves. It may be that this effect is intensified the more dissimilar the individual's group affiliation and that of his neighborhood. To be taunted, jeered at, or rejected by one's peers might well be expected to leave its imprint upon the individual's picture of himself.

But it is probably more than simple prejudice, narrowly

conceived as hostility to members of a group, which is responsible for these results. Beyond this, actual cultural dissimilarity may produce rejection. It is characteristic of cultural groups that they tend to feel united on the basis of shared norms, values, interests, attitudes, perspectives, goals, etc. Ease of communication and a sense of solidarity spring directly from such similarity of thought and feelings. The likelihood that an individual will be accepted into the group is thus a question not only of whether he is socially defined as different by virtue of his group membership, but also of whether he actually is different—in interests, values, "personality" traits—by virtue of the fact that he has, perhaps through his parents and relatives, absorbed the values of his own membership group. For example, a Jewish child may learn from his parents, relatives, etc., that it is extremely important to be a good student in school. If he is raised in a Catholic neighborhood, where, according to our data,[7] less stress is placed upon this quality, then he may be scorned by his peers as a "grind," an "eager beaver," and an "apple polisher." At the same time he may place little value on being "tough," a "good fighter"; these qualities, more highly valued in the group by which he is surrounded, may give him the reputation of being a "sissy." If cultural dissimilarity does have such an effect, then it is likely that the greater the cultural dissimilarity, the greater the effect.

The point, then, is that qualities which may be accepted or admired in one's own group may be rejected by members of another group. Hence, there is a real likelihood that one will feel different when in a dissonant social context, and this sense of difference may lead the individual to question himself, doubt himself, wonder whether he is unworthy.

The same factors may operate to generate anxiety. In

[7] See Chapter 13.

79

Chapter 8, we shall attempt to indicate how a negative self-picture may generate anxiety. It is thus possible that the relationship between the dissonant context and anxiety may be in part mediated through its influence on the self-picture. In addition, the tension generated by prejudice, the threat of attack, the lack of social support, the feeling of isolation, the possible feeling of helplessness could all be expected to contribute to anxiety among those predisposed in that direction.

It is also possible that the effect of contextual dissonance may be heightened by living in a neighborhood chiefly inhabited by people who are, in the broader society, defined as a minority group. To be an "outsider" in a predominantly Catholic or Jewish neighborhood appears to be associated with greater emotional disturbance than to be an "outsider" in a Protestant neighborhood. It is thus possible that Catholics and Jews, defined as "minority groups" in the broader society, develop stronger religious solidarity within their own neighborhoods. Hence, the youngster who lives in a neighborhood chiefly inhabited by members of such solidary religious groups, but who is himself not a member of the group, may experience particularly strong feelings of isolation.

These findings may shed some light on the results of the previous chapter, viz., the absence of a clear relationship between the social prestige of a group and the self-esteem of its members. Groups are, indeed, differentially evaluated in the broader society, but, for the child, a more effective interpersonal environment is the neighborhood. But the social composition of a neighborhood is largely determined by the pattern of ecological segregation; in other words, members of different classes, races, religions, and nationalities tend to live near one another. For the child, acceptance or rejection within the neighborhood may be more important than acceptance or rejection within the broader society. Since, in general, minority group members are probably as likely to band together as majority group members, the minority group child may receive as much social support and acceptance as the majority group child. This may be one reason why, for the child, the prestige of his membership groups in the broader society may have relatively slight effect upon his level of self-acceptance.

PART III
IN THE FAMILY

CHAPTER 5

THE BROKEN FAMILY

THUS far we have considered the relationship of various "secondary groups"—social classes, religious groups, nationality groups—to the individual's self-conception. In the present chapter, and in the two succeeding ones, we turn to one of the child's crucial primary groups—his family. What is the significance of family structure, sibling position, and parental behavior for the child's self-esteem and anxiety levels?

Among the important problems besetting modern society is that of the high frequency of marital rupture, whether expressed in divorce, separation, or separation by death. Family breakup may result from problems of the parents, but it generates problems in the child. It is a common observation that delinquency and emotional disturbance often appear among children from such broken families.

Do children from broken families differ from others in terms of self-esteem and psychosomatic symptoms of anxiety? Let us first consider self-esteem. Table 1 indicates that a somewhat larger proportion of children of divorced or separated parents had low self-esteem than those whose families were intact. Children of separated parents were as likely as children of intact families to have high self-esteem, but were less likely to have medium self-esteem and more likely to have low self-esteem.[1] As a group, children whose parents had been separated by death did not differ much

[1] In this analysis, the children of parents who have been separated at times offer responses similar to those of children from intact families and at other times offer responses similar to those of children from broken families. Because of the limited number of cases available and the inadequacy of the ancillary data, the present investigator has been unable to detect any consistent pattern in their responses.

TABLE 1

Marital Status of Parents and (a)* Self-Esteem, (b)* Psychosomatic Symptoms

	Marital status of natural parents			
Self-Esteem	Living together	Divorced	Separated	Separated by death
High	45%	38%	46%	42%
Medium	25	25	16	27
Low	29	37	38	32
Total percent	100	100	100	100
(Number)	(3871)	(268)	(146)	(402)
Number of psychosomatic symptoms				
Few	52%	34%	44%	45%
Intermediate	15	15	15	18
Many	33	50	40	37
Total percent	100	100	100	100
(Number)	(2670)	(169)	(104)	(270)

from those of intact families. In terms of self-esteem, marital rupture does appear to have some effect, but the differences are generally small.

Marital rupture does, however, appear to be more strongly associated with physiological symptoms of anxiety. Children of divorce, for example, are 18 percent more likely than children from intact families to report four or more psychosomatic symptoms. These results suggest the possibility that divorce, in terms of broad effects, may more conspicuously influence level of anxiety than level of self-esteem.

There is, in fact, good reason for expecting this to be the case. If one's parents are so incompatible that the marriage ends in divorce; if one's mother must struggle to make ends meet without the aid of a husband; if one must undergo the often difficult process of adjustment to a stepparent—these are conditions generating stress, tension, and anxiety but they do not directly challenge the worth of the child. His merit or inadequacy, his virtue or vice, have nothing to do with it.

At the same time, the child's self-esteem becomes entangled in the family rupture in various ways. On the simplest level, of course, the social stigma of divorce may produce a reputation of being strange or different and, to some extent, inferior. Secondly, it is likely that if parental disharmony prevails before the divorce then the parents may well take out their aggression on the child. They may be irritated with him, cold, sarcastic, impatient, caustic, discouraging, contemptuous, or indifferent; such behavior is almost certain to enhance the child's feeling of worthlessness. Finally, the clinical and theoretical work of Horney suggests that early fundamental anxiety in the child will tend ultimately to issue in feelings of self-contempt.[2] (Her theory is discussed later.) Perhaps the surprising thing is not that children of divorce have somewhat lower self-esteem than children from intact families, but that the differences in self-esteem are not still larger.

Do these relatively small differences thus indicate that the broken home has only a minor bearing on the self-esteem of the child? While such a conclusion is in general justified, it is at the same time misleading in the sense that it fails to specify the conditions—and we use this term broadly—under which the marital rupture occurs. Under certain conditions, as we shall see, family breakup is strongly related to self-esteem; under other conditions, it appears to make no difference at all.

Upon what does the effect of the broken family depend?

[2] Karen Horney, *Neurosis and Human Growth*, New York: Norton, 1950.

It depends, first, on *who* has been divorced or widowed; it depends, second, on *when* they were divorced or widowed; and it depends, third, on *what happened after* they were divorced or widowed.

Religion and Divorce

It is a matter of common knowledge that religious groups differ in their attitudes toward divorce. It is thus reasonable to assume that divorce in a Catholic family may represent an experience which is different in nature and intensity from divorce in a Protestant family. For one thing, Catholics in our sample are less likely to be children of divorce than Protestants. In our sample, Jews are even less likely than Catholics to report divorce. It seems likely that divorce among Catholics and Jews occurs in the face of stronger group opposition than divorce among Protestants. It is thus interesting to observe that Catholic and Jewish children of divorce are more likely to have low self-esteem than Catholics and Jews from intact families, but divorce makes almost no difference among Protestant families. (Table 2) Similarly, Catholic and Jewish children of divorce are considerably more likely than their co-religionists from intact families to have many (6 or more) psychosomatic symptoms, whereas this is distinctly less true of Protestants.

The experience of divorce is thus more strongly related to signs of psychic or emotional disturbance among Catholic and Jewish children than among Protestant children. The reasons are hardly obscure. The Catholic Church, of course, rigidly proscribes divorce, and the practice is strongly opposed to the Jewish cultural tradition.

If Catholic and Jewish norms are more strictly opposed to divorce than Protestant norms, then at least three points may be considered: (1) One may perhaps assume that, on the average, the degree of parental disharmony necessary to produce divorce is greater in Catholic or Jewish than in Protestant families. If this is so, then Catholic and

TABLE 2

Divorce and Self-Esteem and Psychosomatic Symptoms, by Religion

Self-Esteem	Catholics		Jews		Protestants	
	Divorced	Intact	Divorced	Intact	Divorced	Intact
High	36%	44%	44%	54%	40%	44%
Medium	24	26	17	24	26	25
Low	40 *	30	39	21	34	32
Total percent	100	100	100	100	100	100
(Number)	(90)	(1583)	(18)	(514)	(112)	(1391)

Number of psychosomatic symptoms

2 or less	27%	49%	30%	56%	42%	53%
3–5	40	36	50	34	41	35
6 or more	33 *	15	20	10	16	12
Total percent	100	100	100	100	100	100
(Number)	(52)	(1097)	(10)	(352)	(73)	(966)

Jewish children of divorce have on the average probably experienced more hectic and anxiety-ridden family lives than Protestant children of divorce. (2) Since divorce in Catholic and Jewish families must be undertaken in opposition to greater social pressure, it may represent a more shocking, a more emotionally violent, experience both for the parents and for the child, thus contributing to emotional disturbance. (3) Since the Catholic and Jewish group norms are more firmly opposed to divorce, the social stigma of divorce is probably greater among Catholics and Jews than among Protestants; hence, the Catholic or Jewish child, already anxiety-ridden by the tension experienced in the home, may be reinforced in his feeling of being different, and less worthy, by the horrified reaction of members of the extended family and by neighborhood co-religionists.

89

But the question may be raised: Perhaps it is not divorce as such which is responsible for the results; perhaps it is due to the fact that Jewish and Catholic adolescents react more negatively to *any* family breakup.

The most obvious way to check this point is to compare Jewish and Catholic children whose families have been broken by death. While we have seen that Jewish and Catholic children of divorce manifest more emotional disturbance than Protestant children of divorce, Table 3 indi-

TABLE 3

Emotional Disturbance of Catholic-Jewish and Protestant Children Whose Families Have Been Broken by Death

	Catholics or Jews	Protestants
Low self-esteem	32%	33%
(Number)	(214)	(141)
Many psychosomatic symptoms		
(more than 3)	36%	39%
(Number)	(144)	(97)

cates that there is no clear difference between these groups if the families have been broken by death. It is, then, not simply family breakup in general, but divorce in particular, that is most closely associated with emotional disturbances among Catholics and Jews.

The Young Divorcee

Just as the significance of marital rupture depends on whose family has been broken, so does it also depend on when the marriage was dissolved. In general, our data suggest that if a woman has married early, has had a child shortly thereafter, and has been divorced a short time later, then her child will have a greater tendency to manifest emotional disturbance. If, on the other hand, both she and her child were older at the time of the marital rupture, then the child's psychological state tends to be just about normal.

While we do not have exact information on the mother's age at the time of the marital rupture, we can approximate her age in the following way: We know approximately how old the mother is now, how old the child is now, and how old the child was at the time of the divorce. Through simple calculation we can determine how long ago the divorce took place and how old the mother was at the time of the divorce.

Table 4 indicates that if the mother was 23 years or less at the time of the divorce, then 22 percent of the children

TABLE 4

Mother's Age When Divorced and Child's Present Psychological State

Child's present self-esteem	Mother's age when divorced		
	23 or under	24–31	32 or over
High	22%	39%	43%
Medium	29	22	27
Low	48	39	29
Total percent	100	100	100
(Number)	(31)	(111)	(106)

* 23 and under vs. 24 and over: Proportion "High."

Number of psychosomatic symptoms			
3 or less	39%	49%	54%
4	6	13	24
5 or more	56	38	22
Total percent	100	100	100
(Number)	(18)	(69)	(68)

have high self-esteem; if she was between 24–31 years old, the proportion is 39 percent; and if she was 32 years or more, the proportion is 43 percent.[3] Similarly, the younger the mother at the time of the divorce, the more frequently did the children report having many psychosomatic symptoms.

Now, as we might expect, the children of young divorcees were also very young at the time of the divorce. Specifically, seven-eighths of these children were three years or less when their mothers and fathers parted. It thus seems to be that a particular combination of life circumstances— a very young divorced mother with a very young child—is especially conducive to the development of emotional disturbance in the child.

But which factor is really crucial in these results? Is the truly decisive factor the child's age at the time of the divorce? It may be that the very young child is extremely impressionable at this time of life and that the turmoil of divorce may have a traumatic effect upon him from which he may not fully recover.

This explanation, it turns out, is not sufficient in itself. Table 5 shows that there is some tendency for children who were young at the time of the divorce to be less likely to have high self-esteem, but the differences are not very large and the trend is somewhat uneven. More to the point, however, is the question: Among all children who were three years or less at the time of the divorce, are those whose mothers were very young more likely to develop low self-esteem than those whose mothers were more mature?

---

[3] It may be asked: Who are these people who experienced early divorce? Our data indicate that they are more likely to be urban, Catholic, women. There is no indication, however, that these characteristics are responsible for the observed differences. Wherever there is a sufficient number of cases available for comparison, children whose mothers were older at the time of the divorce were more likely to have high self-esteem than children whose mothers were younger.

TABLE 5

Child's Age at the Time of Divorce and Present Self-Esteem

| | Child's age at time of divorce | | | |
Self-Esteem	3 years or less	4–6 years	7–9 years	10 years or more
High	33%	43%	38%	43%
Medium	28	24	21	22
Low	39	33	40	35
Total percent	100	100	100	100
(Number)	(103)	(51)	(47)	(60)

Table 6 suggests that this is so. About one-fourth of the children of the very young group, one-third of the intermediate group, and one-half of the more mature group

TABLE 6

Mother's Age at Time of Divorce and Child's Present Self-Esteem, among Children Who Were Very Young at Time of Divorce

| | Children who were 3 years or less at time of divorce | | |
Child's present self-esteem	Mothers 23 years or less at time of divorce	Mothers 24–31 years at time of divorce	Mothers 32 years or over at time of divorce
High	26%	35%	50%
Medium	30	30	25
Low	44	35	25
Total percent	100	100	100
(Number)	(27)	(57)	(12)

had high self-esteem. It is, then, not simply the tender age of the child which is important.

Still another factor must be considered: perhaps these results stem from the fact that these very young divorcees were also very early brides. It is possible that a girl who marries very early tends to be an unstable person or that, because of her youth, she is simply less able to deal with a home or children. It might then not be the divorce as such but the early age of marriage which is at the heart of the matter.

Since we do not know the mother's age at marriage, we must again approach the matter indirectly. Let us consider those mothers whose present age is 37 years or less. Older mothers will not be considered, since we cannot tell which of them were married early and which were married later. But we can be certain that if a woman is now 37 years or less and has a child who is a high school junior or senior (probably between 16 and 18 years old) then this woman married early; probably the majority of these women were in their late teens at the time of the marriage.

If we consider only these young mothers, we find that children's self-esteem is substantially lower if the mother has been divorced than if she has not. Among children of very young women, 53 percent of the children of divorce, but only 33 percent of the children from intact families, had low self-esteem. (Table 7) Indeed, if the woman is now young, married early, had a child soon thereafter, and was soon divorced, the children are twice as likely as average to have low self-esteem. To know that the student's mother is now very young and has been divorced is, in fact, one of the strongest predictors of low self-esteem. Among women with comparable careers who were not divorced, however, the child's self-esteem is practically normal.

We thus see that it is not simply a question of whether

94

TABLE 7

Maternal Divorce and Child's Self-Esteem among
Mothers Who Are Currently Very Young

Child's self-esteem	Mother currently 37 years or younger		
	Divorced		Family not broken
High	27%	✿	44%
Medium	20		23
Low	53		33
Total percent	100		100
(Number)	(55)		(276)

TABLE 8

Mother's and Child's Age at Time of Divorce and
Child's Present Self-Esteem

Self-Esteem	At time of divorce . . .		
	Mother and child both relatively young ‡	Mother and child both relatively mature ‡‡	All others
High	22% ✿	42%	41%
Medium	29	26	24
Low	48	32	35
Total percent	100	100	100
(Number)	(31)	(77)	(140)

‡ Mother 23 years or less and child 6 years or less.
‡‡ Mother 32 years or more and child 7 years or more.

TABLE 9

Mother's Age When Widowed and Child's Present Psychological State

Child's present self-esteem	Mother's age when widowed ‡		
	27 or under	28–34 years	40 or over
High	23%	42%	50%
Medium	50	20	26
Low	27	38	24
Total percent	100	100	100
(Number)	(22)	(45)	(42)

* 27 and under vs. 28 and over: Proportion "High."

Number of psychosomatic symptoms			
3 or less	58%	61%	73%
4	25	25	10
5 or more	17	14	17
Total percent	100	100	100
(Number)	(12)	(28)	(30)

‡ In order to obtain an adequate number of cases for analysis, it has been necessary to use different age cutting points when considering divorcees and widows. The reason is that the average age of widowhood is considerably higher than the average age of divorce.

the mother has been divorced that is crucial; under certain conditions, e.g., older mothers and older children, self-esteem is fairly normal. (Table 8) Similarly, it is not a question of whether the child was very young when the marriage broke up or that the mother married very early. It is, apparently, under a special combination of circumstances—when the mother married early, quickly had a child, and shortly thereafter was divorced—that low self-esteem is especially likely to develop in the child.

96

When we turn from families broken by divorce to those broken by death, somewhat similar results appear, but the differences are less striking. Students whose mothers were relatively young when they were widowed are less likely to have high self-esteem and to be free of psychosomatic symptoms of anxiety. (Table 9) At the same time, they are not conspicuously poorly adjusted, tending, rather, to be in the intermediate category. Similarly, children of widows who are now young are less likely than others to have high self-esteem. (Table 10)

There is little doubt that early divorce or widowhood which leaves the mother with one or more very young children tends to place the mother in a difficult situation. In addition to running the house, caring for the children, etc., she is faced with serious financial problems in the absence of a husband. The mother who feels insecure, anxious, irritable, and frustrated under such circumstances is certain to affect the emotional development of her children. If the woman is older and better capable of handling these

TABLE 10

Present Age of Widow and Child's Self-Esteem

Child's self-esteem	Mother's present age		
	37 or less ‡	38–47	48 or over
High	15%	43%	48%
Medium	45	24	25
Low	40	32	27
Total percent	100	100	100
(Number)	(20)	(145)	(122)

* 37 or under vs. 38 or over: Proportion "High."

‡ The number of mothers who are 37 years or less is too small to permit comparisons of psychosomatic symptoms.

problems, the effect upon the children would in general be less deleterious than if she were younger and more likely to succumb to the strain.

One factor which might operate in favor of the young divorcee or young widow is the greater likelihood of remarriage. And, indeed, our data show that the remarriage rates of these women are relatively high. Even if these women do remarry, however, the self-esteem of their children remains relatively low. Instead of attempting to explain this finding at this point, however, let us turn to the more general question: What is the association between parental remarriage and the child's psychological and emotional development?

Remarriage

Thus far we have asked: To whom does the marital breakup occur and when does it occur? The third question we wish to consider is: What happens after the divorce or death? Is the family reconstituted through remarriage or does it remain a truncated nuclear unit? Let us first consider those children whose parents had been divorced and whose mothers later remarried. (In almost all cases of divorce the children remained with the mother.) What is the association between such remarriage and the child's self-esteem?

Table 11 indicates that children whose mothers remarried tended to have lower self-esteem than those whose mothers did not remarry. We find that 46 percent of the children of divorce who acquired stepfathers had low self-esteem compared with 34 percent of those whose parents did not remarry. Similar results appear when we consider psychosomatic symptoms. It is somewhat surprising to find that parental remarriage, rather than helping the psychological adjustment of the child, is associated with lower self-esteem and greater anxiety.

Now let us consider the case of parental death. As in the

TABLE 11

Self-Esteem of Children and Divorce and Remarriage of Mothers

Self-Esteem of child	Parents divorced, mother remarried	Parents divorced, mother did not remarry	Parents never divorced or separated
High	32%	40%	46%
Medium	22	26	25
Low	46	34	28
Total percent	100	100	100
(Number)	(134)	(92)	(3533)

Number of psychosomatic symptoms

	Parents divorced, mother remarried	Parents divorced, mother did not remarry	Parents never divorced or separated
2 or less	33%	41%	52%
3–4	31	39	27
5 or more	36	20	21
Total percent	100	100	100
(Number)	(86)	(49)	(2439)

case of divorce, we find, the self-esteem level of children tends to be lower if their parents remarried than if they did not. Table 12 shows that if the surviving parent remarried 34 percent have high self-esteem, whereas if the parent did not remarry 46 percent of the children had high self-esteem. This latter group's self-esteem, in fact, is just as high as that of children from intact families.

But does it make a difference to the child's self-esteem whether the father has died and the mother remarried or whether the mother has died and the father remarried? Table 13 suggests that self-esteem appears to be somewhat lower if the mother has died than if the father has died, although the differences are not very large. Similarly the

TABLE 12

Remarriage of Widowed Parents and Child's Self-Esteem

| Self-Esteem | Parent died and surviving spouse . . . | | Parent never divorced or widowed |
	Remarried	Did not remarry	
High	34% *	46%	46%
Medium	27	24	25
Low	39	30	28
Total percent	100	100	100
(Number)	(128)	(223)	(3533)

differences in psychosomatic symptoms between those who acquired stepmothers or stepfathers is small; if they acquired either stepparent, however, then they were clearly more likely to show more anxiety than if their parents did not remarry.

It may be noted that the negative association between remarriage and self-esteem is not simply a reflection of the age of the mother or of the child at the time the marriage was dissolved. Among mothers of equal age or children of equal age, higher self-esteem appears among children whose mothers did not remarry.

These results are surprising since, by and large, one would assume that a surrogate parent is better than no parent at all and that the restoration of an approximation to a normal family life would be better than the abnormality of having but a single parent. A father—even if he is not the biological father—can give the child someone to lean on, to depend on, to turn to for advice and support. He can reduce the sense of strangeness, of difference, which may haunt the child without a father. He can help restore the sense of "normality" which is often conducive to calm self-

TABLE 13

Self-Esteem of Children Whose Families
Have Been Separated by Death

Self-Esteem of child	Acquired step-father	Acquired step-mother	Parent did not remarry	Parents never divorced or separated
High	36%	30%	46%	46%
Medium	28	27	24	25
Low	36	43	30	28
Total percent	100	100	100	100
(Number)	(72)	(56)	(223)	(3533)

* Acquired stepparents vs. parent did not remarry: Proportion "High."

Number of psychosomatic symptoms

	Acquired step-father	Acquired step-mother	Parent did not remarry	Parents never divorced or separated
2 or less	39%	37%	51%	52%
3–4	39	37	29	27
5 or more	23	27	20	21
Total percent	100	100	100	100
(Number)	(45)	(41)	(148)	(2439)

*Acquired stepparents vs. parent did not remarry: Proportion "High."

acceptance. Finally, he can reduce anxiety in the family by his monetary support, thus partly freeing the mother from economic burdens and cares and enabling her to devote a normal amount of time and attention to the children. One would certainly expect the child's self-esteem to respond favorably to these happy circumstances.

But let us consider the matter from another viewpoint. When the father is removed from the family, either through divorce or death, what happens to the mother and child? It is a common observation that when people are faced by a common problem or difficulty, they tend to draw more closely together. They "huddle together for warmth." Both mother and child must share the responsibilities which would ordinarily be assumed by the husband. If the child is old enough, he may be called upon to help financially. If not, his tasks around the house are likely to increase as he seeks in part to relieve his mother of the additional burdens she must face.

The broken family is thus likely to make mother and child more dependent upon one another. The mother must depend upon the child for emotional support and other kinds of help. The child is dependent on the mother for the encouragement, affection, and guidance which both a mother and father can provide. The mother's life thus comes to focus more centrally on the child; he may be a burden, but he is of supreme importance to her. The bond of mother and child is cemented by their common plight.

Then the mother remarries. Conditions of life become easier for both. The point is, however, that the mother's interest shifts, at least in part, to her new husband—to his interests, his needs, his desires. In addition, if, as is often the case, the husband has children from a previous marriage, then the mother devotes part of her attention to her stepchildren.

The child may still retain the affection of his mother, but he is no longer the exclusive center of her universe. She becomes less dependent upon him for emotional and physical support, less involved in his needs. He is now one among several in whom she is interested. To become less important to his mother is likely to diminish the child's feeling of significance.

We also noted above that, in the fatherless family, the child must often assume responsibility for tasks which are not required of a child his age. He may take pride in the fact that he can master these tasks successfully and that his mother is dependent upon his efforts. With remarriage, he is relieved of some of these burdens, for now the mother and father can share these tasks. At the same time his feeling of worth may decrease, for he can no longer take such special pride in these accomplishments. Life may be easier for him, but he may feel meaner, smaller, less significant in this new world created by his mother's remarriage.

Finally, remarriage may require a fairly fundamental readjustment on the part of the child. In the case of a family broken by death, the child may consider it a betrayal of the memory of the departed parent for the widow to remarry. It is not unusual in such cases for the child to feel resentful, if not bitter, toward both the mother and the stepfather. But even without this reaction, the child must still face the difficulty of adjusting to a new parent and perhaps new stepbrothers and stepsisters—in short, to the complex web of relationships which are involved in a new family structure. Inevitably this will contribute to his feelings of anxiety and call into question his picture of himself.

If such difficulties of adjustment do occur, then one might go one step farther to suggest that the longer the child has had a "normal" family life, i.e., the longer he has lived in an intact family, the more difficult will it be for him to adjust to the "new" family resulting from remarriage. If difficulty of adjustment is related to the child's psychological state, then we might advance the following hypothesis: the longer the child has lived in an intact family, the more adversely affected will he be by remarriage. In order to examine this question, we asked our subjects how old they were at the time their families were broken.

Let us compare those children who were 10 years or older when the marriage was dissolved with those children who were 3 years or younger. Among the older group, Table 14 shows, those who acquired stepfathers were 15

TABLE 14

Divorce or Widowhood, Remarriage and Child's Self-Esteem,
by Child's Age at Time of Family Break-up

| | Child's age at time of divorce or death | | | | | |
| | 3 years or less | | 4–9 years | | 10 years or more | |
Self-Esteem	Re-married	Not re-married	Re-married	Not re-married	Re-married	Not re-married
High	32%	37%	33%	46%	32%	49%
Medium	32	27	19	21	27	26
Low	35	37	48	32	41	26
Total percent	100	100	100	100	100	100
(Number)	(71)	(41)	(64)	(56)	(37)	(78)

percent more likely than those who did not acquire stepfathers to have low self-esteem; among the younger group,
those who acquired stepfathers were 2 percent less likely
than those who did not to have low self-esteem. If the child
has lived longer in an intact family, apparently, then the
negative consequences of remarriage are most evident.

We have thus suggested that it is difficult for a child
to adjust to a "new" family, and that the longer he has
been attached to an "old" family the more difficult the adjustment and the more adverse the psychological consequences. It should be emphasized that this does not mean
that children who were older at the time their families
dissolved will have lower self-esteem than children who
were younger; on the contrary, their self-esteem is higher.
The matter may be summarized as follows: If the child
was young when the family dissolved, then he will tend
to have low self-esteem whether or not his mother remarried. If, on the other hand, the child was older at the
time the marriage dissolved, then his self-esteem will be

normal if his mother did not remarry but will be below normal if she did remarry.

Why should children who were older at the time their families broke up be more affected by parental remarriage than children who were younger? It may be that these older children remember their fathers well and remember the normal family lives they have lived throughout a good part of their childhood. In addition, the older the child is at the time of the marital breakup, the more likely it is that he has developed a relationship with his father; and, as we have observed earlier, the father-child relationship is not without importance in the emotional development of the child. It might thus be particularly difficult for older children to adjust to and accept a substitute father or mother. In addition, if the family has been broken by death, the older child may be more likely to resent the remarriage as a betrayal of the memory of the departed parent, which could make him hostile both to his natural surviving parent and to his stepparent.

Discussion

If we return to our original question, "Does the broken home have an effect upon the emotional state of the child?" the best answer would seem to be "It depends." First, it depends on religion: if the child is Catholic or Jewish, there appears to be a clear effect; if the child is Protestant, there appears to be little or no effect. Second, it depends on the mother's age at the time of the marital rupture: if the mother was very young, there appears to be a clear effect; if the mother was older, there appears to be little effect. Third, it depends on remarriage: children whose mothers remarried appear to be more disturbed than those whose mothers did not remarry. The negative effect of remarriage is particularly strong among older children.

These results point to certain reasons why the broken family may be associated with emotional disturbances in the child. The greater significance of divorce among Catholics and Jews than among Protestants, for example, suggests that subcultural norms may play a role in this relationship. Similarly, the apparently more powerful effect of divorce among very young women than among older women suggests that the degree to which the parent is equipped to cope with the strain of raising a family alone may be very important. And the negative effect of parental remarriage, particularly among older children, suggests that the problem of readjustment to new family circumstances may be a significant factor. These findings suggest that the theoretical significance of a relationship may be clarified by studying the conditions under which the relationship does *not* hold as well as the conditions under which it *does* hold.

CHAPTER 6

BIRTH ORDER AND SELF-ESTEEM

ALONG with parents and friends, the child's brothers and sisters constitute an important part of his interpersonal environment. Not only do they exert a direct influence upon him as members of the same household but their very presence necessarily affects his relationship with his parents.

That birth order, or sibship structure, may have an important bearing upon personality development and behavior is strongly suggested by recent research. The evidence indicates that children who vary in ordinal position in the family, or in particular combinations of brothers or sisters, show differences in frequency of the "affiliation motive," in rates of schizophrenia, in rates of duodenal ulcer, in rates of alcoholism, in scientific and political eminence, etc.[1] In this chapter we shall consider the relevance of certain sibling positions to one aspect of adjustment, viz., self-esteem.

If we simply look at the child's birth order in the family, we find little association with self-esteem. What does make a difference is whether the subject has *any* brothers or sisters. Only children, we find, tend to have higher self-esteem than others. It is less important whether one is the first or second or third child in the family than whether one has any siblings at all. Let us, then, concentrate on the only child.

[1] An excellent recent summary of the results of such studies appears in Edith Chen and Sidney Cobb, "Family Structure in Relation to Health and Disease," *Jour. of Chronic Diseases,* Vol. 12, No. 5 (1960), pp. 544–567.

The Only Child

The perils and problems of being an only child are abundant. As far as self-esteem is concerned, however, the advantages appear to outweigh the disadvantages. Whereas 51 percent of the only children had high self-esteem, this was true of 44 percent of children with siblings. (Table 1)

TABLE 1

Self-Esteem of Only Children and Children with Siblings

Self-Esteem	Only children	Children with siblings
High	51% *	44%
Medium	21	26
Low	29	31
Total percent	100	100
(Number)	(521)	(4001)

It is interesting to note, however, that it is the male only children, rather than the female only children, who are especially likely to have high self-esteem. Whereas 54 percent of the only boys had high self-esteem, this was true of 44 percent of the boys with siblings; [2] on the other hand, 47 percent of the only girls had high self-esteem compared with 44 percent of the other girls. Among the girls, in fact, only children are also slightly more likely to

[2] These results are not an artifact of the fact that only boys are more likely to come from the upper classes. In our sample, in fact, only boys and other boys have just about equal distributions in the various class groups. Nor are these results due to religion. Table 3 shows that only Catholic boys have higher self-esteem than other Catholic boys; only Protestant boys have higher self-esteem than other Protestant boys; and only Jewish boys have higher self-esteem than other Jewish boys. Only boys are slightly more likely than other boys in our sample to come from large cities (65 percent to 58 percent), but size of home community is unrelated to self-esteem.

have low self-esteem but are less likely to have intermediate self-esteem. The only girl, apparently, has no general self-esteem advantage over girls with siblings. (Table 2)

While only boys thus have higher self-esteem than other boys and only girls, it may be noted that it is the Jewish only boys who have conspicuously high self-esteem. This is not simply a reflection of the fact that Jewish children

TABLE 2

Birth Order and Self-Esteem by Sex

| Self-Esteem | Males | | | | | | |
	Only child	First child	Second child	Third child	Fourth child	Fifth child	Sixth or later child
High	54%	44%	44%	44%	48%	46%	42%
Medium	21	24	25	26	24	20	30
Low	25	32	31	30	28	34	28
Total percent	100	100	100	100	100	100	100
(Number)	(278)	(919)	(710)	(243)	(94)	(44)	(40)

* Only boys vs. all others: Proportion "High."

| Self-Esteem | Females | | | | | | |
	Only child	First child	Second child	Third child	Fourth child	Fifth child	Sixth or later child
High	47%	44%	44%	43%	42%	35%	48%
Medium	20	26	27	25	34	23	29
Low	32	30	30	33	25	42	23
Total percent	100	100	100	100	100	100	100
(Number)	(234)	(838)	(658)	(258)	(89)	(43)	(31)

generally have higher self-esteem, for Jewish only boys have higher self-esteem than Jewish boys with siblings, and Jewish only boys are significantly more likely than Jewish only girls to have high self-esteem. In the latter case, the difference is especially conspicuous—67 percent of the Jewish only boys, but 47 percent of the Jewish only girls, had high self-esteem. With regard to low self-esteem, the differences are even greater. Fully 41 percent of the Jewish only girls had low self-esteem compared with only 10 percent of the Jewish only boys. (Table 3)

TABLE 3

Religion, Sex, Possession of Siblings, and Self-Esteem

| | Boys | | | | | |
| | Catholics | | Protestants | | Jews | |
Self-Esteem	Only child	Other children	Only child	Other children	Only child	Other children
High	52%	41%	51%	45%	67%	54%
Medium	24	27	19	23	23	24
Low	24	32	30	33	10	23
Total percent	100	100	100	100	100	100
(Number)	(116)	(919)	(98)	(737)	(39)	(233)

| | Girls | | | | | |
| | Catholics | | Protestants | | Jews | |
Self-Esteem	Only child	Other children	Only child	Other children	Only child	Other children
High	52%	43%	47%	41%	47%	52%
Medium	20	25	21	29	12	24
Low	29	31	32	30	41	24
Total percent	100	100	100	100	100	100
(Number)	(66)	(706)	(105)	(700)	(32)	(268)

In Jewish families, then, the position of only child is apparently advantageous to the male but not to the female. Whereas Jewish only boys have higher self-esteem than Jewish boys with siblings, Jewish only girls do not have higher self-esteem than Jewish girls with siblings. Among Catholics and Protestants, on the other hand, the differences between only boys and only girls are much smaller. Only boys do have slightly higher self-esteem than only girls, but the advantage is considerably less than that of Jewish only boys over Jewish only girls.

One might be disposed to interpret this finding as an outcome of the traditional importance attached to the male in Jewish culture. It may be noted however, that, as a group, Jewish boys differ very little from Jewish girls in terms of self-esteem. It is still possible, however, that if there is only one child in the family, then there may be a strong preference for a male. In other words, the general cultural value might be accentuated and sharpened under these special circumstances.

A related factor may lie in the parents' desire for the occupational and social success of their children. If a family has many children, then it need not pin its hopes for advancement on any particular child but may, on the contrary, stake its aspirations on those children who seem to be more promising. If, on the other hand, the family has but one child, then it must pin its hopes on him. If Jewish parents are inordinately interested in the social advancement of their children, then the only boy would tend to be the object of inordinate parental attention. He might be encouraged to do well, might be helped in his work, might be praised for his accomplishments, etc. The conditions generating a heightened concern for the only boy in the Jewish family may also generate a heightened disappointment in the only Jewish girl, for she would epitomize the very frustration of these mobility aspirations.

The more general point, however, is that only boys—

whether Protestant, Catholic, or Jewish—have higher self-esteem levels than other boys of the same religion. In part this may be due to the fact that they probably get more attention from their parents than do boys from large families. While only boys doubtlessly run a greater risk of parental overprotection, they also may experience less neglect. As a general rule, we would expect the only boy to feel that he is an object of importance to his parents, not only because he is the first child but also because his initial feeling of importance is not diminished by the advent of other children.

Sex Distribution of Siblings

Among the most important interpersonal influences in the life of the child are his brothers and sisters. But does it make a difference whether they are brothers or whether they are sisters? And, if so, does it make a difference whether they are mostly older brothers or sisters or younger brothers or sisters? Each of these combinations, considered in relation to the sex of the child, may produce a distinctively different interpersonal environment.

Let us consider boys in families of three or more. (In families of two, no combination of sibling structure appears to bear any relationship to self-esteem.) Among males, we find that if the majority of children are boys, the self-esteem of the respondent tends to be lower than if half or less than half are boys. Among boys in predominantly male families, 41 percent of the boys have high self-esteem; among boys in families in which males are in the minority or in which the sexes are equally distributed, 50 percent have high self-esteem. ("Equal distribution" includes the respondent; if the male respondent is excluded, then "equal distribution" means that most of his siblings are girls.)

The self-esteem of girls, however, is not enhanced by being surrounded by brothers. Whether the girl is surrounded mostly by brothers or by sisters appears to bear little relationship to her level of self-acceptance.

We thus see that boys whose siblings are mostly sisters tend to have higher self-esteem than those who are mostly surrounded by brothers. But if a boy is mostly surrounded by sisters, it may make a difference whether he is an older boy with younger sisters or a younger boy with older sisters. In order to examine this question, we have selected those boys whose siblings were chiefly sisters and have divided them into those who were either in the first half or middle positions in the family and those who were in the second half of the family.

Let us consider this latter group—the younger boys whose older siblings are chiefly or exclusively girls. In many cases they are the first boys in the family after several girls have been born. This is the group, we find, that has the highest self-esteem: 56 percent of them had high self-esteem, compared with 48 percent of older boys with younger sisters and 41 percent of the boys whose siblings were mostly brothers.

It may be noted that this result is not a reflection of a generally higher self-esteem level of younger boys. Table 4 shows that if the family consists mostly of boys, then, as far as self-esteem is concerned, it makes no difference whether the boy is among the earlier born or the later born. The same results also appear when we standardize on social class and religion.

Why is the younger boy in a family consisting mostly of older sisters so unusually likely to have high self-esteem? Certainly there are reasons for expecting the opposite: in identifying with older sisters, for example, he might develop "sissyish" characteristics which would make him an object of contempt to other boys. On the other hand, there are many advantages to this position. Perhaps the most fruitful approach to this question is to consider how

TABLE 4

Proportion of Brothers and Sisters, Ordinal Position and Self-Esteem, among Males (Familes of Three or More Children)

Self-Esteem	No brothers or brothers in the minority		Brothers in the majority or equal	
	Respondent first half or middle of family	Respondent last half of family (younger minority)	Respondent first half or middle of family	Respondent last half of family
High	48%	56%	41%	40%
Medium	24	20	26	28
Low	29	24	34	31
Total percent	100	100	100	100
(Number)	(244)	(127)	(544)	(237)

* Younger minority boys vs. all others: Proportion "High."

each of the other family members is likely to greet the arrival of the boy.

Consider first the father. Having sired several daughters, we might expect the father to be particularly anxious to have a boy. The family status is, after all, chiefly dependent upon the accomplishments of its males and the family hopes for upward social mobility are likely to be pinned on the son. The longer the son's arrival is deferred, therefore, the more eager the father may be to have a boy. Another consideration is the family name—only the boy can carry it on. The name is an important part of the individual's identity, and in this sense the son represents an extension and continuity of the father's identity that may be important to the father. In addition, the father may wish to introduce the boy to some of the high points of his own childhood—baseball or football games, hunting, fishing, etc.—which he cannot recapture in the rearing of girls. These, plus the general cultural prescription that "a man should have a son," may make the father all the more eager to have a boy the longer his arrival is deferred.

Mothers, too, are likely to be anxious to have a boy after having several girls. That the mother does feel unusually warm and affectionate toward the newly arrived boy after having had several daughters is clearly suggested by the study of Sears, Maccoby, and Levin.[3]

These investigators conducted interviews with mothers to learn about the emotional attitudes and behavior toward children in infancy and during the kindergarten period. Table 5 shows that when the new child is a boy, and the family already has girls but no boys, 50 percent of the mothers are classified as very warm toward the child during infancy, whereas if the family already has boys but no girls only 17 percent are classified as very warm. Similarly, if we consider the child at kindergarten age, 43 percent of the mothers are described as very warm to the boy if the family has girls but no boys, compared with 31 percent if the family has boys but no girls. Conversely, the latter are twice as likely as the former to be described as "relatively cold."[4]

It may be noted that girls who come later in the family do not fare as well as boys. When the new child is a girl, mothers are somewhat more likely to be warm toward her in infancy if there are only boys in the family than if there are only girls, but the advantage is considerably less than that of boys with older sisters over boys with older brothers. At kindergarten age, in fact, when the new child is a girl, it makes no difference whether the older children are brothers or sisters.

[3] Robert R. Sears, Eleanor E. Maccoby, and Harry Levin, *Patterns of Child Rearing*, Evanston, Ill.: Row, Peterson and Co., 1957, p. 514.
[4] *Ibid.*

115

TABLE 5 ‡

Mother's Warmth toward Infant and Child: Relationship
to Sexes of Previous Children

Mother's warmth toward child	Family already has . . .			
	Boys, no girls	Girls, no boys	Children of both sexes	No older children
When the new child is a boy	During infancy			
Very warm	17%	50%	30%	34%
Moderately warm	64	42	50	46
Relatively cold	19 *	8	20	20
Total percent	100	100	100	100
(Number)	(42)	(48)	(20)	(90)
When the new child is a boy	At kindergarten age			
Very warm	31%	43%	40%	29%
Moderately warm	21	33	50	38
Relatively cold	48 *	24	10	33
Total percent	100	100	100	100
(Number)	(42)	(49)	(20)	(91)

* Difference between mean scale values.

‡ Table 5 is adapted from Sears, Maccoby, and Levin, *op. cit.*, p. 514.

If maternal affection and warmth are essential for the development of a high level of self-esteem, then we have one good reason why younger boys who have mostly older sisters have higher self-esteem. The mothers are apparently very eager to have these boys and this special affection continues at least through early childhood. The data of Sears, et al., are thus highly consistent with, and help to explain, our results.

Some inferential evidence bearing on the favored position of the younger boy with older sisters is the following: We asked our respondents to indicate who their parents' favorite child was while they were growing up. Most students, of course, reported that their parents had no favorites or that they were the favorite. Let us, however, consider those who cited a younger sibling as the parental favorite. Table 6 shows that girls were more likely to cite

TABLE 6

Boys' and Girls' Description of Parental Favoritism
toward Younger Siblings

	"Who was mother's favorite child?"		"Who was father's favorite child?"	
	Boys	Girls	Boys	Girls
A younger brother	43%	56%	44%	55%
A younger sister	57	44	56	45
Total percent	100	100	100	100
(Number)	(63)	(94)	(94)	(82)

a younger brother, rather than a younger sister, as both the mother's and the father's favorite child, whereas boys were less likely to cite a younger brother as the parental favorite. This is generally consistent with the findings that younger boys with older brothers do not have high self-esteem but younger boys with older sisters do have high self-esteem. It is interesting to note that this description of parental favoritism refers to children who are not in our sample.

How are the older sisters likely to react to the arrival of a boy? For one thing they may become caught up in the enthusiasm of the father and mother for the boy and may tend to indulge him and lavish affection on him. Girls are also probably more likely than boys to greet any new child in the family with interest and affection, since this new object provides them with an opportunity to rehearse their mother roles. There may, furthermore, be less hostility between older sisters and younger brothers because parents are less likely to make invidious distinctions between them. For example, the athletic skill of the younger boy may be compared favorably or unfavorably to the older boy, but not to the older girl. It is no blow to her pride to know that her younger brother is athletically superior to her. Conversely, the looks of a younger girl may be compared favorably or unfavorably to her own, but not the looks of a younger boy. We would suggest that much of what goes under the heading of sibling rivalry actually stems from invidious comparisons, and unequal affection and approval, of parents toward children; that these invidious comparisons are especially likely to be made between children of the same sex; and that sibling rivalry may thus be considerably less between children of opposite sexes.

We thus see that for the self-esteem of the male, it is more advantageous for him to be surrounded by sisters than by brothers, and that this is especially true if he is one of the younger children in the family. As far as the older boy is concerned, it makes less difference to him whether the younger children are boys or girls, although there is still some advantage if they are girls, since they may represent less of a threat and offer fewer opportunities for invidious comparisons.

With regard to girls, there does seem to be more advantage in being a first girl after several boys than in being a girl chiefly with older sisters, especially in families of three or four, but the difference is not so striking as among the boys. This is, in fact, precisely in accord with the data of Sears, Maccoby, and Levin. In general, to introduce a new sex into the family after several children have been born appears to elicit greater maternal warmth (Sears, et al.) and higher self-esteem, but the advantage is greater among the boys.

We will refer to these boys who are in the second half of the family and whose siblings are mostly sisters as the "younger minority boys." (The term "minority" is not used here in the sense of minority religion or minority race, but as minority sex in families of three or more children.) These younger minority boys, we have noted, are more likely to have high self-esteem. But it appears to be a special kind of high self-esteem which characterizes these boys, viz., an unconditional self-acceptance. It is this subject to which we now turn.

Unconditional Self-Acceptance

Some years ago Margaret Mead suggested that one of the characteristics of American middle-class child-rearing practices was the pattern of "conditional love." [5] Instead of accepting the child for what he is, Mead suggested, American parents show an affection for the child when he outstrips others in some competitive enterprise and feel disappointed and distressed when he lags behind.

What this observation suggests is that people may also be characterized by conditional or unconditional self-acceptance. "Conditional self-acceptance" would be indicated if self-esteem varied directly with some objective measure of success or failure. "Unconditional self-acceptance" would be expressed if people tended to have high self-esteem irrespective of their objective performance.

One important measure of objective performance among high school students is one's school grade average. Our data indicate that the higher the student's grade average, the more likely he is to have a high level of self-acceptance. The question may thus be raised: Do younger minority boys have higher self-esteem because they have higher

[5] Margaret Mead, *And Keep Your Powder Dry*, New York: Morrow, 1942.

119

grades? The answer is—emphatically not. As a group, younger minority boys have distinctly lower grades than other boys. Only 24 percent of them are A or B students compared with 34 percent of the other boys. The younger minority boys have higher self-esteem not because of their grades, but in spite of their grades. (Table 7)

TABLE 7

Sex Distribution of Siblings, Ordinal Position, and Grades, among Males (Families of Three or More Children)

| | No brothers or brothers in the minority | | Brothers in the majority or equal | |
| | Respondent in first half or middle of family | Respondent in last half of family (younger minority) | Respondent in first half or middle of family | Respondent in last half of family |
Grade average				
A–B	34%	24%	32%	36%
C	47	57	48	40
D–F	18	19	20	25
Total percent	100	100	100	100
(Number)	(233)	(118)	(536)	(230)

* Younger minority boys vs. all others: Proportion A–B.

The central point is this: The self-esteem of the younger minority boy is less dependent upon, and less influenced by, his grades in school than are other boys. Table 8, for example, shows that grades are clearly related to self-esteem in each group except the younger minority boys. In this last group, but in no other group, students with low grades have unusually high self-esteem levels. In other words, while the self-esteem of other groups appears to

TABLE 8

Sex Distribution of Siblings, Ordinal Position, Grades, and Self-Esteem, among Boys (Families of Three or More Children)

	No brothers or brothers in the minority					
	Respondent in first half or middle of family Grades			Respondent in last half of family (younger minority) Grades		
Self-Esteem	A–B	C	D–F	A–B	C	D–F
High	56%	45%	41%	46%	60%	64%
Medium	20	27	27	19	18	18
Low	24	28	32	35	22	18
Total percent	100	100	100	100	100	100
(Number)	(79)	(104)	(41)	(26)	(65)	(22)

	Brothers in the majority or equal					
	* Respondent in first half or middle of family Grades			* Respondent in last half of family Grades		
Self-Esteem	A–B	C	D–F	A–B	C	D–F
High	51%	40%	29%	42%	44%	30%
Medium	26	27	18	32	33	20
Low	23	32	53	26	23	50
Total percent	100	100	100	100	100	100
(Number)	(168)	(240)	(102)	(78)	(86)	(56)

121

be highly dependent upon their academic performance, the self-esteem of the younger minority boys appears to be completely independent of their academic performance.

Since this is so, one may ask whether the self-esteem of younger minority boys is indifferent to other types of performance as well. The student's relationship with his peers would be an important area of his social performance.

First, let us consider the individual's participation in formal high school groups. Such participation in itself, of course, cannot be considered a sign of interpersonal success, since membership is open and voluntary. Nevertheless, in differentiating those who do or do not like to join groups, it may at the same time roughly reflect those whose histories of interpersonal relations with peers have been more or less satisfactory. As we shall see in Chapter 10, those students who participate more in groups tend to have higher self-esteem. It is thus interesting to note that while it is generally true that boys who are active participants have higher self-esteem, it is not true of younger minority boys. Whether they participate a great deal or very little in high school activities, their self-esteem remains the same. (Table 9) This suggests that, among younger minority boys, self-esteem may be relatively impervious to, and independent of, intensity of social participation.

More to the point, however, is the question of leadership, particularly whether one feels that one is a leader. Let us first consider the question of informal opinion leadership. Such self-designated opinion leadership has been shown in other studies to be closely associated with leadership as designated by others.[6] We thus asked our respondents: "Compared with other students in this school, are you more or less likely than they are to be asked your views on student government or topics of general high

[6] Elihu Katz and Paul F. Lazarsfeld, *Personal Influence*, Glencoe, Ill.: The Free Press, 1955.

TABLE 9

Sex Distribution of Siblings, Ordinal Position, Participation
in High School Clubs, and Self-Esteem, Among Males
(Families of Three or More)

	Club membership			
	Younger minority boys		Other boys	
Self-Esteem	Belong to no clubs	Belong to some clubs	Belong to no clubs	Belong to some clubs
High	83%	50%	38% *	50%
Medium	11	19	28	23
Low	6	31	35	26
Total percent	100	100	100	100
(Number)	(18)	(16)	(211)	(145)

	Hours spent in extra-curricular activities			
Self-Esteem	One or less	Two or more	One or less	Two or more
High	67%	60%	38%	46%
Medium	20	20	26	26
Low	13	20	36	28
Total percent	100	100	100	100
(Number)	(15)	(15)	(135)	(182)

school interest?" Another question, which may reflect either
formal or informal leadership, was: "How often do you
find yourself taking a position of leadership in a high school
group you are with?"

Despite the small number of cases, the following suggestive finding may be noted: Whereas those who say they
are "less likely" than others to be asked their opinions and

who "never" take a position of leadership tend to have lower self-esteem than those who indicate that they are leaders, this is not true among younger minority boys. (Table 10) In this group, those who say they are not leaders are just as likely as those who claim they are leaders to have high self-esteem. The younger minority boy, even if he does not consider himself a peer-group leader, tends to have high self-esteem, whereas this is not generally true of other boys.

Now let us consider the question of actual formal group leadership—whether the individual has ever held an elected position in a high school club or organization. We asked our respondents whether they had ever held a position as president or chairman of a school club or organization and whether they had ever held any other elected positions in such organizations, such as vice-president, secretary, treasurer, committee member, etc. For the total sam-

TABLE 10

Sex Distribution of Siblings, Ordinal Position, Self-Designated Leadership and Self-Esteem, Among Males
(Families of Three or More)

| | Likely to be asked your views by others . . . | | | |
| | Younger minority boys | | Other boys | |
Self-Esteem	Less likely	More or equally likely	Less likely	More or equally likely
High	70%	62%	34% *	49%
Medium	30	12	27	25
Low	—	25	39	26
Total percent	100	100	100	100
(Number)	(10)	(24)	(129)	(211)

ple of boys, the experience of having been a president or other elected officer of a club is positively related to self-esteem.[7] For the younger minority boy, those who have held the position of president have higher self-esteem than those who have not, but those who have held other elected positions do not have higher self-esteem than those who have not.

We thus see that for younger minority boys, unlike other boys, it appears to make no difference to their self-esteem whether their school grade averages are high or low, whether they join many or few clubs, whether they feel they are informal leaders or followers, or whether they have held secondary elected positions in school clubs; the only difference appears to be whether they have been elected president. This suggests that with the exception of outstanding social success, social or intellectual success or failure bears little relationship to the self-esteem of the younger minority boys. Of special interest are the younger minority boys who have failed—who have low grades, participate in few activities, do not consider themselves leaders, have held no elective offices. These boys have self-esteem as high as, or higher than, the other boys who have succeeded and, with the exception of election to the presidency, as high or higher than younger minority boys who are successful. These are the boys who epitomize most sharply the conception of unconditional self-acceptance. Unlike other boys their self-esteem appears to be relatively impervious to, or independent of, their objective accomplishments.

Discussion

We have suggested that the younger-minority boy, unlike other youngsters, tends to develop a type of self-esteem which is not based on competitive achievement, upon outdoing others, upon social or academic success.

[7] See Chapter 10.

Rather, it is a fundamental feeling of worth deriving from the care, love, and affection of his significant others. In his early years, at least, everything is working in his favor. The father is eager for his arrival, the mother treats him with inordinate affection, the sisters regard him as something precious. Is it any wonder that he should grow up feeling that he is a person of worth?

It should be noted, however, that the younger-minority boys have significantly lower grades in school than other boys. It may thus be that a solid, unshakeable feeling of self-acceptance may be a deterrent to accomplishment. Part of the motivation to work hard in school may be the need to prove one's worth both to other people and to oneself.

This situation clearly contains the seeds of a dilemma— whether it is better for a child to accept himself unconditionally or to be academically successful. Obviously the decision is based upon one's values. Most parents would probably say, and believe, that they would rather that their child be happy than successful.

But the issue is not so easily resolved. For one thing, youngsters who are academically successful are more likely to have high self-esteem. Their self-esteem level may influence their performance, e.g., through reduction of "test anxiety," but it is also probably true that their external success will enhance their self-esteem levels. It may be a conditional self-esteem, but it is nonetheless an important factor in mental health and human happiness. Furthermore, the youngster who does well in high school is more likely to go on to college and ultimately to end up in a more prestigious occupation, to have a higher standard of living, etc. The sense of success, abetted by the respect he is granted by others, may well culminate in an increased feeling of worth in adult years. Some measure of uncertainty about one's worth may in the long run—the very long run—produce a very firm feeling of self-esteem. Objective accomplishment—the successful mastery of difficulties—affords a firm foundation for self-respect.

The solution, of course, must lie in giving careful consideration to the potentialities of the particular child. If his native abilities are modest, he should still be accepted and respected for what he is; the parent who wants him to be otherwise sows in the child the seeds of self-doubt. If he is working below his potentialities, it is necessary to consider ways of motivating him to improve his performance. Parental misjudgment of the child's abilities is likely to produce under-achievement, on the one hand, or undue anxiety, on the other.

CHAPTER 7

PARENTAL INTEREST AND CHILDREN'S SELF-CONCEPTIONS

IN THE previous two chapters we dealt with certain aspects of the structure of the family—whether the family is intact, has been dissolved, has been reconstituted, etc., and the nature and distribution of children in the family. The significance of these structural properties, of course, lies in the fact that they are translated into typical experiences; but it is not always possible to specify what these experiences are. It seems relevant at this point to attempt to step across the threshold into the home and try to learn more about interaction in the family. Specifically, can we gain information about how parents feel and behave toward their children?

In dealing with the types of parental behavior which might be considered relevant for child development, research studies have run the gamut from such specific child-rearing practices as breast-feeding or bottle-feeding, time of bladder and bowel-training, and time of weaning, to such broad categories of parental behavior as emotional support, intrusiveness, and punitiveness.[1] One point which has been relatively neglected, however, is the simple question: How interested is the parent in the child? Is the child an object of importance to the psychic and emotional life of the parent? Beyond this, what is the relationship between such parental interest or indifference and the child's feeling of self-worth? Is it more deleterious to have parents who are indifferent but nonpunitive or parents

[1] Urie Bronfenbrenner, "Socialization and Social Class through Time and Space," in E. E. Maccoby, T. M. Newcomb, and E. L. Hartley, eds., *Readings in Social Psychology*, Third Edition, New York: Holt, 1958, pp. 400–425.

who are interested in the child but hostile toward him? These are some of the questions to which the present chapter is directed.

Indicators of parental interest. Two conspicuous methodological difficulties stand out in attempting to obtain a measure of parental interest in the child: (1) since the possibilities of expressing such interest exist in an almost infinite number of parent-child interactions through the years, it is difficult to select a sample of such expressions of interest which will satisfactorily reflect the whole; and (2) since the questionnaires are directed toward the children, we face the problem of inferring the parental attitudes and behavior from the child's reports.

In light of these problems, our procedure in constructing the questionnaires was to index parental interest indirectly by selecting three recurrent but diverse areas of life which represented fairly specific points of contact between parent and child. We selected recurrent situations in order to obtain a wider sampling of interaction than reports of single specific events. We selected diverse situations on the assumption that idiosyncratic factors might determine behavior in any specific situation but that this danger would be reduced if several diverse situations were considered. We approached the matter indirectly by asking about objective behavior in order to reduce bias; in each case an effort was made to give the questions a relatively "neutral" or "objective" slant. Finally, we used three diverse situations in order to observe whether the use of different indicators of the same concept ("interest in the child") would yield essentially the same results. If so, it would reduce the danger that the result was merely an artifact of the particular measure used. It is the consistency of the data in these three areas, then, rather than the adequacy of any particular measure, upon which the brunt of the present argument rests.

129

The three areas of life selected for examination were: (1) relationships with friends; (2) reactions to the child's academic performance; and (3) responsiveness to the child at the dinner table. Since the types of inferences to be drawn vary with each of these three areas of parent-child interaction, we will deal with each separately.

Parents' Knowledge of the Child's Friends

During the period of middle childhood, a child's emotions tend to be deeply involved in his friends; indeed, friends may be the child's main ego-extensions. The parents' reactions to the child's friends may thus be an indirect indicator of their interest in the child.

In order to examine this question, we attempted to rivet the student's attention to a recurrent situation and to hold the image of what went on in these situations in the forefront of his attention. The instructions were as follows:

> We would like you to think back to a specific period of your childhood, namely, when you were in the 5th and 6th grades. For most children this would be about the age of 10 or 11. Try to keep this period generally in mind when answering the following questions. Although your feelings and experiences may have varied, try to answer the questions in terms of your *average* or *typical* experiences at this time.

After asking whether the child had many friends, whether he visited them in their homes and whether they visited him in his home, we asked: "During this period, did your mother know who most of your friends were?"

Table 1 indicates that there is little difference in the self-esteem of those who said their mothers knew "all" or "most" of their friends, but that the self-esteem of these respondents is substantially higher than those who said

TABLE 1

* Reports of Mother's Knowledge of Child's Friends and Subject's Self-Esteem

Respondent's self-esteem	"During this period (age 10 or 11) did your mother know who most of your friends were?"				
	All of them	Most of them	Some of them	None, or almost none	Don't know or can't remember
High	47%	45%	33%	30%	27%
Medium	23	24	27	15	38
Low	29	31	41	55	35
Total percent	100	100	100	100	100
(Number)	(848)	(559)	(113)	(20)	(26)

their mothers knew "some" or "none" of their friends.[2] It should be noted, however, that only 8 percent said their mothers knew "some" or "none" of their friends. These responses thus appear to indicate an extreme lack of interest. It is among this exceptional group that low self-esteem is particularly likely to appear.

The question is, however: Is the student's report of his mother's knowledge of friends fairly realistic or is it entirely determined by the student's bias? In other words, it is possible that students feel that their mothers should

[2] Except as noted, all the two-variable relationships presented in this chapter are maintained for boys and girls separately. Due to the small number of indifferent responses in some social classes, it has not been possible to control on social class for each table. However, in the final summary table (Table 10), in which the various indifferent responses are combined to provide a larger number of cases, social class (and various other factors to be mentioned) does not account for the relationship between reported parental indifference and self-esteem.

have known the child's friends—that this would be the "good," "right," "proper" thing to do. It may thus be that students who hold negative attitudes toward their mothers will report that their mothers knew few of their friends. In this case, the relationship cited above might simply reflect an association between unfavorable attitudes toward one's mother and one's self-esteem.

In order to check on this possibility, we have selected two questions which may reflect the student's attitude toward his mother. The first question, dealing with the past, is: "When you were about 10 or 11 years old, to whom were you most likely to talk about personal things?" The second question, dealing with the present, is: "When your parents disagree, whose side are you usually on—your mother's or your father's?" Table 2 shows that those respondents who

TABLE 2

† Reports of Mother's Knowledge of Child's Friends and
Subject's Self-Esteem, by Tendency to Confide
in Others

	Most likely to talk about personal things to . . .					
	Mother		Other person		No one or can't remember	
	Mother knew friends . . .					
Respondent's self-esteem	All or most	Some or none	All or most	Some or none	All or most	Some or none
High	51%	39%	41%	34%	46%	29%
Medium	23	32	26	20	21	30
Low	26	29	33	46	34	41
Total percent	100	100	100	100	100	100
(Number)	(539)	(41)	(537)	(55)	(195)	(27)

said their mothers knew most of their friends had higher self-esteem than those who said she knew few, irrespective of whether they confided in their mothers, in someone else, or in no one in childhood.[3] Similarly, Table 3 in-

TABLE 3

† Reports of Mother's Knowledge of Child's Friends and Subject's Self-Esteem, by Identification with Parents

	Student currently identifies chiefly with . . .					
	Mother		Father		Both equally	
	Mother knew friends . . .					
Respondent's self-esteem	All or most	Some or none	All or most	Some or none	All or most	Some or none
High	43%	32%	39%	27%	52%	39%
Medium	23	22	29	33	22	29
Low	34	45	32	40	26	32
Total percent	100	100	100	100	100	100
(Number)	(381)	(40)	(185)	(15)	(407)	(31)

dicates that the same relationship is maintained irrespective of whether the respondent currently sides with his mother, his father, or both equally in parental disagreements. The results, then, do not appear to be attributable to the student's past recollections of, or present attitudes toward, his mother.

[3] Table 2 indicates that within each subclassification (or partial association) created by the introduction of the test factor, the direction, and generally the size, of the relationship between maternal interest and self-esteem is maintained. Within each partial association, however, the differences are no longer statistically significant because of the reduction in the number of cases. This statement also applies to Tables 3 and 4.

Another possibility must, however, be considered, namely, that it may not be the child's attitude toward his mother in general, but his recollection of how she behaved toward his friends in particular, that colors his recollection of whether she knew his friends. We thus asked those students who said their mothers knew any of their friends: "How did she usually act toward them?" Table 4

TABLE 4

† Reports of Mother's Knowledge of Child's Friends and Subject's Self-Esteem, by Mother's Behavior toward Friends

	How mother acted toward child's friends . . .					
	Very friendly		Fairly friendly		Not friendly	
	Mother knew child's friends					
Respondent's self-esteem	All or most	Some or none	All or most	Some or none	All or most	Some or none
High	48%	34%	45%	33%	32%	21%
Medium	23	24	26	28	29	26
Low	29	41	29	39	40	53
Total percent	100	100	100	100	100	100
(Number)	(1091)	(58)	(259)	(51)	(38)	(19)

shows that irrespective of whether the students said their mothers were friendly or not friendly, those who said their mothers knew all or most of their friends had higher self-esteem than those who said their mothers knew some or none of their friends. Their recollection of whether their mothers knew their friends is, then, not simply a reflection of their favorable or unfavorable memories of their mother's behavior toward their friends.

We thus see that irrespective of whether the child says he did or did not chiefly confide in his mother, irrespective of whether he identifies with her, with his father, or with both equally, and irrespective of whether he says she was friendly or unfriendly to his mates, the student who reports that his mother knew most of his friends tends to have higher self-esteem than the one who does not. It is likely, then, that the reported differential knowledge of friends does not simply reflect the student's biased perception of, or attitudes toward, his mother. Such differential knowledge probably represents a reflection of the mother's interest in the child and in his ego-extensions.

It should be mentioned that those students who said their mothers knew few of their friends but were friendly toward them were actually slightly less likely to have high self-esteem than those who said their mothers knew most of their friends but were unfriendly (41 percent to 34 percent). This difference is not statistically significant, but it does suggest the possibility that simple interest (as reflected in knowledge of friends) may be even more important than parental pleasantness or unpleasantness (as reflected in parental friendliness). While this finding is at best suggestive, it is relevant in the light of other findings to be presented later.

Now let us consider the father's knowledge of the child's friends. Once again we find that parental interest is not strongly associated with self-esteem except for the extreme group who said their father knew "none, or almost none" of their friends. This small group—8 percent of the respondents—was clearly more likely to have low self-esteem than those who reported that their fathers knew some, most, or all of their friends. (Table 5) This difference obtains even when mother's knowledge of friends is held constant. Both exceptional maternal indifference and ex-

TABLE 5

* Reports of Father's Knowledge of Child's Friends and Subject's Self-Esteem

	"During this period (age 10 or 11) did your father know who most of your friends were?"				
Respondent's self-esteem	All of them	Most of them	Some of them	None, or almost none	Don't know or can't remember
High	49%	46%	41%	35%	34%
Medium	22	25	26	20	32
Low	28	29	33	46	34
Total percent	100	100	100	100	100
(Number)	(366)	(534)	(431)	(123)	(41)

ceptional paternal indifference thus appear to be associated with low self-esteem in the child.

Academic Performance

We now turn to a second recurrent but fairly specific point of contact between parent and child which may serve as an indicator of parental interest in the child, viz., the parents' response to the child's performance in school. While it is possible for the parent to be generally oblivious to what happens to the child in school, at one point the totality of performance is tightly summarized for him on a single sheet—the report card. His response to the report card, then, may importantly epitomize his attitude toward the child's achievements and qualities.

In order to learn something about the parents' typical reactions, we asked our respondents: "When you were in the 5th and 6th grades in school, what did your *mother* usually do when you brought home a report card with high grades? (Check as many as apply.)"[4] We then asked: "How about when you brought home a report card from the 5th or 6th grades which contained low marks? What did your mother *usually* do then? (Check as many as apply.)"[5] The same questions were asked about the father's reactions.

Let us consider first the parents' reactions to poor grades, since the issue is more sharply highlighted in this regard. The parental response to poor grades may roughly be divided into three types: (1) The punitive reactions—scolding the child, criticizing him, depriving him of something he wants; (2) the supportive reactions—praising him for the subjects in which he did do well, trying to help him in subjects in which he was doing poorly, or discussing the reasons for his poor performance; and (3) the indifferent reactions—paying no attention to grades, simply taking poor report cards for granted, or not even looking at the report card.

In terms of Mead's[6] principle of reflected appraisals, our expectations would be obvious: those students whose parents were critical or punitive would have the lowest self-esteem; those whose parents were supportive and helpful would have the highest self-esteem; and those whose parents were indifferent would be in-between. The results,

[4] The alternatives offered were: did not receive any report cards with high grades; praised you; gave you something you wanted; paid no attention to it; told you that you should be able to do even better; took good report cards for granted; did not see your report cards; other (What?); can't remember.

[5] The alternatives presented were: did not receive any report cards with low grades; scolded you; criticized you; deprived you of something you wanted; praised you for subjects in which you were doing well; paid no attention to it; took bad report cards for granted; tried to help you in subjects in which you were doing poorly; discussed with you the reasons for poor performance; didn't see your report cards; other (What?); can't remember.

[6] George Herbert Mead, *op. cit.*, Part II.

however, do not bear out these expectations. Table 6 indicates that it is not the punitive responses which are most closely related to low self-esteem, but the indifferent ones. Once again, we find, the proportion who give the indiffer-

TABLE 6

Report of Parental Reaction to Low Marks and Subject's
Self-Esteem ‡

Respondent's self-esteem	* Mother's reaction			
	Supportive and punitive	Supportive only	Punitive only	Indifferent
High	49%	44%	34%	26%
Medium	25	25	25	13
Low	26	30	41	61
Total percent	100	100	100	100
(Number)	(178)	(533)	(228)	(23)

Respondent's self-esteem	* Father's reaction			
	Supportive and punitive	Supportive only	Punitive only	Indifferent
High	47%	46%	36%	34%
Medium	28	25	24	19
Low	25	30	40	47
Total percent	100	100	100	100
(Number)	(139)	(413)	(241)	(85)

‡ In this table both boys and girls who report indifferent responses are more likely than those who report punitive or supportive responses to have low self-esteem. The boys who report indifferent responses, however, are less likely than other boys to have medium self-esteem and slightly more likely to have high self-esteem. Since the boys' responses are based upon only 10 cases (mother's reaction) and 41 cases (father's reaction), it is uncertain whether this is a meaningful difference or a matter of chance fluctuation.

ent responses is very small. We may thus assume that such responses represent rather extreme indifference. Those who do report such indifference, however, not only have lower self-esteem than those who report supportive responses but are also somewhat lower than those who report punitive responses.

It is interesting to note that those students who report only supportive responses do not differ from those who report both supportive and punitive responses. Both groups, however, have higher self-esteem than those who report only punitive responses; those who report indifferent responses, as noted, are lowest in self-esteem.

Another possible indication of parental indifference is the following: We asked our respondents whether their marks in the 5th and 6th grades were above or below average, and then inquired: "(If your marks were average or below average) Was your mother satisfied with your grades in school?" As we would expect, those students who said that their mothers were satisfied even when their grades were average or below average had higher self-esteem than those who reported that their mothers were dissatisfied. More interesting, however, is the fact that the lowest self-esteem appears not among those who report that their mothers were dissatisfied but among those who said "She seldom commented on my marks." It should be pointed out that less than 4 percent gave this last response. Among this small group, however, fully 52 percent had low self-esteem, compared with 38 percent of those who said their mothers were dissatisfied, 30 percent of those who said their mothers were fairly satisfied, and 24 percent of those who said their mothers were very satisfied. (Table 7) Once again we see that maternal indifference is more highly predictive of low self-esteem than overt dissatisfaction.

When we turn to parents' reactions to high grades, our analysis is restricted for the following reason: we cannot

139

TABLE 7

* Mother's Satisfaction with Child's Grades and Subject's Self-Esteem

| | "(If your marks were average or below average) Was your mother satisfied with your grades in school?" | | | | |
Respondent's self-esteem	Yes, very satisfied	Yes, fairly satisfied	No, not satisfied	Seldom com- mented on my marks	Don't know
High	48%	45%	38%	28%	35%
Medium	27	24	24	20	25
Low	24	30	38	52	40
Total percent	100	100	100	100	100
(Number)	(221)	(438)	(372)	(40)	(40)

compare punitive responses with indifferent ones because a parent will rarely chastise or punish his child for doing well in school. We can, then, only classify the parental responses as supportive (praised you, gave you something you wanted) or indifferent (paid no attention to it, did not see report cards). As we would expect, those students who reported that their mothers and fathers gave supportive responses had higher self-esteem than those who reported indifferent responses.

While many people are inclined to treat the report card as a trivial part of life, it holds a special and almost unique significance in the development of the self-concept. Among the myriad criteria upon which an individual's worth may be judged, the report card is almost the only objective, unequivocal measure of a certain aspect of the individual's worth. Whether a person is kind, courageous, principled, likeable, etc., may be matters of opinion, with much variation, subjective interpretation, or distortion of facts; but

140

a report card is a black-and-white, strictly measurable and comparable characterization of the individual. With due recognition of the different degrees of importance attached to it, we would argue that total parental indifference to the report card is very difficult, and, as our respondents indicate, it is actually very rare.

It may thus be that most parents who are totally uninterested in the child's school performance are likely to be uninterested in the child. The parent may be punitive —may scold the child, deprive him of something, etc.—if he does poorly in school, but at least he is interested, concerned, involved with the child. Apparently more than deprecation and chastisement, and certainly more than praise or support, such indifference is associated with lower self-esteem in the child.

Participation in Mealtime Conversations

The discussion of knowledge of friends and reactions to report cards referred to recurrent situations in the past. We now turn to an everyday recurrent situation in the present which may reflect parental interest in the child, viz., family interaction at the evening meal. The responses to these items are somewhat more subjective in nature, although, as above, we have tried to make the question fairly neutral and indirect. Although in this area the questions are probably more "contaminated" than in the "friends" and "report card" situations, they are so close to our central theme that they may merit presentation.

The importance of the evening meal lies in the fact that it is a constant, persistent, frequent point of contact between parents and children. What goes on at the dinner table not only represents a great multitude of interactions but may well epitomize the total range of parent-child interactions which occurs in other areas of life.

In order to learn something about what goes on at the dinner table, we asked our respondents:

1) Do all the members of your family eat the evening meal together?
2) (If your family usually or always eats together) how often do you participate actively in the meal-time conversation?
3) As far as you can tell, how interested are the other family members in what you have to say on such occasions?

Fewer than 6 percent of the respondents said that they "rarely or never" participated in the mealtime conversation and an equally small proportion of those who did participate felt that others were "not interested" in what they had to say. Tables 8 and 9 indicate that these re-

TABLE 8

* Frequency of Respondent's Participation in Mealtime Conversation, and Self-Esteem

| Respondent's self-esteem | "(If your family usually or always eats together) How often do you participate actively in the mealtime conversation?" | | | |
	Always	Usually	Sometimes	Rarely or never
High	52%	45%	33%	32%
Medium	23	27	25	16
Low	25	28	42	52
Total percent	100	100	100	100
(Number)	(697)	(446)	(173)	(89)

spondents were considerably more likely than others to have low self-esteem.

The student's belief that others are interested in him is thus closely related to his self-conception. His self-con-

TABLE 9

* Subject's Estimate of Family's Interest in His Opinions,
and Self-Esteem

Respondent's self-esteem	"As far as you can tell, how interested are the other family members in what you have to say on such occasions?"			
	Very interested	Fairly interested	Not interested	Don't know
High	56%	43%	19%	37%
Medium	23	26	20	17
Low	21	30	61	46
Total percent	100	100	100	100
(Number)	(432)	(833)	(79)	(108)

ception, of course, undoubtedly contributes to his belief that others are interested. The child who thinks little of himself is automatically inclined to assume that others are uninterested in his opinions and activities. At the same time it is likely that something in the actual attitudes and behavior of others toward him contributes to his belief that they are or are not interested in what he has to say. The student has, after all, interacted with his family tens of thousands of times. He has thus been exposed to almost innumerable signs as to whether others are interested in what he has to say: the stifled or open yawn when he speaks, the interruption or changing of the subject, the look of distractedness when he expresses an opinion; or, on the other hand, the light of interest when he presents his views, the responses appropriate to his comment, the encouragement to continue, the request for his opinion on a subject which others have initiated—all these are clear and unmistakable signs of whether others are interested in what the individual has to say. Thus, while the individual's self-conception undoubtedly influences his belief that others are interested in his views, it seems unlikely that something in their actual attitudes and behavior has not contributed at least in some measure to his appraisal of their level of interest.

Summary Measure of "Interest in the Child"

In order to learn something about parental interest in the child, we have focused upon three recurrent sets of life experiences—friends, report cards, dinner conversations. While no one of these areas of interaction may in itself be an adequate reflector of parental interest in the child, the consistency of the results in all three areas suggests that there may be a real relationship between parental indifference and low self-esteem in the child.

It should be noted that reports of parental indifference are clearly the exception; very few students indicate that their parents gave the "uninterested" or "indifferent" response to any of these items, let alone most of them. In order to provide the most liberal interpretation of parental indifference, we have combined all those who reported any lack of interest on the part of their parents. Twenty percent of the sample did report such indifference. This is an exceptional, but not an insignificant, group; it is also large enough to enable us to introduce certain controls. Table 10 indicates that 44 percent of these students had low self-esteem, compared with 26 percent of the others.

It may be noted that this association between parental indifference and children's self-esteem is not an artifact of associated status or role characteristics. In other words, whether one belongs to the upper, upper-middle, lower-middle, or lower social classes; [7] whether one is a Protest-

[7] The number of indifferent responses in the upper class is, however, very small, and the difference in this subgroup therefore cannot be considered reliable.

TABLE 10

"Parental Interest" Index and Subject's Self-Esteem

	Parental interest	
Respondent's self-esteem	No evidence of lack of interest	Some evidence of lack of interest
High	49% *	29%
Medium	25	26
Low	26	44
Total percent	100	100
(Number)	(945)	(241)

ant, Catholic, or Jew; whether one is male or female; whether one lives in a large city, a medium sized community, or a small town—whichever of these conditions obtain, the result is essentially the same: if the parents manifest indifference to the child, that child is less likely to have a high level of self-regard.

Similarly, we find that it is not simply a question of whether parents were strict or lenient with the child or whether the respondent feels that the punishment he received as a child was generally deserved or undeserved. Whether the student says that his parents were stricter or less strict than others or whether he says that the punishment he received was generally deserved, partly deserved and partly undeserved, or generally undeserved, the result is the same: students who report a lack of parental interest have lower self-esteem than others. In fact, students who reported a lack of parental interest but who felt that the punishment in childhood was deserved had somewhat lower self-esteem than those who indicated that their parents were interested but who felt their punishment in childhood was generally undeserved.

Discussion

These data thus suggest that extreme parental indifference is associated with lower self-esteem in the child and, in fact, seems to be even more deleterious than punitive parental reactions. It may be that even if the mother is only sufficiently interested in the child to chastise or berate him, even if she is discourteous enough to be unpleasant to his friends, this level of interest is associated with higher self-esteem than is maternal indifference.

Of course, it is probably not simply interest per se which accounts for the observed relationships. Very likely such lack of interest in the child goes along with lack of love, a failure to treat the child with respect, a failure to give him encouragement, a tendency to consider the child something of a nuisance and to treat him with irritation, impatience, and anger. But whatever other kinds of parental behavior may be reflected in these indicators, they probably at least reflect the idea that the child is important to someone else, that others consider him of worth, of value, of concern. The feeling that one is important to a significant other is probably essential to the development of a feeling of self-worth.

PART IV
PSYCHOLOGICAL AND INTER-
PERSONAL CORRELATES

CHAPTER 8

SELF-ESTEEM AND ANXIETY

THUS far we have focused on certain external social factors—broad social group memberships, neighborhood dissonance, family breakup, sibling structure, parental interest—which appear to be associated with the child's self-esteem. We shall now shift our attention to a consideration of what goes on in the mind of the adolescent with low self-esteem. In later chapters we shall ask about the bearing of this psychological state upon socially significant attitudes and behavior.

That anxiety represents an important, if not central, element of neurosis is widely acknowledged. In Chapter 2 we noted that the lower the subject's self-esteem level, the more likely was he to report experiencing various physiological indicators of anxiety—hand trembling, nervousness, insomnia, heart pounding, pressures or pains in the head, fingernail biting, shortness of breath when not exercising or working hard, palmar perspiration, sick headaches, and nightmares. People with low self-esteem were also more likely to report that they had suffered from "nervousness," "loss of appetite," "insomnia," and "headache" during the past five years.

In addition to these psychophysiological indicators, Fromm-Reichmann [1] has suggested that anxiety is manifested by (1) "interference with thinking processes and concentration," (2) "a frequently object-less feeling of uncertainty and helplessness," (3) "intellectual and emotional preoccupation," and (4) "blocking of communication." Some of our items appear to reflect these states in

[1] Frieda Fromm-Reichmann, "Psychiatric aspects of anxiety," in M. R. Stein, A. J. Vidich, and D. M. White, eds., *Identity and Anxiety*, Glencoe, Ill.: The Free Press, 1960, pp. 129–130.

some measure. The statement "I find it hard to keep my mind on a single task or job" appears to indicate an interference with concentration. "I feel anxious about something or someone all the time" suggests a feeling of uncertainty. "At times I have been worried beyond reason about something that really did not matter" would appear to reflect intellectual and emotional preoccupation. And a negative response to the statement "I find it easy to make talk when I meet new people" would suggest a blockage of communication. All of these indicators are, to be sure, very crude measures of the concepts advanced by Fromm-Reichmann. It is interesting to note, however, that with regard to every one of the indicators of anxiety cited, people low in self-esteem were conspicuously more likely than those with high self-esteem to report having such experiences. While each of these indicators is undoubtedly questionable in itself, the results are perfectly consistent.

Contributory Factors

Given the association between self-esteem and anxiety, the question arises: Does low self-esteem tend to generate anxiety or does anxiety tend to generate low self-esteem? Horney, on the basis of her clinical and theoretical work, has taken the position that anxiety is of central significance; in her view, anxiety sets in motion a complex chain of psychological events which produces, among other consequences, self-hatred and self-contempt.[2] Briefly, Horney contends that the child, through a variety of adverse circumstances in the family, develops a fundamental fear, a basic anxiety. In order to cope with this anxiety, he retreats into the world of imagination where he creates an idealized image which gives him a sense of strength and confidence. This image is so admirable and flattering that

[2] Karen Horney, *Neurosis and Human Growth, op. cit.*

when the individual compares it with his actual self, this latter self is so pale and inferior by comparison that he feels a hatred and contempt for it.[3]

According to this theory, then, anxiety tends to generate low self-esteem. And, indeed, our data are entirely consistent with Horney's interpretation. There is reason to believe, however, that the opposite sequence may also occur, viz., that low self-esteem may generate anxiety. This can occur for reasons quite different from those advanced by Horney. This point will constitute the central focus of this chapter. In the analysis which follows, we shall attempt to specify certain factors associated with low self-esteem which may be expected to create anxiety. Four such factors will be considered: (1) instability of self-image; (2) the "presenting self"; (3) vulnerability; and (4) feelings of isolation. We will suggest that low self-esteem contributes to these four conditions; that these conditions in turn tend to generate anxiety; and that if we control on these factors, the relationship of self-esteem to anxiety will decrease.

Instability of the self-image. One possible reason why people with low self-esteem experience an inordinate amount of anxiety is that they tend to have shifting and unstable self-pictures. Table 1 shows the relationship between the individual's score on the self-esteem scale and

[3] We would suggest that it is equally plausible to assume that the idealized image would arise in response to low self-esteem. In Horney's view, the individual attempts to cope with anxiety by raising himself above others in his imagination. It appears to us, however, that an individual will seek to raise himself above others if he fears that he is inferior to them. It seems unlikely that the *anxious* person would seek to raise himself above others if he really considered himself to be a worthy, highly adequate person. On the other hand, it is understandable that he should want to raise himself above others if he actually considered himself below them, that he should create in his imagination a worthy person if, in the cold light of reality, he considered himself unworthy.

his score on a "stability of self-picture" scale.[4] Two points should be made about this table. The first is that the least stability is found among those who have rather low self-esteem, but not the lowest. The relationship is somewhat curvilinear, with the trough appearing among those who have fairly low self-esteem (score 4 on the self-esteem scale). In other words, people who hold rather negative opinions of themselves, but who are not absolutely, unequivocally, consistently self-deprecatory, appear to have the most changeable pictures of themselves.

TABLE 1

* Self-Esteem and Stability of Self-Picture

"Stability of self-picture" score	Self-Esteem						
	High 0	1	2	3	4	5	Low 6
Very stable	71%	46%	34%	20%	15%	18%	21%
Intermediate	20	28	32	31	29	27	37
Very unstable	9	26	33	49	56	55	42
Total percent	100	100	100	100	100	100	100
(Number)	(484)	(811)	(741)	(461)	(247)	(121)	(38)

The other point is this: People with low self-esteem are much more likely than those with high self-esteem to have unstable self-conceptions. At the extremes, the students with high self-esteem were three-and-one-half times as likely as those with low self-esteem to have "very stable" self-pictures and the latter were four times as likely as the former to be "very unstable."

But are people with unstable self-pictures more likely to experience anxiety? Frame of reference theory would

[4] A description of this scale appears in Appendix D-2.

lead us to expect this to be the case. Sherif [5] has provided striking demonstrations that it is characteristic of the human mind to assimilate new experiences or stimuli into already existing frames of reference. It seems reasonable to assume that the individual's self-attitude is probably the major single anchorage point to which new stimuli are related. If, however, a person has unclear, unstable, uncertain opinions, attitudes, and perceptions of himself— if he simply is not sure of what he is like—then he is deprived of his most valuable frame of reference; this deprivation is almost certainly anxiety-provoking.

The results are consistent with this reasoning. Table 2

TABLE 2

* Stability of Self-Image and Frequency of Report
of Psychosomatic Symptoms

Number of psychosomatic symptoms	"Stability of Self" Scale					
	Stable 0	1	2	3	4	Unstable 5
2 or less	66%	58%	49%	39%	32%	32%
3	13	15	14	19	15	14
4 or more	21	27	36	42	53	54
Total percent	100	100	100	100	100	100
(Number)	(388)	(760)	(848)	(633)	(239)	(91)

shows that the more uncertain the individual is about what he is like, the more does he tend to report experiencing many physiological symptoms of anxiety.

We thus see that people with low self-esteem have less stable self-pictures; that people with unstable self-pictures

[5] Muzafer Sherif, *The Psychology of Social Norms*, New York: Harper, 1936.

have more psychosomatic symptoms; and that people with low self-esteem have more psychosomatic symptoms. But in order to be able to say that people with low self-esteem are more anxious because their self-pictures are more unstable, it is necessary to show that were they not more unstable—were the stability of all groups in fact equal—then they would not have more psychosomatic symptoms than others (or that the difference between the groups would decrease). In order to examine this question, we have equated the stability of all self-esteem groups by "standardizing" on stability.

Table 3 indicates that were all groups equal in stability, the relationship between self-esteem and psychosomatic symptoms would decrease, although it would still remain strong. Originally, for example, those with the highest self-esteem were 50.2 percent more likely than those with the lowest self-esteem to have few psychosomatic symptoms. If both groups were equally stable, however, the difference would be 47.5 percent. These data would suggest that stability is a "contributory factor" in accounting for the relationship between self-esteem and anxiety, although it does not appear to be a very powerful factor.

The "presenting self." Another factor which may contribute to the association between self-esteem and anxiety is the tendency for people with low self-esteem to present a false front or face to the world.[6] The "false front" is essentially a coping mechanism; its central aim is to overcome the feeling of worthlessness by convincing others—the outside world—that one is worthy.

Our respondents were asked to agree or disagree with the following statements: "I often find myself 'putting on an act' to impress people" and "I tend to put up a 'front'

[6] For a discussion of false fronts in the economic or prestige areas, see Erving Goffman, *The Presentation of Self in Everyday Life,* Edinburgh: University of Edinburgh, Social Sciences Research Center, 1956.

TABLE 3

† Original Relationship Between Self-Esteem and
Psychosomatic Symptoms and Relationship
Which Would Appear If All Self-Esteem
Groups Were Average in Stability

| | Original relationship | | | | | |
| | Self-Esteem | | | | | |
Psychosomatic symptoms	High 0	1	2	3	4	Low 5–6
2 or less	69.6%	58.0%	46.5%	40.1%	28.6%	19.4%
3–4	19.5	26.0	28.2	33.6	31.4	31.0
5 or more	10.9	16.1	25.3	26.3	40.0	49.7
Total percent	100.0	100.0	100.0	100.0	100.0	100.0
(Number)	(477)	(796)	(724)	(456)	(245)	(155)

Relationship standardized on stability of self-picture

| | Self-Esteem | | | | | |
Psychosomatic symptoms	High 0	1	2	3	4	Low 5–6
2 or less	66.2%	57.0%	47.0%	42.3%	28.3%	18.7%
3–4	21.2	25.8	27.9	32.7	34.0	31.0
5 or more	12.6	17.2	25.0	25.0	37.7	50.3
Total percent	100.0	100.0	100.0	100.0	100.0	100.0
(Number)	(477)	(796)	(724)	(456)	(245)	(155)

to people." In each case, the lower the self-esteem, the more likely is the respondent to agree with the statement. If the responses to both questions are combined, it is found that people with low self-esteem are nearly six times as likely as those with high self-esteem to agree with both

TABLE 4

* Self-Esteem and Tendency to Present Façade to Others

Agreement with two statements reflecting presentation of façade	Self-Esteem						
	High 0	1	2	3	4	5	Low 6
Agree with both	6%	11%	14%	21%	26%	34%	34%
Agree with one	13	17	22	21	24	23	26
Agree with neither	80	71	64	58	50	42	40
Total percent	100	100	100	100	100	100	100
(Number)	(484)	(816)	(725)	(452)	(245)	(120)	(38)

statements. (Table 4) It seems clear that the person who accepts himself feels less need to present a false front to the outside world.

What is anxiety-provoking about the presentation of a façade? At least two factors may be suggested. The first is that putting on an act tends to be a strain. To act cheerful when one is sad, sympathetic when one is indifferent, friendly when one is hostile, courageous when one is timid—all this by sheer force of will and self-control—can hardly be other than a constant strain. The second source of tension lies in the possibility that one will make a false step, reveal some inconsistency, let the guise slip. Table 5 indicates that respondents who say they present a façade to the world are more likely to report psychosomatic symptoms.

Since people with low self-esteem are more likely to present a false front to others and since people who present a false front manifest more symptoms of anxiety, we might assume that one reason people with low self-esteem show more anxiety is because of their tendency to present a false front.

TABLE 5

* The "Presenting Self" and Psychosomatic Symptoms

Number of psychosomatic symptoms	Statements reflecting presentation of façade		
	Agree with both	Agree with one	Agree with neither
2 or less	36%	46%	54%
3–4	27	29	27
5 or more	35	25	19
Total percent	100	100	100
(Number)	(445)	(565)	(1937)

The data appear to accord with this interpretation. We find that if respondents who vary in self-esteem did not differ in their tendency to put up a front to others—if they were all average in this regard—then the relationship of self-esteem to psychosomatic symptoms of anxiety would be somewhat reduced. Specifically, 70.2 percent of those with the highest self-esteem have fewer than three psychosomatic symptoms; if these people were as likely as those with low self-esteem to put on an act with others, however, 63.7 percent would have fewer than three psychosomatic symptoms—a decrease of 6.5 percent. We may thus infer that one reason people with high self-esteem have fewer anxiety symptoms is that few of them feel impelled to present a false front to the world.

Vulnerability. In light of the widely accepted assumption that the sentiment of self-regard is important to the emotional life of the individual, it can be assumed that negative self-opinions are rarely accepted with equanimity. Hence, we would expect the person with low self-esteem to be inordinately sensitive to any evidence in the experience of his daily life which testified to his inadequacy, incompetence, or worthlessness. To use Horney's felicitous term, they are highly *vulnerable*.[7]

Several items of evidence testify to this vulnerability. People with low self-esteem, we find, (1) are much more likely to be sensitive to criticism, to be deeply disturbed when they are laughed at, scolded, blamed, criticized, etc.[8] (Table 6); (2) are much more likely to be bothered

TABLE 6

* Self-Esteem and Sensitivity to Criticism or Attack

"Sensitivity to criticism" scale	Self-Esteem						
	High 0	1	2	3	4	5	Low 6
Highly sensitive	26%	32%	39%	45%	60%	53%	68%
Not sensitive	74	68	61	55	40	47	32
Total percent	100	100	100	100	100	100	100
(Number)	(469)	(781)	(710)	(439)	(231)	(114)	(37)

if others have a poor opinion of them; (3) are much more likely to be deeply disturbed if they do poorly at some task they have undertaken; (4) are much more likely to be disturbed when they become aware of some fault or inadequacy in themselves. In addition, among the normal volunteers described earlier, low self-esteem subjects are more likely to be described by nurses as "touchy and easily hurt." (Table 7)

It is also interesting to note that more vulnerable people have higher anxiety levels. Consider the "sensitivity to criticism" scale. Three-fifths of the highly sensitive stu-

[7] *Neurosis and Human Growth*, especially Chap. 5.

[8] A description of the "sensitivity to criticism" scale appears in Appendix D-4.

TABLE 7

* Self-Esteem of Normal Volunteers and
Nurses' Descriptions of Them as
"Touchy and Easily Hurt"

Nurses' descriptions as "touchy and easily hurt"	Self-Esteem		
	High	Medium	Low
Yes	4%	13%	17%
Undecided	9	13	42
No	87	73	42
Total percent	100	100	100
(Number)	(23)	(15)	(12)

dents reported a large number of psychosomatic symptoms compared with only one-fifth of those who were not sensitive to criticism. (Table 8) Similarly, those who were bothered by the negative opinions of others and who were disturbed at failure or the awareness of inadequacies in

TABLE 8

* Sensitivity to Criticism and Psychosomatic Symptoms

Number of psychosomatic symptoms	"Sensitivity to criticism" score			
	Low 0	1	2	High 3
2 or fewer	67%	55%	40%	26%
3	12	15	18	14
4 or more	21	29	42	59
Total percent	100	100	100	100
(Number)	(306)	(1446)	(782)	(311)

themselves tended to report more psychosomatic symptoms.

If the anxiety of low self-esteem people is due in part to their greater vulnerability, then it would follow that if they were not so vulnerable, they would not experience so many symptoms of anxiety. And Table 9 shows that

TABLE 9

† Self-Esteem and Psychosomatic Symptoms: (A) Original Relationship; and (B) Relationship Standardized on Sensitivity to Criticism

A. Original relationship			
Number of psychosomatic symptoms	Self-Esteem		
	High	Medium	Low
2 or less	62.0%	43.6%	25.5%
3–4	24.1	30.5	31.9
5 or more	13.9	26.0	42.6
Total percent	100.0	100.0	100.0
(Number)	(1229)	(1129)	(376)

B. Relationship standardized on sensitivity to criticism			
Number of psychosomatic symptoms	Self-Esteem		
	High	Medium	Low
2 or less	60.4%	44.3%	29.1%
3–4	24.5	30.2	33.3
5 or more	15.1	25.5	37.6
Total percent	100.0	100.0	100.0
(Number)	(1229)	(1129)	(376)

this is so. If we standardize all self-esteem groups on sensitivity to criticism, then the original difference of 36.5

percent between the two extreme groups decreases to 31.3 percent.

Feelings of psychic isolation. The adolescent afflicted with pangs of self-contempt may develop at least two solutions to the problem of feelings of worthlessness: (1) he may retreat into the world of imagination where he can dream of himself as worthy, and (2) he may put up a false front to others to convince them that he is worthy. But as is so often the case with neurotic solutions, they may generate consequences more devastating than those they were designed to alleviate. One of these consequences would appear to be the development of feelings of isolation.

Both these factors—the private world of daydreaming and the public pose—tend to separate the person with low self-esteem from others. He cannot share himself with others fully, freely, and spontaneously. For these reasons we would expect such people to experience a fundamental feeling of loneliness.

Our respondents were asked: "Do you think most people know the kind of person you really are, or do you feel that most people do not know what really goes on underneath?" Table 10 indicates that slightly over one out of every three respondents with the highest self-esteem felt that others did not understand what they were really like underneath whereas this was true of fully five out of six people with the least self-esteem. With perfect regularity, a decreasing level of self-esteem is accompanied by an increasing proportion who feel misunderstood by others.

It is no wonder, then, that these people come to be afflicted with a haunting sense of isolation and loneliness. "Would you say that you tend to be a lonely person?" the respondents were asked. Without exception, the lower the individual's level of self-esteem, the more likely is he to be afflicted with pangs of loneliness. Only 35 percent of those with the least self-esteem said that they were "not lonely,"

161

TABLE 10

* Self-Esteem and Belief That Others Know
How One Really Feels

"Do you think most people know the kind of person you really are, or do you feel that most people do not know what really goes on underneath?"	Self-Esteem						
	High 0	1	2	3	4	5	Low 6
Most do not know what goes on underneath	36%	50%	54%	64%	73%	74%	84%
Most know the kind of person I really am	64	50	46	36	27	26	16
Total percent	100	100	100	100	100	100	100
(Number)	(507)	(860)	(786)	(503)	(264)	(124)	(38)

compared with fully 86 percent of those possessing the highest self-esteem level. (Table 11)

The feeling of loneliness is, then, not just a matter of being physically alone. A person is lonely who cannot make contact with others, communicate with them, get through to them, share feelings, ideas, and enthusiasms with them; and these are things the person with low self-esteem has difficulty in doing because of his involvement in his private world of imagination and his public pose.

Given the fact that low self-esteem may contribute to a feeling of isolation, the question may be raised: Why should feelings of isolation be associated with anxiety? We would suggest that the person who stands alone lacks social support; thus, he is more likely to feel threatened by the powerful sea of forces which surround him. He can never

TABLE 11

* Self-Esteem and Loneliness

"Would you say that you tend to be a lonely person?"	Self-Esteem						
	High 0	1	2	3	4	5	Low 6
Very lonely	1%	2%	2%	4%	8%	20%	22%
Fairly lonely	13	19	26	35	42	37	43
Not lonely	86	79	72	60	49	43	35
Total percent	100	100	100	100	100	100	100
(Number)	(520)	(878)	(798)	(506)	(269)	(125)	(37)

share himself with another completely, and he can never feel the strength and reassurance which comes from such sharing and support. Hence, threats, dangers, or problems which others can work out with friends or relatives must be faced by him alone, and are therefore felt to be inordinately dangerous and anxiety-provoking.

Table 12 shows that people who feel lonely and isolated

TABLE 12

* Feelings of Loneliness and Psychosomatic Symptoms

Number of psychosomatic symptoms	"Would you say that you tend to be a lonely person?"		
	Very lonely	Fairly lonely	Not lonely
2 or less	22%	37%	56%
3–4	31	31	26
5 or more	47	31	18
Total percent	100	100	100
(Number)	(124)	(818)	(2280)

163

do indeed manifest more physiological symptoms of anxiety. Similarly, people who feel misunderstood are more likely to manifest these physiological symptoms of anxiety. Students who felt that others knew what they were really like underneath had fewer psychosomatic symptoms than those who felt that their inner lives were closed to others.

It is thus not surprising to find that if feelings of isolation are controlled, the relationship between self-esteem and anxiety decreases. (Table 13) Whereas those with high self-esteem are 36.3 percent more likely than those with low self-esteem to have few psychosomatic symptoms, the data show that if both groups did not differ in feelings of isolation, the difference would be reduced to 31.3 percent.

Joint effect. In the foregoing discussion, four factors which may contribute to the association between self-esteem and anxiety have been suggested; none of these factors completely accounts for the relationship, but each appears to contribute to it. Due to the limited number of cases, it is not possible to control on all four factors simultaneously, but we have been able to control on three of them. Table 14-A shows the original relationship between self-esteem and psychosomatic symptoms and Table 14-B shows this relationship when it is standardized simultaneously on feelings of isolation, sensitivity to criticism, and instability of self-image. It will be seen that the original difference of 36.8 percent decreases to 26.7 percent. These three factors considered jointly, then, make a fairly substantial contribution to the original relationship, although they by no means entirely account for it.

To say that the joint impact of the several "explanatory" factors cited here is stronger than the impact of each considered individually is not to deny that each explanatory variable may to some extent be contaminated by the others. For example, if we show that sensitivity to criticism partly accounts for the relationship of self-esteem to

TABLE 13

† Self-Esteem and Psychosomatic Symptoms: (A) Original
Relationship; and (B) Relationship Standardized
on Feelings of Loneliness

A. Original relationship			
Number of psychosomatic symptoms	Self-Esteem		
	High	Medium	Low
2 or less	62.4%	44.2%	26.1%
3–4	23.5	30.1	31.5
5 or more	14.0	25.7	42.4
Total percent	100.0	100.0	100.0
(Number)	(1374)	(1279)	(425)

B. Relationship standardized on feelings of loneliness			
Number of psychosomatic symptoms	Self-Esteem		
	High	Medium	Low
2 or less	60.5%	44.7%	29.2%
3–4	24.0	29.8	32.0
5 or more	15.5	25.5	38.8
Total percent	100.0	100.0	100.0
(Number)	(1374)	(1279)	(425)

psychosomatic symptoms, we cannot be certain that sensitivity to criticism may not be reflecting at the same time,
say, instability of self-image or psychic isolation. We have,
at least, guarded against the danger to the following extent. Every explanatory variable considered in this chapter has been related to psychosomatic symptoms controlling
separately on every other variable, including self-esteem.

165

TABLE 14

† Self-Esteem and Psychosomatic Symptoms: (A) Original
Relationship; and (B) Relationship Standardized
on Three Test Factors

A. Original relationship

Number of psychosomatic symptoms	Self-Esteem		
	High	Medium	Low
2 or less	69.5%	52.3%	32.7%
3–4	19.9	27.3	32.7
5 or more	10.6	20.4	34.6
Total percent	100.0	100.0	100.0
(Number)	(452)	(1420)	(789)

B. Standardized relationship

Number of psychosomatic symptoms	Self-Esteem		
	High	Medium	Low
2 or less	65.4%	51.3%	38.7%
3–4	21.3	27.4	32.9
5 or more	13.3	21.7	28.9
Total percent	100.0	100.0	100.0
(Number)	(452)	(1420)	(789)

It turns out that each of these factors is related to psychosomatic symptoms independently of the others.[9]

To summarize: four factors associated with self-esteem which might be expected to contribute to anxiety have been suggested: the instability of the self-image, the pre-

[9] Space limitations prevent us from presenting the 32 tables upon which this statement is based.

senting self, vulnerability, and feelings of isolation. Self-esteem was found to be related to each of these factors; each of these factors was related to psychosomatic symptoms of anxiety; and when each of these factors was controlled the relationship of self-esteem to anxiety decreased to some degree. This would suggest that these four factors contributed in some measure to the relationship between self-esteem and anxiety.

On the basis of these results, it seems reasonable to assume that not only is low self-esteem a psychologically distressing state in itself but it also tends to set in motion a train of events which leads to a state at least equally distressing, viz., feelings of anxiety.

CHAPTER 9

INTERPERSONAL ATTITUDES AND BEHAVIOR

THE cement of social life does not primarily consist of grand passions or cosmic philosophies; it consists of casual conversations, small talk, the easy interchange of ideas, the sharing of minor enthusiasms. The individual's self-conception plays an important role in such interaction. What a person thinks of himself, then, is not an imprisoned, encapsulated attitude which has no relevance beyond the borders of his psyche; on the contrary, it extends out into his relationships with other people—guiding, modifying, and controlling them in accordance with its own inexorable logic.

In this chapter, we will ask: What is the relationship between a person's feelings about himself and his feelings about other people? How does his self-conception influence his behavioral orientation toward the world? What is the association between his self-esteem and the impression he makes on others?

The present discussion will focus on the person with extremely low self-esteem. Since the phrase "the person with extremely low self-esteem" is rather cumbersome, we will call this person the *egophobe* and his opposite number the *egophile*. Admittedly these terms are unaesthetic and somewhat misleading, but no superior alternative suggests itself. So long as the terms *egophobe* and *egophile* are recognized as referring to those who have very low and very high scores on our self-esteem scale, there is no sacrifice of meaning. At the same time, this usage not only has the advantage of brevity and ease of expression but it also highlights the central purpose of this chapter, viz., to describe pure types or ideal types. Few real people will, of course, possess all the characteristics of the pure type, but these characteristics will be found in greater abundance among egophobes than egophiles. Our purpose, then, will be to present a composite portrait of the egophobe's interpersonal feelings as well as the impression he makes on others.

In the New York State study, it was not possible to identify those with extremely high and extremely low self-esteem, since the questionnaires were anonymous. However, in an independent study of achievement and creativity conducted by Dr. Albert Caron among nearly 1,300 high school students in the Washington, D.C. area, our self-esteem scale was utilized. We then selected out 18 students who had extremely low self-esteem (scores 5 or 6 on the scale) and 18 students who had extremely high self-esteem (score 0 on the scale). These students came to the investigator's office, completed questionnaires similar to those administered to the New York State students, and were then interviewed for periods ranging between one and one-and-a-half hours. The interviews were recorded on tape. These interviews proved to be a valuable supplement to the quantitative data derived from the New York State study. On the basis of these combined data we shall attempt to paint a portrait of the egophobe's attitudes and feelings toward other people.

Interpersonal Vulnerability

As we noted in the previous chapter, one of the outstanding feelings of the egophobe is a sense of interpersonal threat. He is, for example, much more likely to say that "criticism or scolding hurts me terribly"; much more likely to say that he feels deeply disturbed "when anyone laughs at you or blames you for something you have done wrong"; much more likely to say that he is "extremely sensitive" to criticism.

Since, as we shall see, the egophobe feels that others do not like him very much, we might expect him to adopt

169

the defensive reaction of saying that it does not matter to him what others think. On the contrary, however, he is considerably more likely to say that he is deeply concerned with others' reactions to him. When asked "How much does it bother you to find that someone has a poor opinion of you?" 63 percent of the egophobes, but only 39 percent of the egophiles, say that it "bothers me very much." (Table 1) It may also be remembered from the previous chap-

TABLE 1

* Self-Esteem and Distress at Negative
Evaluations by Others

"How much does it bother you to find that someone has a poor opinion of you?"	Self-Esteem						
	High 0	1	2	3	4	5	Low 6
Bothers me very much	39%	42%	46%	48%	54%	53%	63%
Bothers me somewhat	37	36	40	36	33	30	18
Bothers me very little	24	21	15	16	14	17	18
Total percent	100	100	100	100	100	100	100
(Number)	(520)	(873)	(795)	(505)	(267)	(124)	(38)

ter that normal volunteers with low self-esteem were more likely to be described by nurses as "touchy and easily hurt." Apparently the egophobe's sensitivity to criticism, reproach, slights, etc., tends to be visible to, or suspected by, outside observers.

If the egophobe is as hypersensitive to criticism, ridicule, or chastisement as these data suggest, we would expect this to impart a tense and dangerous coloring to his interpersonal relations. For example, one egophobic girl described her distaste for competition in the following terms: ". . . in a job where there is competition you can run over other people. . . . I don't want to hurt other people because I've been hurt, and I don't feel it's right to hurt other people. [Q: When you say you've been hurt, what do you have in mind?] Well, most of my life people have made fun of me. People have humiliated me in front of other people." At this point the respondent had difficulty in holding back tears.

The egophobe's lack of confidence in his own judgment often leads him to assume that the critics are right. As one girl noted: "Like when I'm in school and somebody says 'I don't like the clothes you are wearing.' So I say that I am going to stop wearing the clothes, and won't wear the two pieces together again. Then in class somebody says, 'You're so dumb that you don't know the answer to this simple question.' And that hurts me. It's not many times that people do criticize me, but when it happens it does degrade me."

Interpersonal Awkwardness

The egophobe not only tends to say that he feels threatened by other people but he is also likely to describe his interpersonal relations as awkward and difficult. Difficult interpersonal relations, however, may be expressed in different ways. One kind of difficulty takes the form of fighting, squabbling, or resisting other people. Another form is manifested in awkwardness, uneasiness, or avoidance. While we have no evidence regarding the first type of interpersonal difficulty, the egophobe clearly considers himself awkward and uneasy in his interpersonal relationships.

For example, three out of four egophiles said that "I find it easy to make talk when I meet new people," compared with only about one out of three egophobes. Similarly, when asked "Would you say that you are the sort of person who finds it easier or harder to make friends than most people?" over one out of four egophobes, compared with one out of twenty egophiles, said "harder." (Table 2)

The egophobe also has a somewhat greater tendency to

171

TABLE 2

* Self-Esteem and Interpersonal Awkwardness

	Self-Esteem						
Difficulty in making talk and in making friends	High 0	1	2	3	4	5	Low 6
Easy to make talk and easy to make friends	70%	72%	61%	56%	45%	35%	29%
Either hard to make talk or hard to make friends	27	23	31	31	40	40	50
Hard to make talk *and* hard to make friends	3	6	8	13	15	24	21
Total percent	100	100	100	100	100	100	100
(Number)	(252)	(389)	(363)	(213)	(119)	(59)	(24)

say that "I tend to be a rather shy person." (Table 3) Here
the differences are not so clear and consistent as in some
of the other tables; in other words, shyness does not
characterize all egophobes nor is it absent among egophiles. In general, however, egophobes show a somewhat
greater tendency to describe themselves as shy. It may also

TABLE 3

* Self-Esteem and Shyness

	Self-Esteem						
"I tend to be a rather shy person"	High 0	1	2	3	4	5	Low 6
Agree	33%	41%	48%	48%	55%	62%	55%
Disagree	67	59	52	52	45	38	45
Total percent	100	100	100	100	100	100	100
(Number)	(510)	(872)	(789)	(508)	(263)	(126)	(38)

be noted that nurses were less likely to deny that ego-phobic normal volunteers were "easily embarrassed" and "shy." (Table 4)

TABLE 4

Self-Esteem and Description as "Easily Embarrassed" and "Shy," among Normal Volunteers

	Self-Esteem		
Described by nurses as . . .	High	Medium	Low
"Easily embarrassed"			
Yes	4%	7%	17%
Undecided	13	13	33
No	83	80	50
Total percent	100	100	100
(Number)	(23)	(15)	(12)
"Shy"			
Yes	13%	40%	25%
Undecided	9	7	25
No	78	53	50
Total percent	100	100	100
(Number)	(23)	(15)	(12)

The egophobe's awkwardness and inhibition in his relationships with others in some cases appears to lead him to avoid other people, or at least to fail to take the initiative in establishing contacts with them. Whereas two-fifths of the egophobes said that "I prefer to pass by school friends, or people I know but have not seen for a long time, unless they speak to me first," only one out of every eight egophiles agreed with this statement. (Table 5)

TABLE 5

* Self-Esteem and Failure to Initiate Conversations

"I prefer to pass by school friends, or people I know but have not seen for a long time, unless they speak to me first"	Self-Esteem						
	High 0	1	2	3	4	5	Low 6
Agree	12%	16%	16%	24%	24%	36%	41%
Disagree	88	84	84	76	76	64	59
Total percent	100	100	100	100	100	100	100
(Number)	(521)	(882)	(796)	(509)	(268)	(127)	(39)

This failure to initiate contacts is suggested by the boy who said: "Well, I guess I sort of shy away from people . . . I don't feel like knowing a lot of people. I get mixed up. I won't go up to someone and say: 'Hi, my name is _____.' I'll have to be approached by somebody and be introduced and probably get to know the person better." And a girl, describing her changing reactions to people, said: "But sometimes people I've known for a long time, and have been associated with, I'll see them and I'll just go away someplace rather than strike up an old acquaintance . . ."

Self-consciousness and vulnerability in human relationships appear to play a role in this relative absence of initiative. One boy, contrasting his earlier with his present reactions, said: ". . . when you are small it's much easier making friends, because you don't feel you are going to embarrass yourself meeting new people . . . But when you get older it's not so easy. You begin to think what a fool you can make of yourself in the eyes of a person you don't know. I kind of become shy and withdrawn."

174

One girl, describing her mother as shy about meeting new people, was asked whether she was also shy. "I would say so, [with] people my own age I am . . . my father brings business associates home sometimes and I'm not too shy about that, except after I've met them, I kind of withdraw with a book into a small corner. I don't like to take part in conversations with people I don't know."

Some egophobes report that their first reaction to new situations is one of tension. One girl, in reference to social activities, said: ". . . I'd rather go with girls than with boys. Sometimes I'm real anxious about meeting people. It worries me and I get tensed up about it . . . And I was surprised that I wasn't tensed up about this interview, and I thought I would be. I thought I would be petrified, and I'm not."

At times such awkwardness and tension may produce an interference with communication. In its mild form, it may be manifested in a hesitancy to express one's views. As one egophobe expressed it: ". . . I am kind of hesitant in a large group of people. I'm kind of shy . . . I don't know what a crowd does to me . . . I get all quiet . . . I have always been that way."

At times, however, this interference with communication may become quite serious. One girl, explaining why she discussed public affairs very little, said: "Because I don't like to talk about it. I don't like to say anything. I don't have anything to say. Every time I say anything, the words just don't come out right. [Q: Is that typical when there are other discussions, too?] Yes. I don't know how to talk to people. What I say doesn't come out what I mean . . . I might be wrong in what I say, and then it will start something. So I just keep things to myself."

In sum, the egophobe does not tend to see his relationships with people as easy, smooth, fluid, spontaneous. In many cases he withdraws from social relationships, or at least does not make contact on his own initiative. Apparently, he tends to be too self-conscious, guarded, and uncertain to enable him to engage in spontaneous communication.

Assumptions Regarding Others' Reactions

Cooley has observed that we do not see ourselves as others see us but as we imagine they see us.[1] The attitudes and feelings of others toward us are never available to us in immediate experience, but, rather, reach us through the sieve of our own perceptual mechanisms and defenses.

The individual's opinion of himself is thus likely to be importantly influenced by what he imagines others think of him. At the same time, he is also likely to attribute to others the opinion he holds of himself. Both processes are doubtlessly circular and mutually reinforcing. It is thus not surprising to find that those people who consider themselves unworthy are more inclined to feel that others share this opinion of them. As noted in Chapter 2, we asked our respondents: "What do you think most people think of you?" Whereas one out of four egophobes said that others thought poorly of them, this was true of only one out of a hundred people with high self-esteem.

There is evidence to suggest, however, that the egophobe is not simply reading into the reactions of others feelings which have no basis in reality. It will be recalled from Chapter 2, for example, that nurses who were asked to describe normal volunteers were less likely to characterize the egophobes as "well thought of," "makes good impression," "often admired," and "respected by others." In many cases, the egophobe may be quite correct in assuming that others do not value him highly.

The egophobe is not only more disposed to feel that others lack respect for him (an assumption which may not be incorrect) but is also more likely to be convinced that

---

[1] *Human Nature and the Social Order,* p. 152.

he lacks "likeable" qualities. For example, when asked to characterize themselves in terms of a series of descriptive adjectives, egophobes were consistently less likely to consider themselves well-liked and well-respected. They were less likely to describe themselves as "easy to get along with," "able to get along with all kinds of people," "well-respected and looked up to by others," "pleasant," "likeable," "popular," "good-natured," and "well-liked by many different people." (Table 6) They were more likely to characterize themselves as "dreamy," "emotional," and "temperamental."

TABLE 6

Self-Esteem and Interpersonal Trait Descriptions

Proportion describing them- selves as very or fairly . . .	Self-Esteem						
	High 0	1	2	3	4	5	Low 6
(Number)	(198)	(361)	(294)	(200)	(87)	(50)	(18)
* Easy to get along with	95%	92%	89%	89%	85%	75%	56%
* Able to get along with all kinds of people	94	94	89	89	84	77	50
* Well-respected and looked up to by others	87	82	73	74	62	56	22
* Pleasant	96	92	92	90	88	76	44
* Likeable	95	92	92	86	79	67	50
* Popular	89	81	82	75	66	62	22
* Good-natured	98	94	91	93	90	81	62
* Well-liked by many different people	93	88	81	79	69	66	25

The fact that egophobes are less likely to feel that others like them does not mean, however, that they are unconcerned with whether others like them. On the contrary, those normal volunteers with low and medium self-esteem more often gave the impression that they were very "anxious to be approved of," "eager to get along with others," and "wants everyone to like him." (Table 7)

TABLE 7

Self-Esteem and Desire to Please among Normal Volunteers

	Self-Esteem		
Described by nurses . . .	High	Medium	Low
* "Very anxious to be approved of"			
(Number)	(23)	(15)	(12)
Yes	22%	47%	42%
Undecided	17	27	33
No	61	27	25
"Eager to get along with others"			
Yes	35%	53%	58%
Undecided	17	20	8
No	48	27	33
"Wants everyone to like him"			
Yes	17%	40%	25%
Undecided	30	20	33
No	52	40	42

The egophobe, then, tends to assume that others do not like him very much, that he lacks the friendly, sociable qualities which others find appealing. He does not, however, respond by dismissing the importance of interpersonal success, but, on the contrary, often makes special efforts to gain it. His misfortune lies in the fact that those people are often most popular who do not strive for popularity.

178

One impression emerging from the interviews is that the egophobes were much less likely to consider themselves interesting or important to others. An egophobic boy whose parents had died and who now lived with his married sister and brother-in-law said: "Well, I can't expect them to be interested in me. Of course, they have their own children. And I really don't expect it from them. I just kind of live with them. I wouldn't talk over my affairs with them because I know they aren't interested." A girl said: "I can help others with their problems, but I guess I feel I bore others when I talk about mine."

The Façade

As noted in the previous chapter, people with low self-esteem are much more likely to say that they tend to put up a "front" or "façade" to others which covers their real feelings. One boy was asked whether most people knew what he was like underneath. He replied: "Nobody knows, really, except my parents. Mostly I'm just sort of happy-go-lucky. Just recently I went on a blind date with this girl . . . She was a lot of fun, had a terrific sense of humor, and could talk about anything you wanted to talk about—the intellectual sort of type—and we just hit if off so great. Then she said, when we were dancing: 'You know, Dick, you're not so happy-go-lucky, really. Deep down inside you're very serious.'"

A girl reported: "I don't know why, but I have always tried to hide—I've never said anything outright that would give anybody my real feelings—that I was unhappy. Usually I am a relatively gay person. Yet my teachers—if I have been quiet in class or something like that—will ask me after class what happened, because I'm usually such a gay person. And being as I'm not usually happy, I'm deceiving people in that point." The pose of cheerfulness is also expressed by the boy who said: "I don't say that much. Most of the time I'm just joking. And most of the people think that is what I do all the time."

It is interesting to note that while egophobes generally tend to rate themselves lower on most desirable characteristics, they nevertheless rate themselves as highly as others on "having a good sense of humor." They are, however, probably less successful in deceiving others than they think. It is interesting to note, for example, that egophobic normal volunteers were less likely to be described by nurses as "straightforward and direct." (Table 8) In this sense, the

TABLE 8

Self-Esteem and Description as "Straightforward and Direct" among Normal Volunteers

	Self-Esteem		
Described by nurses as . . .	High	Medium	Low
"straightforward and direct"			
Yes	39%	13%	8%
Undecided	30	47	33
No	30	40	58
Total percent	100	100	100
(Number)	(23)	(15)	(12)

attempt to impress others by putting on an act is to some extent self-defeating.

Faith in People

With regard to the relationship between self-attitudes and attitudes toward others, two conflicting points of view have been advanced. The first approach, implicit in the work of Freud, is that the individual who loves himself more will thereby love others less. This is suggested by

180

Freud's economic conception of the libido and his theory of object cathexis. Given a certain "fund" or "quantum" of libido, the person who invests this energy in himself will have less available for others. Fromm notes: "According to Freud, the more love I turn toward the outside world the less love is left for myself, and vice versa." [2]

The opposite point of view has been propounded by Fromm.[3] In Fromm's view, the individual's attitude toward humanity, toward human nature, is one of the central axioms of his life theory. If he trusts and respects human nature, then he will trust and respect himself, since he is himself a member of the human race. If he hates and despises others, then he will have a fundamental contempt for himself.

In the present investigation we related our scale of self-esteem to a scale of "misanthropy" or "faith-in-people." [4] Table 9 indicates that as self-esteem decreases, the pro-

TABLE 9

＊ Self-Esteem and Faith in People

"Faith-in-people" scale	Self-Esteem						
	High 0	1	2	3	4	5	Low 6
High	45%	38%	32%	30%	27%	12%	23%
Medium	25	28	27	22	25	26	13
Low	30	34	42	47	48	62	63
Total percent	100	100	100	100	100	100	100
(Number)	(407)	(706)	(621)	(392)	(206)	(105)	(30)

[2] Erich Fromm, *Man For Himself,* New York: Rinehart, 1947, p. 128.

[3] *Ibid.,* Chap. IV, p. 1.

[4] A description of this scale appears in Appendix D-3. The relationship of misanthropy to other attitudes is presented in Morris Rosen-

portion having high faith in people (with one exception) decreases and the proportion with low faith in people increases regularly.

Among the normal volunteers, too, the skepticism toward human nature is more apparent among egophobes. They were more likely to be described by nurses as "skeptical" and "able to doubt others." (Table 10)

TABLE 10

Self-Esteem and Skepticism among Normal Volunteers

	Self-Esteem		
Described by nurses as . . .	High	Medium	Low
* "Skeptical"			
(Number)	(23)	(15)	(12)
Yes	17%	13%	33%
Undecided	13	20	50
No	70	67	17
"Able to doubt others"			
Yes	35%	20%	58%
Undecided	22	33	33
No	43	47	8

Among some egophobes this low faith in people takes the form of contempt for the great mass of humanity; among others, mistrust; and among still others, hostility. An illustration of a contemptuous attitude is afforded by an egophobic boy who said: "Well, a lot of people think I'm a

berg, "Misanthropy and Political Ideology," *Amer. Soc. Rev.*, Vol. XXI (1956), pp. 690–695, and "Misanthropy and Attitudes Toward International Affairs," *Conflict Resolution*, Vol. 1 (1957), pp. 340–345.

cynic, which I am . . . As far as I can see, everything is a big farce, the whole civilization we have built up is like a house of cards, somebody will blow on it some day and everything will fall down. I say this and most people don't approve. They think that America is the greatest country, that nothing can destroy America, *and the human race is good*, and everybody is a fine guy and so forth. I don't think it's at all true . . ."

A girl generalized her experience with another to include her entire sex. "Boys seem to be more honest than girls," she said. "Girls are sometimes rather sneaky about the whole thing, and I don't like that. If a girl doesn't like another girl, there are always sneaky little comments." She reported that her girl friend had become jealous because she had dated a boy of whom the friend was fond. "And I didn't like it, but she was still sweet . . . I would have liked to talk the whole thing out and got it over with, but everybody wants to play sneaky games." And another girl opined: "Everybody's out, in a way, to get what they can out of life for themselves, and a lot of people cut corners."

Detachment and Isolation

In the discussion of self-esteem and anxiety, we noted that the egophobe tends, relatively speaking, to describe himself as separated from people. This would be expected on the basis of various things he says about himself—that he feels threatened by others; that he feels others do not like or respect him very much; that he distrusts others; that he does not openly reveal himself to others, etc. Such a person would tend to "keep himself to himself."

And the egophobes do, indeed, say that this is so. When asked, "Do you think most people know the kind of person you really are, or do you feel that most people do not know what really goes on underneath?" 84 percent of the egophobes, but only 36 percent of the egophiles, replied: "Most do not know what goes on underneath."

This tendency to avoid revealing oneself was reported in the previous section by the egophobic girl who said "I've never said anything outright that would give anybody my real feelings . . ."; and the student who said "And being as I'm not usually happy, I'm deceiving people in that point." Another girl, discussing her relationship with her father, reported: "Yes, he'll ask me why my mother is so moody today. Usually I can explain it because she usually tells me about her feelings, *but I don't tell her too much about mine.*" Another girl said: "I guess most people know part of my feelings—I mean surface feelings. But I don't discuss things I consider big."

It is of some interest to note that egophobes are more likely to report that this detachment, this lack of intimacy, has characterized them for a long time. We asked our respondents to think back to when they were 10 or 11 years old and to indicate in whom they were most likely to confide about personal matters at that time. Egophobes were considerably more likely than others to say that "I never talked about personal things to anyone."

In view of the threatening nature of interpersonal relationships and their often unsuccessful and unsatisfactory character, many egophobes show a marked preference for being alone. "Well, I just don't have any friends or anything, so I just stay by myself," one egophobe said. [Q: How about when you were a child?] "No, I never really had any close friends." A low self-esteem boy said "You could say I'm antisocial, but I don't really put too much stock in [friends] . . . I do prefer to be alone, I don't know, because I like to think . . . I don't feel really comfortable with people. Usually I go out on excursions on the nature trail behind the house, and I usually spend the whole day there when I have it. Just lay down on the grass quietly."

One apparent result of all this, as noted earlier, is a haunting sense of isolation and loneliness. Whereas only 14 percent of the egophiles said that they were very or fairly lonely, this was true of fully 65 percent of the egophobes.

Assertiveness or Docility

Do people with low self-esteem tend to assert themselves, dominate others, and control people; or do they, on the contrary, tend to exhibit qualities of submissiveness and docility? Here we will confine our attention to the nurses' descriptions of the normal volunteers; due to the small number of cases, these results must generally be interpreted with caution. It is interesting to note, nevertheless, that egophobes are more likely than egophiles to be described as: easily led; usually gives in; lets others make decisions; too easily influenced; lacks self-confidence. Egophiles, on the other hand, are more likely to be described in the following terms: can be strict if necessary; firm but just; likes to compete with others; stern but fair. It may be noted that some of the "assertive" qualities attributed to egophiles by the nurses are not entirely flattering. Whatever the evaluation of these qualities, however, egophobes tend more to be seen as docile and yielding and tend less to be described as dominant and assertive. (Table 11)

TABLE 11

Self-Esteem and Submissiveness or Assertiveness,
Among Normal Volunteers

Traits of submissiveness or docility (nurses' descriptions)	Self-Esteem		
	High	Medium	Low
(Number)	(23)	(15)	(12)
Easily led			
Yes	4%	20%	17%
Undecided	22	27	25
No	74	53	58

185

Traits of submissiveness or docility (nurses' descriptions)	Self-Esteem		
	High	Medium	Low
Usually gives in			
Yes	9%	7%	25%
Undecided	17	27	25
No	74	67	50
Lets others make decisions			
Yes	4%	13%	17%
Undecided	26	27	33
No	70	60	50
Too easily influenced			
Yes	9%	13%	8%
Undecided	22	13	50
No	70	73	42
Lacks self-confidence			
Yes	9%	27%	25%
Undecided	22	7	33
No	70	67	42

Traits of dominance and assertiveness (nurses' descriptions)

	High	Medium	Low
Can be strict if necessary			
Yes	39%	20%	17%
Undecided	30	33	33
No	30	47	50
Firm but just			
Yes	35%	13%	—
Undecided	26	27	42
No	39	60	58
Likes to compete with others			
Yes	17%	33%	8%
Undecided	43	20	25
No	39	47	67
Stern but fair			
Yes	13%	7%	—
Undecided	39	27	25
No	48	67	75

Discussion

In this chapter we have focused on certain interpersonal qualities of the person with low self-esteem—as he sees these qualities in himself and as others see these qualities in him. According to the egophobe's report, he is more vulnerable in interpersonal relations (deeply hurt by criticism, blame, or scolding); he is relatively awkward with others (finds it hard to make talk, does not initiate contacts, etc.); he assumes others think poorly of him or do not particularly like him; he has low faith in human nature; he tends to put up a "front" to people; and he feels relatively isolated and lonely. In addition, nurses describe the egophobic normal volunteers as being less respected by others and as being relatively submissive and lacking in assertiveness.

Both kinds of data employed in this chapter—the individual's subjective feelings about people and the objective descriptions made by nurses—have important implications for social behavior. To an important extent the egophobe's level and nature of participation in social life will be importantly influenced by his subjective feelings about others, the mechanisms he adopts to deal with them, the beliefs he has concerning others' attitudes toward him, etc. Whether the egophobe is right or wrong about these things—whether he is accurately reading or is misreading the effect he has on others—these are the assumptions upon which he operates; these are the thoughts and feelings that guide his actions. Similarly, the egophobe's participation in social life will be influenced by others' reactions toward him. From the sociological viewpoint, then, these subjective elements are not simply trivia, curiosities, or irrelevancies. On the contrary, we will attempt to show in the next three chapters how these interpersonal attitudes and reactions may have a definite bearing upon social attitudes and behavior in several important institutional areas. People act on the basis of their assumptions of what they are like, and these actions, in turn, have characteristic consequences for their lives in society.

PART V
SOCIAL CONSEQUENCES

CHAPTER 10

PARTICIPATION AND LEADERSHIP IN THE HIGH SCHOOL COMMUNITY

IN THE previous chapter, we were chiefly concerned with interpersonal attitudes and the impression which the individual makes on others. Now we wish to examine some of the social consequences of these attitudes and impressions. One major area of interpersonal relationships in the life of the student is his participation and leadership in the high school community. Interpersonal success in the high school is, of course, both a cause and a consequence of self-esteem, probably involving a reinforcing and spiraling effect. In this chapter, we shall examine the data from one perspective—the perspective of the possible effect of self-esteem on high school participation. In doing so, we do not mean to imply that self-esteem may not also in part be a consequence of such interaction.

If one wished to learn something about the nature and extent of a student's network of social relationships in the high school, one might begin by asking the following kinds of questions: Does the student have a group of friends and acquaintances with whom he engages in ordinary day-to-day conversation? If so, does he speak up forcefully and emphatically in such discussions or is he the quiet one in the group? Do friends and acquaintances seek him out, ask his advice, solicit his opinion? Does he join school clubs—the French Club, the Chess Club, the Young Republicans? Does he go out for the teams, join the Debating Society, work on the Yearbook, play in the orchestra, join the Glee Club? If so, what is his role in such organizations? Is it a dynamic, active role which catapults him into a position of leadership, or does he remain a passive member who goes along with the group? How about the classroom? Is he an alert and lively participant who makes an impression on his peers, or is he one of the inconspicuous, nearly invisible, members of the class who simply occupies a seat? If we can answer these questions about a student, we would have a solid foundation for determining the kind of "social force" he is in the high school, for judging his social or interpersonal impact.

Broadly speaking, three "social environments" within which participation and leadership may occur can be distinguished: 1) informal voluntary groupings, such as cliques, gangs, friendship groupings, etc.; 2) formal voluntary groupings, such as teams, clubs, and other organizations; and 3) formal involuntary groupings, such as academic classes. Concerning each of these types of groupings, we will, wherever possible, ask: First, is the student a member of the group? Second, if so, is he an active, energetic contributor and participant? Third, does this active participation thrust him into a position of leadership?

Membership in Voluntary Formal Organizations

In general, voluntary formal organizations may be classified into two types: inclusive and exclusive groups. Inclusive groups, such as political parties, attempt to attract to their ranks the largest number of appropriate and qualified members; exclusive groups, such as private clubs, seek to keep their numbers small, to restrict their base, to keep *out* many of those who aspire to membership. In American high schools, most voluntary organizations are of the inclusive type. Students are encouraged to join groups, and a group often counts itself successful in the degree to which it succeeds in attracting a large number of members.

Since high school clubs are, by and large, open to all and inclined to welcome new members, we may ask: How is the individual's self-conception related to his membership in school organizations? We thus asked our subjects: "About how many hours do you spend, in an average week, on extracurricular activities in school?" We find that 52 percent of those with the least self-esteem participated in extracurricular activities one hour per week or less compared with 36 percent of those with the highest level of self-esteem. Understandably, this result is paralleled by the number of extracurricular activities in which these students take part. Forty percent of the lowest self-esteem respondents took part in no such activities compared with 27 percent of those with the highest level of self-respect.

We have combined the responses to these two items into an index of participation in extracurricular activities. "High" participation refers to those who join in three or more activities or who spend 5 or more hours a week at such activities; "medium" participation refers to those who join one or two activities or who spend less than 5 hours a week at such activities; and "low" participation refers to those who participate in no activities. Table 1 shows that

TABLE 1

* Self-Esteem and Participation in
Extracurricular Activities

Participation in extracurricular activities	Self-Esteem						
	High 0	1	2	3	4	5	Low 6
High	49%	48%	45%	41%	39%	29%	15%
Medium	25	27	27	25	22	34	45
Low	26	25	28	34	39	37	40
Total percent	100	100	100	100	100	100	100
(Number)	(216)	(333)	(288)	(196)	(108)	(41)	(20)

the lower the individual's self-esteem, the less likely is he to be a highly active participant.

"Extracurricular activities" is, of course, a broad term,

encompassing a wide variety of activities. Let us, then, focus on one type of school organization—the club. Table 2

TABLE 2

* Self-Esteem and Membership in School Clubs

Number of clubs	Self-Esteem						
	High 0	1	2	3	4	5	Low 6
None	38%	41%	48%	50%	50%	63%	70%
One	28	24	24	24	22	12	13
Two	14	16	15	13	15	18	13
Three or more	19	19	14	14	14	7	4
Total percent	100	100	100	100	100	100	100
(Number)	(271)	(414)	(378)	(246)	(130)	(60)	(23)

shows a striking relationship between self-esteem and club membership. Seventy percent of the egophobes, but only 38 percent of the egophiles, belonged to no clubs; conversely the high self-esteem people were much more likely than others to be a member of several school clubs.

Club membership is, of course, only one type of extracurricular activity. Other activities would include membership on an athletic team, the school newspaper or yearbook staff, the cheer leader squad, etc. It is apparently, club membership—the Spanish Club, Chess Club, Hiking Club, etc.—that is most conspicuously related to self-esteem.

It is interesting to note that one of the few groups in which people with low self-esteem are more likely than those with high self-esteem to be members is the Glee Club or Choir. Attention is directed to the fact that in such groups there is probably less normal time or scope for spontaneous interaction. In addition, the individual mem-

194

ber's contribution does not tend to be unique, but tends to be buried or integrated in the collective effort. Furthermore, it does not tend to be spontaneous but is controlled by the director and the implacable dictates of the music. In such a group environment, people with low self-esteem appear to be more comfortable.

TABLE 3

Self-Esteem and Membership in Glee Club or Choir

"Since you entered high school, have you ever belonged to . . . glee club or choir?"	Self-Esteem						
	High 0	1	2	3	4	5	Low 6
Yes	18%	20%	21%	22%	30%	28%	33%
No	82	80	79	78	70	72	67
Total percent	100	100	100	100	100	100	100
(Number)	(277)	(425)	(395)	(250)	(128)	(64)	(24)

Leadership in Club and Class

Joining clubs which are open to all comers is one thing, but rising to positions of leadership in such groups is quite another. Social psychologists have long sought the combination which would unlock the secret of personality factors in leadership, but thus far the solution has largely eluded them. While the problem is complex and, as Gibb [1] has pointed out, often dependent on the particular situation and special conditions of the group, our data indicate that, within formal and informal high school groups, the individual's conception of himself is associated with such leadership.

[1] Cecil A. Gibb, "Leadership," Chap. 24 in Gardner Lindzey, ed., *Handbook of Social Psychology*, Vol. II, Cambridge, Mass.: Addison-Wesley, 1954.

Table 4 indicates that 78 percent of those with least self-esteem had never held a position as president or chairman

TABLE 4

Self-Esteem and Frequency of Election as President
or Chairman of School Organization

President or chairman of club or organization	Self-Esteem						
	High 0	1	2	3	4	5	Low 6
Never	56%	62%	66%	68%	64%	70%	78%
Once	20	17	15	17	19	20	13
Twice or more	24	20	18	15	18	10	9
Total percent	100	100	100	100	100	100	100
(Number)	(269)	(414)	(376)	(245)	(129)	(61)	(23)

of a club or school organization, compared with 56 percent of those with the highest self-esteem level.[2]

This relationship becomes somewhat sharper and more even when we ask our respondents whether they have ever held *any* elected position in a club or school organization—whether president, chairman, secretary, treasurer, committee member, etc. Three-fifths of the highest self-esteem respondents have held some elected post in a club or school organization, compared with slightly over one-third of those

[2] These differences do not stem entirely from the lower participation rates of the egophobes. If we eliminate those who currently belong to no clubs and consider only those who belong to one club and those who belong to two or more clubs, we still find that those with lower self-esteem are less likely to be leaders. We cannot, of course, completely equalize on total high school participation, since many of these students have been members and leaders of clubs or school organizations in the past. As an approximation, we have controlled on club membership in the present.

196

with the least self-esteem. With one minor exception, each step down the self-esteem scale is matched by a decreasing proportion of group officers. (Table 5)

TABLE 5

* Self-Esteem and Election to Officerial Post
in Club or School Organization

Ever held any elected position	Self-Esteem						
	High 0	1	2	3	4	5	Low 6
Held elected position	60%	59%	52%	49%	49%	42%	36%
Never held elected position	40	41	48	51	51	58	64
Total percent	100	100	100	100	100	100	100
(Number)	(247)	(385)	(343)	(223)	(111)	(53)	(22)

Now let us consider a group of which all students are members whether they like it or not—the classroom group. We find that just as students with low self-esteem are less likely than others to become club leaders, so are they less likely to be elected to such positions by their peers in the classroom. The relationship to self-esteem in the classroom, however, is less uniform and pronounced than in voluntary organizations. We asked our respondents whether they had ever held any elected office in their homeroom class—either as president, vice-president, secretary, treasurer, etc. Since such posts are necessarily scarce, it is understandable that only a small number of people had held these positions. Nevertheless, as self-esteem decreases, the proportion who report being elected to such offices also tends to go down. (Table 6)

It would, of course, have been highly desirable to obtain

197

TABLE 6

* Self-Esteem and Election to Position as Homeroom Officer

	Self-Esteem						
Elected as home-room officers	High 0	1	2	3	4	5	Low 6
Never elected	62%	65%	68%	73%	72%	83%	74%
Elected at least once	38	35	32	27	28	17	26
Total percent (Number)	100 (259)	100 (392)	100 (352)	100 (231)	100 (116)	100 (59)	100 (23)

sociometric ratings of these students, but this could not be done because the New York State questionnaires were anonymous. We did, however, conduct a small pilot investigation with 272 high school seniors from two high schools in the vicinity of Washington, D.C. In this study, respondents signed their names, and sociometric data about them were obtained.

The results of this study were reported in Chapter 2. It will be recalled that people with low self-esteem: (1) were less likely to be selected as a leader by two or more of their classmates; (2) were judged as less likely to be actually chosen by others if an election were held; (3) were less likely to be described as active participants in classroom discussions; and (4) were more likely to be described as relatively subdued and inactive in classroom discussions.

These sociometric data clearly indicate a relationship between a self-designated personality characteristic and the individual's "social impact." Whether the same relationships would have been found in our larger sample of ten high schools must, of course, remain unknown. Of the two schools used in this pilot study, one was chiefly upper middle class, the other chiefly working class. All students were seniors. There is no apparent basis for considering the combined results atypical.

Participation and Leadership in Informal Groups

The warp and woof of any social fabric consists of the small, intimate, informal, face-to-face, voluntary groupings which generally fall under the heading of "primary groups." In the high school these are variously called friendship groups, cliques, gangs, "crowds," "potlucks," etc. They have no formal structure, no elected leader, charter, or constitution, no official criteria for membership; relationships are personal, noninstrumental, noncontractual, noneconomic. A major motivation for joining such groups is simply the pleasure of human association.

Just as people with low self-esteem are less likely to join formal groups and become leaders in them, so are they less likely to participate actively in informal groups and assume positions of informal leadership. This conclusion is based upon the responses to four questions: (1) how often the student engaged in "discussions of matters of student government or general high school interest"; (2) what part he took in such discussions—whether he played an "active" role in such discussions (i.e., took an equal share in the conversation or tried to convince others) or a "passive" role (i.e., usually just listened or "once in a while" expressed an opinion); (3) whether he was more or less likely than other students "to be asked your views on student government or topics of general high school interest"; [3] and (4) how often he found himself taking a

[3] This question, with some variation, has frequently been used in research on "opinion leadership." Other studies have indicated that answers to this question are usually quite accurate; people who designate themselves as opinion leaders tend to be so designated by others. See Elihu Katz and Paul F. Lazarsfeld, *Personal Influence*, Glencoe, Ill.: The Free Press, 1955, pp. 149–161.

position of leadership in high school groups. The results of all four items are in agreement. (Tables 7–10) People

TABLE 7

* Self-Esteem and Participation in Discussions of Matters of Student Government or General High School Interest

	Self-Esteem						
Engage in discussions . . .	High 0	1	2	3	4	5	Low 6
Very often or quite often	26%	24%	22%	17%	15%	12%	8%
Occasionally	41	40	37	40	43	25	46
Rarely or never	33	36	41	43	43	62	46
Total percent	100	100	100	100	100	100	100
(Number)	(264)	(412)	(374)	(234)	(122)	(64)	(24)

TABLE 8

* Self-Esteem and "Active" or "Passive" Responses to Discussions of High School Matters

	Self-Esteem						
Participation in discussions	High 0	1	2	3	4	5	Low 6
"Active"	77%	74%	61%	63%	58%	54%	26%
"Passive"	23	26	39	37	42	46	74
Total percent	100	100	100	100	100	100	100
(Number)	(256)	(395)	(362)	(227)	(118)	(57)	(23)

with low self-esteem were less likely to describe themselves as frequent and active participants and as informal opinion leaders.

TABLE 9

* Self-Esteem and Opinion Leadership

"... more or less likely to be asked your views about student government or matters of general high school interest?"	Self-Esteem						
	High 0	1	2	3	4	5	Low 6
More likely	15%	13%	12%	9%	9%	14%	—
About the same	64	58	50	44	43	28	38%
Less likely	21	29	38	47	48	58	63
Total percent	100	100	100	100	100	100	100
(Number)	(266)	(404)	(373)	(234)	(118)	(64)	(24)

TABLE 10

* Self-Esteem and Tendency to Assume Group Leadership

"How often take position of leadership in high school group you are with?"	Self-Esteem						
	High 0	1	2	3	4	5	Low 6
Often or sometimes	58%	55%	46%	45%	39%	33%	21%
Rarely	30	31	36	34	35	26	38
Never	13	14	18	21	26	41	42
Total percent	100	100	100	100	100	100	100
(Number)	(261)	(396)	(365)	(228)	(118)	(61)	(24)

In light of the foregoing data, it is difficult to escape the conclusion that people lacking self-respect do not stir up much of a social breeze in the high school. They participate in fewer extracurricular activities (especially clubs); spend less time at such activities; are less often elected as president, chairman, or other officer of clubs or school organizations; are less often elected as homeroom officers; are less popular with their classmates (as determined by sociometric methods); participate less in classroom discussions; participate less frequently and actively in casual, informal conversations with schoolmates; are less often opinion leaders; and are less likely to "take a position of leadership in a group you are with." Even if we independently control (by standardization) on social class, religion, and school grades, students with low self-esteem are less likely than those with high self-esteem to be active participants in formal groups, to be active and frequent participants in informal discussions, to be informal opinion leaders, and to be formal group leaders. Whether the group is formal or informal, voluntary or involuntary, the person with low self-esteem tends to be a relatively impotent social force.

Interpersonal Attitudes and Impact

Why is the person with low self-esteem relatively unlikely to join clubs, to participate actively in informal groups, to be chosen as a leader? The answer to this question has already been anticipated in the previous chapter; the reason, in other words, lies chiefly in his attitudes toward people and in the impression he makes on them.

Let us, for the moment, confine our attention to participation in extracurricular activities. Participation in such activities is a voluntary matter; an important motivation is simply the satisfaction of doing things with others. Now it is obvious that if a person tends to distrust others and if, furthermore, he assumes they dislike him, then he would tend to avoid such groups. But these attitudes, we have seen, are characteristic of the egophobe—he has low "faith-in-people" and he believes that other people have a poor opinion of him.

In order to determine whether these factors contribute

to the lower participation level of the egophobes, we have examined the relationship of self-esteem to participation in extracurricular activities, standardizing simultaneously on these two attitudes.

Table 11 indicates that if those high and low in self-esteem did not differ in their faith in people and their notions of others' opinions of them, then the proportion who were relatively inactive participants in extracurricular activities would be the same. Even when these two attitudes are standardized, however, egophiles are still more likely to be highly active participants. The difference between the two groups is, however, reduced. Originally, egophiles are 22 percent more likely than egophobes to be highly active participants; when these two groups are equalized in terms of the test factors, this difference is reduced to 13.9 percent, a reduction of about three-eighths in the size of the original difference. This would suggest that part of the explanation for the lower participation level of the egophobes is that they doubt that other people like and respect them and that they themselves do not have a very high opinion of other people.

Now let us consider the question of leadership. Two factors which are almost certain to have a bearing upon one's selection as a leader are assertiveness and popularity. In this connection, let us recall how nurses described the egophobic normal volunteers. Egophobes were more likely to be described as submissive (easily led, usually gives in, lets others make decisions, too easily influenced, lacks self-confidence) and were less likely to be described as assertive (can be strict if necessary, firm but just, likes to compete with others, stern but fair). In addition, egophobes were less likely to be described as well-thought of, makes good impression, often admired, respected by others.

If the egophobic high school students are like the egophobic normal volunteers, then the reasons for their failure to be elected to positions of high school leadership are

TABLE 11

† Self-Esteem and Participation in Extracurricular
Activities: (A) Original Relationship and (B)
Relationship Standardized on "What Others
Think of You" and "Faith in People"

A. Original relationship

Extracurricular activities score	Self-Esteem		
	High	Medium	Low
Low	27.4%	28.4%	40.9%
Medium	25.7	27.9	34.0
High	47.0	43.7	25.0
Total percent	100.0	100.0	100.0
(Number)	(413)	(426)	(44)

B. Standardized relationship

Extracurricular activities score	Self-Esteem		
	High	Medium	Low
Low	28.5%	27.0%	27.8%
Medium	25.4	29.0	40.0
High	45.9	44.6	32.0
Total percent	100.0	100.0	100.0
(Number)	(413)	(426)	(44)

Since certain groups were not represented in the high and the low self-esteem categories, the total percent for the 0–1 self-esteem group was 97.4 and the total percent for the 5–6 category was 94.3. In order to achieve comparability, these results have been recomputed on a base of 100.0 percent.

obvious: (1) they are less likely to arouse the respect and affection of others; and (2) their low self-esteem makes them relatively submissive or unassertive in their dealings with others—a quality also negatively associated with leadership. The egophobe thus manifests that peculiar combination of qualities which is least likely to make him a leader among his peers. It is thus apparent that the individual's self-conception is not only associated with his attitudes toward other people, it is also associated with his actions in social life and with the *position* he comes to occupy in his high school peer groups.

CHAPTER 11

SELF-ESTEEM AND CONCERN WITH PUBLIC AFFAIRS

JUST as the individual's self-conception may bear upon his participation in the narrower world of the high school, so may it bear upon his interest and activity in the broader realm of public affairs. There are, however, alternative theories concerning the relationship of self-esteem to political participation.

One point of view, effectively advanced by Lasswell, is that the central motivation behind the striving for political power is to compensate for deprivation or feelings of inadequacy. "The accentuation of power is to be understood as a compensatory reaction against low estimates of the self . . . ," he says.[1] Fromm, in focusing on the citizen's participation in mass political movements, has suggested that men who feel isolated and insignificant in a mass society may tend to join such movements in order to gain a sense of strength and a feeling of belonging through association with powerful and solidary political groups.[2]

On the other hand, there is also reason to expect people consumed with feelings of inadequacy to dissociate themselves from the political realm. Lasswell himself points out that, "At the same time adverse estimates of the self must not be overwhelming, or the resort to power will be blocked by sentiments of utter hopelessness. . . ."[3] Similarly, Goldhamer has suggested that political apathy may be due to the fact that the individual is so exhausted by his inner

[1] Harold D. Lasswell, "Power and Personality" in H. Eulau, S. J. Eldersveld, and M. Janowitz, eds., *Political Behavior*, Glencoe, Ill.: The Free Press, 1956, p. 101.

[2] Erich Fromm, *Escape From Freedom*, New York: Rinehart, 1941, Parts V and VI.

[3] *Op. cit.*, p. 101.

conflicts that he has no energy left for public affairs.[4] And Horney's concept of "neurotic egocentricity"[5] is also in accord with this conclusion. In this view the individual suffering from crippling or incapacitating emotional problems is so wrapped up in his inner world that remote matters of broad scope are unreal or irrelevant to him.

The aim of this chapter is to examine the relationship of self-esteem to two important expressions of political interest and participation: (1) concern with, and attention to, public affairs as reflected in interest in political matters, exposure to public affairs communications in the mass media, and concrete knowledge of public figures; and (2) participation in discussion of national and international affairs, including the quantity and quality of such participation.[6]

Self-Esteem and Apathy Toward Public Affairs

Do young people afflicted with feelings of inadequacy and a sense of worthlessness immerse themselves in national and international affairs or do such matters tend to have little meaning for them? Our data indicate that people with low self-esteem are relatively uninterested in public affairs. They are less likely than others to say that they are interested in political matters;[7] (Table 1) they are

[4] Herbert Goldhamer, "Public Opinion and Personality," *Amer. Jour. of Sociol.*, Vol. 55 (1950), p. 350.

[5] *Neurosis and Human Growth.*

[6] A consideration of the various manifestations of political involvement appears in Robert E. Lane, *Political Life*, Glencoe, Ill.: The Free Press, 1959.

[7] Among adults this expression of interest in political campaigns was shown to be a consistent and valid response. In P. F. Lazarsfeld, B. Berelson, and H. Gaudet, *The People's Choice*, New York: Columbia University Press, 1948, it was shown that people who said they were very interested "(a) had more opinions on issues involved in the election; (b) participated more in election events; and (c) exposed themselves more to the stream of political communications." (P. 41.)

TABLE 1

* Self-Esteem and Interest in National or International Affairs

Interest in national or international affairs	Self-Esteem						
	High 0	1	2	3	4	5	Low 6
Great deal of interest	31%	27%	26%	25%	24%	21%	—
Moderate interest	50	53	50	45	45	47	58%
Mild interest	19	21	24	30	32	32	42
Total percent	100	100	100	100	100	100	100
(Number)	(241)	(359)	(330)	(200)	(101)	(53)	(24)

TABLE 2

* Self-Esteem and Exposure to Public Affairs Communications in the Mass Media

Exposure to mass communications ‡	Self-Esteem						
	High 0	1	2	3	4	5	Low 6
High	24%	23%	15%	15%	13%	10%	—
Medium	48	50	53	44	45	47	54
Low	28	27	32	41	42	43	46
Total percent	100	100	100	100	100	100	100
(Number)	(237)	(351)	(321)	(198)	(98)	(53)	(24)

‡ "High" exposure to communications refers to those who pay a great deal of attention to public affairs in the newspapers and on radio or television; "low" refers to those who pay little attention to public affairs in the press and on the air; and "medium" refers to those who are high on one and low on the other.

less likely to report that they follow news of national or international importance in the newspapers or on the radio or television; (Table 2) and, on an objective test of knowledge of current political figures, they are less likely to identify these figures correctly. (Table 3)

TABLE 3

* Self-Esteem and Correct Identification of Figures
of National and International Importance

Number of correct identifications	Self-Esteem						
	High 0	1	2	3	4	5	Low 6
Eight or more correct	36%	32%	22%	25%	25%	22%	20%
Six or seven correct	26	27	30	30	32	32	10
Five or fewer correct	38	41	48	45	43	46	70
Total percent	100	100	100	100	100	100	100
(Number)	(211)	(301)	(284)	(163)	(84)	(41)	(20)

Similar results appear when we consider a different aspect of political involvement, viz., participation in political discussion. As we would expect on the basis of our discussion of the egophobe's interpersonal attitudes, students with low self-esteem are less likely to say that they participate in such discussions frequently (i.e., that they discuss national or international affairs "a great deal"), and are also less likely to report that they engage in such discussions actively (i.e., that they take an equal share in the conversation or try to convince others of their views).

We have combined these two items—the one dealing with frequency of participation, the other with passivity or activity of participation—into an index of "intensity of political discussion" (see Appendix D-9). Table 4 shows

TABLE 4

* Self-Esteem and "Intensity of Political Discussion"

"Intensity of discussion" index	Self-Esteem						
	High 0	1	2	3	4	5	Low 6
High	53%	46%	37%	40%	36%	35%	14%
Medium	27	33	37	33	33	35	36
Low	20	21	25	27	31	29	50
Total percent	100	100	100	100	100	100	100
(Number)	(221)	(316)	(295)	(174)	(91)	(48)	(22)

that the lower the individual's self-esteem level, the less likely is he to rank high on this index. Whereas 53 percent of the egophiles were both frequent and active participants, this was true of only 14 percent of the egophobes.

Just as the egophobe is less likely to be an opinion leader with regard to high school affairs, so is he less likely to be a political opinion leader. Our respondents were asked: "Compared with the people you know, are you more or less likely than any of them to be asked your views about public affairs?" [8] Forty-six percent of those with the lowest self-esteem, but only 13 percent of those with the highest self-esteem, said they were less likely to be asked their views. (Table 5) Similarly 62 percent of those with the lowest self-esteem, compared with 23 percent of those with the highest self-esteem, said that they "rarely or never" took the lead in political discussions with their peers.

[8] Such self-proclaimed opinion leadership has been shown to be related to other forms of political involvement in Lazarsfeld, Berelson, and Gaudet, *op. cit.*, pp. 49–51.

210

CONCERN WITH PUBLIC AFFAIRS

TABLE 5

* Self-Esteem and Self-Designated Opinion Leadership

More or less likely than others to be asked views?	Self-Esteem						
	High 0	1	2	3	4	5	Low 6
More	8%	13%	10%	8%	5%	6%	4%
Same	78	72	71	65	75	51	50
Less	13	16	19	27	20	43	46
Total percent	100	100	100	100	100	100	100
(Number)	(227)	(336)	(310)	(188)	(97)	(51)	(22)

These findings are not without broad social significance, because a considerable body of evidence has accumulated to suggest that interpersonal, face-to-face communications may be the single most important source of influence in the political realm.[9]

The adolescent with low self-esteem thus appears to manifest the behavior characteristic of the politically apathetic citizen. He expresses a relative lack of interest in matters of national or international import; he is less likely to follow such questions in the press and on the air; and he manifests greater ignorance of such subjects on an objective test of knowledge. In addition, he appears to participate less frequently than others in discussions of na-

[9] Lazarsfeld, Berelson, and Gaudet, *op. cit.*, Chaps. 15–16; B. Berelson, P. F. Lazarsfeld, and W. McPhee, *Voting*, Chicago: University of Chicago, 1954, Chap. 6; E. Katz and P. F. Lazarsfeld, *Personal Influence*, Glencoe, Ill.: The Free Press, 1955, show that people of higher status tend to be public affairs opinion leaders. Social status, however, does not account for the relationship between self-esteem and opinion leadership in the present study. In fact, the relationship between self-esteem and all of the indicators of political involvement is maintained when social class, grades, and religion are independently controlled by means of standardization.

211

tional or international questions; he is unlikely to assume a forceful or dominant role in such discussions; and he is unlikely to be called upon by others for his advice and opinion on such matters.

Why should this be so? In discussing this question, let us first consider why students with low self-esteem are less likely to *discuss* public affairs. Later we will return to the question of why they are *less interested.*

Before turning to these questions, however, it is necessary to take account of the fact that students with high self-esteem may be more likely to discuss public affairs simply because they are more interested. In fact, we find the following to be the case: Students with high self-esteem who are uninterested in public affairs are not more likely than equally uninterested low self-esteem people to engage in political discussions. (Table 6) And this appears to be a rational response. If an individual is not interested in public affairs, why should he discuss them? It is only if a person is interested in public affairs that his silence in such discussions requires explanation. The following section, then, deals with the question: Why, among students who are interested in public affairs, are people with low self-esteem less likely than those with high self-esteem to express their views to others?

In a general way, the answer to this question has already been suggested in our earlier discussion of the egophobe's interpersonal attitudes. The question we wish to raise at this point is: Among these various interpersonal attitudes, which are most crucial in accounting for the egophobe's relatively low level of informal political discussion? [10] Our data suggest that three attitudes are of decisive importance:

[10] In this section we are dealing only with students who are interested in politics. This has reduced the number of cases available for analysis, particularly among those with low self-esteem. For this reason, we have combined categories 5 and 6 on the self-esteem scale.

TABLE 6

Self-Esteem and "Intensity of Political Discussion" among
Those Equally Interested in Public Affairs

"Intensity of political discussion"	* Interested					
	Self-Esteem					
	High 0	1	2	3	4	Low 5–6
High	63%	56%	46%	53%	44%	43%
Medium	26	32	37	32	30	30
Low	11	12	17	15	25	27
Total percent	100	100	100	100	100	100
(Number)	(182)	(254)	(226)	(123)	(63)	(44)

"Intensity of political discussion"	Not Interested					
	Self-Esteem					
	High 0	1	2	3	4	Low 5–6
High	5%	5%	11%	8%	12%	4%
Medium	34	38	37	34	42	48
Low	60	57	52	58	46	48
Total percent	100	100	100	100	100	100
(Number)	(38)	(58)	(65)	(50)	(26)	(25)

Interpersonal threat. People with low self-esteem, we find, are more likely than others to say that they would be "deeply disturbed" if someone were to laugh at them for their political opinions; are more likely to report that in discussions of public affairs "I often prefer to say nothing at all than to say something that will make a bad impression"; and are more likely to say that they avoid ex-

pressing opinions "that will make people angry with me."
These three items have been combined into a score of
"interpersonal threat" (see Appendix D-8). Table 7 shows

TABLE 7

* Self-Esteem and Interpersonal Threat among
Interested Students

Interpersonal threat score		Self-Esteem					
		High 0	1	2	3	4	Low 5–6
Not threatened	(0)	38%	35%	29%	29%	21%	10%
	(1)	30	28	32	33	36	31
	(2)	20	22	26	25	18	33
Threatened	(3)	12	15	13	14	25	26
Total percent		100	100	100	100	100	100
(Number)		(171)	(239)	(210)	(117)	(56)	(39)

that the lower the self-esteem, the more likely is the respondent to say that he feels threatened by discussions
of public affairs. And our data indicate that the more
threatened the individual feels, the more inhibited he appears to be in discussing public affairs.

Lack of confidence in interpersonal impact. A second
reason why people with low self-esteem are less likely to
participate frequently and actively in political discussions
is that they appear to be more doubtful that they have
anything worthwhile to contribute. They are, for example,
more likely to say that they often have opinions about public affairs which they would like to express but feel too
unsure of themselves to express these ideas; they are less
likely to agree that "If I were to present my ideas on public affairs to a group of strangers, I believe they would be

impressed by my views"; and they are more likely to say that most people's opinions on public affairs are sounder than their own.

We have combined these three items into an index of "confidence in interpersonal impact." Table 8 shows that

TABLE 8

* Self-Esteem and Confidence in Interpersonal Impact among Interested Students

Confidence in interpersonal impact	Self-Esteem					
	High 0	1	2	3	4	Low 5–6
High (0)	32%	23%	18%	14%	6%	6%
(1)	33	34	37	28	35	24
(2)	24	22	26	33	35	26
Low (3)	11	20	19	24	24	44
Total percent	100	100	100	100	100	100
(Number)	(147)	(206)	(182)	(102)	(49)	(34)

the lower the individual's level of self-esteem, the less confidence does he have that what he has to contribute has merit or would be perceived by others as having merit.

Self-consciousness. We would expect the egophobe to be relatively self-conscious when talking to others. In particular, he is likely to be absorbed in the following kinds of questions: What do others think of me? How do they evaluate me? What impression am I making? Such self-consciousness is, of course, fatal to spontaneity; the result, inevitably, is blockage and inhibition in setting forth his ideas.

It is thus not surprising to find that people with low self-esteem are more likely to say that, when a number of

215

people are discussing public affairs, "I am often a little self-conscious about talking up in front of everyone." (Table 9)

TABLE 9

* Self-Esteem and Self-Consciousness among Interested Students

"When a number of people are together talking about public affairs, I am often a little self-conscious about talking up in front of everyone"	Self-Esteem					
	High 0	1	2	3	4	Low 5–6
Agree	25%	39%	48%	52%	49%	71%
Disagree	75	62	52	48	51	29
Total percent	100	100	100	100	100	100
(Number)	(173)	(252)	(217)	(122)	(57)	(42)

We have thus suggested three reasons why people with low self-esteem, even though they are interested, are less likely to talk politics: (1) they feel threatened by others; (2) they doubt whether they have much worthwhile to contribute; and (3) they are self-conscious about talking up in front of others. We find, in fact, that when we control (standardize) on each of these factors, the relationship between self-esteem and discussion of public affairs decreases substantially. (It should be noted, incidentally, that each of these factors is related to political discussion independently of the other two factors.) Since each of these factors exercises an effect independent of the others, then we would expect their joint effect—their cumulative impact—to be particularly strong. Table 10 shows the rela-

TABLE 10

† Self-Esteem and Intensity of Discussion among Interested Students: (A) Original Relationship, and (B) Relationship Standardized on Interpersonal Threat, Lack of Confidence in Interpersonal Impact, and Self-Consciousness

A. Original relationship

Intensity of discussion	Self-Esteem		
	High	Medium	Low
High	56.2%	44.7%	30.9%
Medium	26.9	32.2	34.1
Low	16.9	23.0	35.0
Total percent	100.0	100.0	100.0
(Number)	(491)	(409)	(123)

B. Standardized relationship

Intensity of discussion	Self-Esteem		
	High	Medium	Low
High	43.4%	39.0%	43.9%
Medium	33.6	36.0	30.8
Low	23.2	24.8	25.1
Total percent	100.0	100.0	100.0
(Number)	(491)	(409)	(123)

tionship between self-esteem and intensity of discussion standardized on all three factors simultaneously. Originally, we see, 56.2 percent of those with high self-esteem were active discussants, whereas this was true of only 30.9 percent of those with low self-esteem—a difference of 25.3

217

percent. When we standardize on the three contributory factors, however, the relationship disappears completely. These results suggest the following conclusion: were it not for the fact that politically interested people with low self-esteem felt more threatened, lacked confidence in their impact, and were more self-conscious, they would be just as likely as those with high self-esteem to engage actively in discussions of public affairs.

Self-Esteem and Interest in Public Affairs

Given these reasons for the low self-esteem person's passivity in discussions of public affairs, some questions which spring to mind are: Why is he less interested in public affairs? Why does he pay less attention to these issues in the press? We can understand why he is more fearful of speaking his mind in front of others, but surely there can be no threat in being interested in public affairs.

One general factor appears to be that the psychological problems of the person with low self-esteem tend to turn his interests inward. As Berelson has noted, one of the personality prerequisites for effective democratic participation is "a reasonable amount of freedom from anxiety so that political affairs can be attended to. . . ."[11]

For example, people with low self-esteem are more likely than others to retreat into a private world of daydreaming. Whereas 59 percent of them were high on a Guttman scale of daydreaming,[12] this was true of only 13 percent of those with high self-esteem. (Table 11) In fact, when we control on daydreaming, the original difference in interest of 17.4 percent between those high and low in self-esteem is reduced to 10.1 percent. (Table 12)

Several other items of evidence suggest that the over-

[11] Bernard Berelson, "Democratic Theory and Public Opinion," *Pub. Opin. Qtrly.*, Vol. 16, No. 3 (1952), p. 315.

[12] See Appendix D-6 for a description of this scale.

TABLE 11

* Self-Esteem and Tendency to Daydream

"Tendency to daydream" scale	Self-Esteem						
	High 0	1	2	3	4	5	Low 6
Low	71%	59%	56%	45%	32%	24%	24%
Medium	16	22	21	21	26	23	16
High	13	19	23	34	42	53	60
Total percent	100	100	100	100	100	100	100
(Number)	(475)	(794)	(724)	(456)	(234)	(117)	(37)

whelming absorption in his own psychological problems tends to distract the egophobe from matters of broader social import. He is, for example, much more likely to say that he is too concerned with his inner problems to devote much attention to the broader problems of the world and to agree that "I often find that I am distracted from public affairs by my personal problems." (Table 13) And, in fact, when we standardize on the combined responses to these two items, we find a clear-cut decrease in the size of the relationship between self-esteem and interest in public affairs. In terms of proportions uninterested, the difference between those with high and low self-esteem is 21.0 percent; if these groups are standardized on "concern with personal problems," however, the difference is reduced to 6.3 percent. (Table 14)

Similar results appear if we consider exposure to the mass media. Whereas the difference in the tendency to follow public affairs in the mass media between the extreme self-esteem groups is 18 percent, this difference is reduced to 9.4 percent when the relationship is standardized on "concern with personal problems."

219

TABLE 12

† Self-Esteem and Interest in Public Affairs: (A) Original
Relationship and (B) Relationship Standardized on
"Tendency to Daydream" Scale

A. Original relationship

Interest in public affairs	Self-Esteem					
	High 0	1	2	3	4	Low 5–6
Great	31.5%	27.4%	25.4%	25.0%	24.2%	14.1%
Moderate	50.4	51.9	51.4	43.9	43.2	49.3
Mild	18.1	20.6	23.2	31.1	32.6	36.6
Total percent	100.0	100.0	100.0	100.0	100.0	100.0
(Number)	(232)	(339)	(315)	(196)	(95)	(71)

B. Standardized relationship

Interest in public affairs	Self-Esteem					
	High 0	1	2	3	4	Low 5–6
Great	30.3%	27.5%	25.2%	25.3%	21.2%	20.2%
Moderate	49.8	51.3	51.5	43.9	44.7	47.3
Mild	19.9	21.2	23.2	30.8	34.1	32.4
Total percent	100.0	100.0	100.0	100.0	100.0	100.0
(Number)	(232)	(339)	(315)	(196)	(95)	(71)

While the data are too complex to enable us to establish
a strict cause-and-effect relationship, they nevertheless indicate that were people with low self-esteem not more
likely to say that they were concerned with their own
problems, they would not have such a low level of interest
in, and exposure to, public affairs.

* Self-Esteem and Concern with Own Problems

Concern with personal problems	Self-Esteem					
	High 0	1	2	3	4	Low 5–6
Low	55%	44%	42%	35%	34%	20%
Intermediate	32	37	37	36	38	38
High	13	18	20	29	28	42
Total percent	100	100	100	100	100	100
(Number)	(200)	(280)	(261)	(156)	(79)	(61)

Discussion

While theoretical grounds exist for expecting the individual's feelings of inadequacy both to stimulate and to inhibit involvement in public affairs, our data are consistent in indicating a predominantly inhibitory effect. People with low self-esteem are less likely to express interest in public affairs, to follow such affairs in the mass media, to possess concrete knowledge of such matters, to discuss them actively and frequently in peer groups, or to be public affairs opinion leaders. We have suggested certain factors stemming from the nature of low self-esteem which may deaden interest in affairs of the external world or, if interest is aroused, may reduce the likelihood of expressing one's views.

The problem of self-esteem is a very different one when seen from the viewpoint of the individual than when considered from the perspective of society. From the viewpoint of the individual, fundamental self-hatred is a tragedy of no mean proportions, compounded of depression, tension, and anxiety, and in various ways warping the lives of those afflicted with it. From the viewpoint of society, it

SOCIAL CONSEQUENCES
TABLE 14

† Self-Esteem and Interest in Public Affairs: (A) Original
Relationship, and (B) Relationship Standardized on
"Concern with Own Problems" Score

A. Original relationship

Interest in public affairs	Self-Esteem					
	High 0	1	2	3	4	Low 5–6
Great	32.5%	28.3%	27.7%	28.2%	26.9%	13.6%
Moderate	50.0	54.1	51.6	43.6	39.7	47.5
Mild	18.0	17.8	20.7	28.2	33.3	39.0
Total percent	100.0	100.0	100.0	100.0	100.0	100.0
(Number)	(200)	(280)	(261)	(156)	(79)	(61)

B. Standardized relationship

Interest in public affairs	Self-Esteem					
	High 0	1	2	3	4	Low 5–6
Great	28.4%	27.0%	27.1%	30.6%	29.6%	16.9%
Moderate	49.0	54.1	51.6	43.9	41.0	54.2
Mild	22.2	18.9	20.9	25.6	30.7	28.5
Total percent	100.0	100.0	100.0	100.0	100.0	100.0
(Number)	(200)	(280)	(261)	(156)	(79)	(61)

has clear implications for the operation of a democratic
system of society.[13] For if democracy provides a mechanism by which citizens can have their wills translated into
political policy, then it becomes farcical to speak of democ-

[13] Berelson, *ibid.*, cites "a fairly good measure of self-esteem" as one
of the personality prerequisites for effective democratic participation.

222

racy if it is based upon an ignorant, uninterested, and uninfluential electorate. Hence those social conditions and family experiences, some of which have been discussed in earlier chapters, which operate to destroy the child's sense of his own worth are at the same time undermining the personality prerequisites of a democratic society. The main reassurance lies in the fact that, at least according to our data, many more adolescents appear to be characterized by a fundamental feeling of self-acceptance than seem to be afflicted with feelings of self-rejection.

CHAPTER 12

———◆———

OCCUPATIONAL ORIENTATION

ONE of the most striking characteristics of the American occupational structure is its almost incredible degree of specialization. The *Dictionary of Occupational Titles* presents detailed descriptions of over 23,000 occupations. While we can hardly expect to predict an individual's precise occupational choice on the basis of his self-esteem alone, we can nevertheless examine the relationship of self-esteem to the individual's general orientation toward the world of work, particularly his values, aspirations, and expectations.

Just as interpersonal relationships enter into high school participation and discussions of public affairs, so do they enter into one's occupational orientation. Self-esteem, we find, appears to be related to one particular aspect of interpersonal relationships, viz., the avoidance of power and conflict. Specifically, egophobes are more inclined than others to avoid positions which will make them (1) subordinate to others, (2) superordinate to others, or (3) place them in competition with others. They do not mind helping people, but they are anxious to avoid power relationships with co-workers.

The individual's occupational values may be considered. We asked our respondents to indicate which values they would hope to satisfy in an "ideal job." Ten alternatives were offered; the respondent was asked to rank these as "highly important, of medium importance, of little or no importance, irrelevant, or even distasteful." [1] Most of these alternatives did not show a clear and consistent relation-

[1] A complete description of these occupational values appears in Morris Rosenberg, *Occupations and Values,* Glencoe, Ill.: The Free Press, 1957, pp. 141–142.

ship to self-esteem. Two, however, did—the two dealing most directly with power. One of the alternatives read: "The ideal job for me would have to . . . give me a chance to exercise leadership." Table 1 indicates that adolescents

TABLE 1

* Self-Esteem and Desire for Leadership in Ideal Job

Importance attached to "chance to exercise leadership"	Self-Esteem						
	High 0	1	2	3	4	5	Low 6
Low	27%	22%	22%	32%	39%	43%	50%
Medium	50	53	55	50	42	33	33
High	24	25	23	19	19	24	17
Total percent	100	100	100	100	100	100	100
(Number)	(207)	(345)	(294)	(188)	(95)	(51)	(12)

varying in self-esteem do not differ much in considering this value highly important, but they differ quite substantially in considering it low in importance. With one exception, the lower the self-esteem, the more likely is the individual to consider the opportunity to exercise leadership "low in importance, irrelevant, or even distasteful." In other words, people with high self-esteem do not particularly desire leadership in their work, but neither do they especially reject it; people with low self-esteem, on the other hand, tend definitely and emphatically to reject it.

We might assume that someone who is loathe to dominate others at work would be more anxious to submit to them. But such is not the case. Those people who do not want to tell others what to do also do not want others to tell them what to do. With regard to the value: "The ideal job for me would have to . . . leave me relatively free of supervision by others," we find that students with high self-esteem and those of moderate self-esteem do not differ substantially in the importance they attach to this value, but people with low self-esteem are clearly more likely to emphasize it. (Table 2) In other words, people with low

TABLE 2

Self-Esteem and Desire for Freedom from Supervision

Importance attached to "leave me free of supervision"	Self-Esteem						
	High 0	1	2	3	4	5	Low 6
High	22%	26%	27%	23%	24%	35%	58%
Medium	49	51	52	51	54	45	25
Low	29	24	22	26	22	20	17
Total percent	100	100	100	100	100	100	100
(Number)	(207)	(347)	(295)	(191)	(95)	(51)	(12)

* Score 5–6 vs. score 0–4: Proportion "High importance."

self-esteem are more reluctant than others to enter into a power relationship either as a power-wielder or as a power-subject. Those people with high and medium self-esteem do not differ greatly in terms of these values.

Indeed, the egophobe confronted with these alternatives may often experience conflict. When asked whether, in his work, he would prefer to tell others what to do or to have others tell him what to do, an egophobic boy replied: "Well, I didn't exactly like either one of them. But I'm never good at telling other people what to do. Actually, I'm never sure enough of myself to be able to tell anybody else what to do. I think I get action when I do, but I don't like it because I think there are too many other people who are qualified to tell people what to do. And I don't like being bossed around either. But I take bossing around much easier than a lot of people would. Because I know the position I'm in."

As with power, so with conflict. We asked our respondents: "Which of the following kinds of jobs would you prefer to have?"

_____One which involves competition with others.
_____One involving little or no competition.

With almost perfect uniformity, Table 3 shows, the lower

TABLE 3

* Self-Esteem and Preference for Competition at Work

| Kind of job preferred | Self-Esteem | | | | | | |
	High 0	1	2	3	4	5	Low 6
Involves competition	70%	62%	59%	60%	51%	47%	42%
Little or no competition	30	38	41	40	49	53	58
Total percent	100	100	100	100	100	100	100
(Number)	(190)	(321)	(268)	(173)	(88)	(49)	(12)

the self-esteem, the less enthusiastic is the individual about the prospect of competition in his future work. Seventy percent of the egophiles, but only 42 percent of the egophobes, preferred a job which involved competition with others. If a competitive situation often involves conflict with others seeking the same scarce resources, then it would appear that low self-esteem produces an aversion to conflict in the world of work.

One egophobic girl expressed her feelings as follows:

227

"I can't stand the competition. If I worked in a place where they sell on commission, I'd probably quit before long because people would be grabbing for the sale before I got to it . . . I think that if someone else wants something, they should have it." Her ideal solution enabled her to avoid dominating or being dominated by others, for she said: "I would like to be somewhere where maybe I would have a small department of my own." And an egophobic boy said: "I don't like a lot of competition. I don't like it when people are always going to beat me." Another girl expressed her feeling about competition with the statement: "It doesn't appeal to me. I want a job where you can do your job, help somebody else, and not always have to make enemies to get ahead."

Students with high self-esteem, on the other hand, tend to view competition as a challenge and an opportunity for self-realization. One girl expressed it this way: "Well, I think competition, first of all, adds spice to work. And second, it will make you work harder . . . I think you should try to reach a goal—that kind of competition." Another girl expressed her enthusiasm for competition by inquiring: "Well, how can you know how well you can really do something if you just plod along all by yourself? If other people are doing it, then you can see if you are doing it well and maybe do it better than they are." Another student said, "Oh, I think competition would be better. I think so because in competition you want to improve yourself to get ahead instead of staying on the same level . . ."

More than other people, then, the egophobe prefers not to dominate other people, to be dominated by them, or to pit himself against them.[2] And these findings are consistent with what we know of the egophobe. A leader must make decisions, assume responsibility, guide and direct the

[2] These results are not due to social class, grades, sex, or religion.

actions of others. For someone such as the egophobe who is inordinately sensitive to criticism, this is difficult to do. People may laugh at his decisions, criticize his manner, point out what he did wrong, or express hostility toward him. The egophobe may also avoid the leadership position because he lacks confidence in his own judgment; under these circumstances, to make decisions which have consequences for others may be almost agonizing.

But if fear of interpersonal criticism makes him reluctant to assume a dominant position in relation to others, it may make him equally reluctant to work under the supervision of others. To be supervised by others means to be judged by them. The egophobe may be reproached by his superiors if he makes mistakes; for someone so sensitive to criticism, this may be a painful experience.

Finally, the egophobe's relative reluctance to engage in competition is probably associated with his fear of failure. We find, for example, that he is less likely than others to agree that "Generally speaking, I would rather try something and fail than not try at all" and more likely to say "I do not like to put my abilities to the test." In other words, he appears to experience a "failure of nerve."[3] By avoiding competition, the low self-esteem person (1) reduces the threat of failing to measure up to others and (2) avoids the possible hostility of others if he surpasses them.

The decision to select an occupation is, of course, a complex one, subject to a wide variety of influences. As the egophobe surveys the vast array of occupational alternatives which are theoretically available to him, apparently one of the considerations which he brings to bear in weighing and balancing occupational alternatives is: Does it in-

[3] Edna F. Heidbreder, "The Normal Inferiority Complex," *Jour. Abn. and Soc. Psych.*, Vol. 22 (1927), p. 248, defines the failure of nerve as "an unwillingness to put one's self to the test because of fear of an unfavorable outcome, which would be intolerable."

volve relationships of power and competition? If, in his opinion, it does, then he is more likely to be negatively disposed toward the occupation.

Occupational Aspirations and Expectations

The student in the stage of late adolescence who reflects on the world of work is projecting his vision into the long future. As one would expect, young people who judge and evaluate themselves differently also foresee different occupational futures. Specifically, the egophobe's vision tends to be one of anticipated occupational frustration.

The concept of frustration implies a relationship between two elements—desires and fulfillment. One is not frustrated if one fails to attain what one does not want or if one succeeds in attaining what one does want. It is the failure to fulfill one's desires that is the essence of frustration. As William James noted, one could as easily increase one's self-esteem by reducing one's aspirations as by increasing one's achievements.[4]

If we speak of anticipated success, then self-esteem may be a cause as well as a consequence of frustration. The paradox resides in the fact that the same conditions which produce a strong desire for occupational success also produce a weak expectation of success. First let us consider the individual's desire for success. We asked our respondents: "How important to you, personally, is it to get ahead in life?" Table 4 indicates that those with low self-esteem are as likely as those with high self-esteem to consider it "very important" to get ahead. Those with low self-esteem are somewhat more likely to say it is unimportant and somewhat less likely to say it is "fairly important."[5]

[4] *Op. cit.*, pp. 310–311.

[5] Other evidence suggesting that personality factors may be behind the desire for upward social mobility is presented by Russell R. Dynes, Alfred C. Clarke and Simon Dinitz, "Levels of Occupational Aspira-

TABLE 4

* Self-Esteem and Desire to Get Ahead in Life

". . . important to get ahead in life?"	Self-Esteem						
	High 0	1	2	3	4	5	Low 6
Very important	64%	61%	63%	64%	64%	66%	60%
Fairly important	30	35	33	30	32	23	26
Not very important or very unimportant	5	4	4	6	4	11	13
Total percent	100	100	100	100	100	100	100
(Number)	(521)	(877)	(793)	(510)	(267)	(123)	(38)

But if egophobes, as a group, are as likely to want to get ahead, they are clearly less likely to expect to get ahead. For when asked: "How successful do you expect to be in your work?" people with low self-esteem were considerably less likely to say "above average" or "outstandingly successful." (Table 5) The egophobe's attitude toward the world of work thus appears to be one of anticipated occupational frustration. It should be emphasized that it is not simply anticipated failure, which might be accepted with equanimity if the desire for success were low, but anticipated frustration.

Additional evidence regarding this anticipated frustration appears in the study conducted with high school seniors in the Washington, D.C., area. There we find that

tion: Some Aspects of Family Experience As a Variable," *Amer. Soc. Rev.*, Vol. 21 (1956), pp. 212–215. They showed that those who said they had experienced rejection by their parents, who were less attached to their parents, and who were unhappy in childhood were "high aspirers," i.e., were more willing to make various personal sacrifices as a price for attaining occupational success.

TABLE 5

* Self-Esteem and Expectations of Occupational Success

"How successful do you expect to be in your work?"	Self-Esteem						
	High 0	1	2	3	4	5	Low 6
Average or below average	15%	21%	28%	29%	31%	38%	46%
Above average	58	60	57	58	53	42	54
Outstandingly successful	28	19	15	13	17	21	—
Total percent	100	100	100	100	100	100	100
(Number)	(212)	(375)	(330)	(208)	(108)	(53)	(11)

students with low self-esteem were considerably more likely to say that "I would like to get ahead in life, but I don't think I will ever get ahead as far as I would like," more likely to agree that "I doubt that I will be as successful as most people seem to be," and more likely to agree that "I doubt if I will get ahead as far as I would really like." (Table 6) In each case the differences are clear and substantial. The egophobe's occupational prospects are, in his general view, extremely cloudy.

These are, however, general statements, perhaps as much expressing a mood as venturing a prediction. Actually, the egophobe's anticipated occupational frustration is founded on the evaluation of more specific qualities of the self and the occupation. The prospect of success or failure in the occupational realm is dependent upon the relationship between two judgments: (1) what personal qualities are essential for success in a given field and (2) the degree to which one feels one possesses these particular qualities. For example, a person may feel that the "ability to work hard" is necessary for success in his chosen field.

TABLE 6

Self-Esteem and Anticipated Occupational Frustration

* "I would like to get ahead in life, but I don't think I will ever get ahead as far as I would like."	Self-Esteem		
	High	Medium	Low
Agree	28%	50%	69%
Disagree	72	50	31
Total percent	100	100	100
(Number)	(86)	(139)	(32)
* "I doubt if I will be as successful as most people seem to be."			
Agree	6%	13%	31%
Disagree	94	87	69
Total percent	100	100	100
(Number)	(83)	(137)	(32)
* "I doubt if I will get ahead in life as far as I would really like."			
Agree	28%	56%	78%
Disagree	71	44	22
Total percent	100	100	100
(Number)	(82)	(136)	(32)

If he feels he possesses this quality, then he is more likely to expect to be successful, and vice versa. On the other hand, he may feel he possesses this quality but may still anticipate failure because he does not consider this quality essential, whereas other qualities which he lacks are deemed essential. Or he may expect to be successful de-

233

spite his belief that he lacks this ability since he considers it unimportant for the work. Anticipated occupational success, then, is a function of the relationship between the occupational image and the self-image.

We asked the respondents from the Washington area the following question: "When you think of the qualities that you think will get a young person ahead today, which of the following ones would you say are *essential?* In Column A check as many as you feel are essential." Our respondents were then instructed: "Now GO BACK and check in Column B the qualities which you think you, *yourself,* are good at or possess to a high degree."

Let us consider the proportion in each self-esteem category who believe a quality is essential for success in their chosen field and are convinced that they possess this quality to a high degree. Table 7 indicates that with regard to every quality save one, students with high self-esteem who considered a particular quality essential for success were more likely than those with low self-esteem to feel that they possessed the quality to a high degree. In most cases the differences are very large. The most conspicuous differences, obviously, appear with regard to qualities involving confidence or assurance. Sixty-eight percent of the egophiles, but only 4 percent of the egophobes who considered "self-confidence" essential felt they possessed this quality; the corresponding proportions for "being sure of yourself" were 58 percent and 4 percent. Next in line were the various interpersonal skills: "ability to express yourself" (a 36-percent difference); "ability to make a good impression" (a 30-percent difference); "feeling at ease with different people" (a 33-percent difference); and having "good social poise" (an 18-percent difference). These are followed by factors relating to talent, control, and effort: "practical knowledge," "organizing and administrative ability," "talent, intelligence, and skill," and "hard work and effort." Egophobes are even less likely to feel that they

TABLE 7

Self-Esteem and Conviction That One Possesses Certain
Qualities among Those Who Consider These
Qualities Essential for Success

Consider this quality essential for success	Self-Esteem		
	High	Medium	Low
	(Proportions who believe they *do* possess the quality among those who consider it essential)		
* Ability to express yourself	63%	52%	37%
(Number) a	(85)	(137)	(30)
Leadership ability	47	41	22
(Number)	(75)	(119)	(23)
* Talent, intelligence, or skill	80	69	57
(Number)	(82)	(130)	(28)
* Ability to make good impression	78	60	48
(Number)	(68)	(103)	(21)
* Hard work and effort	65	69	44
(Number)	(84)	(138)	(27)
Organizing and administrative ability	46	38	29
(Number)	(63)	(103)	(17)
Good luck	41	45	10
(Number)	(17)	(29)	(10)
* Self-confidence	68	40	4
(Number)	(79)	(131)	(27)
Having good social poise	58	44	40
(Number)	(52)	(79)	(15)
* Feeling at ease with different people	71	54	38
(Number)	(66)	(125)	(26)
* Practical knowledge	76	75	48
(Number)	(74)	(126)	(25)
* Being sure of oneself	58	37	4
(Number)	(70)	(118)	(24)

a Number represents the individuals who consider the quality essential.

have "good luck," indicating that, in their eyes, even fate is against them.

The only quality considered essential for success which low self-esteem people feel they possess as much as others is "knowing the right people." Within the American value system, this is indeed a dubious distinction and a modest claim.

The egophobe thus tends to feel that he lacks the qualities essential for success in his chosen occupation. But his anticipated occupational frustration begins even earlier than that: it begins in a more frequent conviction that he will never even be able to enter his desired occupation in the first place. This is illustrated in the responses to the following two questions: "What business or profession would you most like to go into? [occupation or kind of work]," and "What business or profession do you realistically think you are most apt to go into [as your life career]?" In terms of this criterion, over four-fifths of the respondents expected to be occupationally satisfied, that is, expected to enter the occupations they desired. A small proportion, however, do not make such a sanguine prediction. We may classify those who do not expect to enter the fields they desire as "occupationally frustrated," and those who do expect to end up in their desired fields as "occupationally satisfied." (Those who had not made up their minds are omitted.) Table 8 shows that the lower the self-esteem, the larger the proportion who anticipate frustration of their occupational desires. At the extremes, twice as many egophobes as egophiles do not expect to do the kind of work they want.

It would thus appear that people with low self-esteem are sufficiently a part of their culture to want what most other people want—occupational success—but their low estimates of their own abilities or other relevant qualities make them dubious that they will succeed in achieving what all value. Nor do their compulsive desires for ap-

TABLE 8

Self-Esteem and Anticipated Occupational Frustration

Occupation desired and occupation expected	Self-Esteem						
	High 0	1	2	3	4	5	Low 6
Anticipated occupational frustration	12%	12%	14%	17%	20%	21%	27%
Anticipated occupational satisfaction	88	88	86	83	80	79	73
Total percent	100	100	100	100	100	100	100
(Number)	(188)	(328)	(269)	(172)	(91)	(42)	(11)

proval permit them to so lower their "pretensions" that a harmony between their aspirations and expectations can be achieved.

Discussion

Most writers on American society have postulated a general desire for upward social mobility. The legends of Horatio Alger and Abe Lincoln glorify the young man who rises from the humblest origins to a position of great prestige, power, or wealth. The desire for success may, however, mean different things to different people. Some want to get ahead in life in order to attain security, which is considered important for a happy family life. Some value advancement for the opportunity it may give them to make a contribution to society or to help specific people. Some are driven to seek social advancement by an urge for power, others by a desire for leisure, comfort, material possessions. The range of needs which may potentially be satisfied by upward social mobility is very wide indeed.

It seems likely that the egophobe's interest in upward social mobility is particularly in social prestige; such prestige, at once reflecting and commanding the respect and admiration of others, would serve to enhance his self-esteem. Support for this view is afforded by data from our Washington area study. We found, for example, that egophobes were much more likely to say that "If I were to have a higher position in society, I think I would have a better opinion of myself" and to agree that "The best way I can think of to get people to think well of me is to be successful." In other words, while the desire for upward social mobility is fairly general and personally imperative in American society, the egophobe is apparently more likely to see it as standing in the service of ego-enhancement than in terms of its contribution to other values.

If the egophobe's desire for success is understandable in terms of his motivational system, his expectation of failure is an almost inevitable consequence of his self-conception. A person who considers himself relatively worthless is generally unlikely to expect to shake the world.

The egophobe's view of his occupational future is thus not only one of anticipated failure, but of anticipated occupational frustration. The egophile, of course, is also anxious to get ahead, but it is probable that it is not a matter of such strong psychological urgency to him. His relatively fortunate situation is thus reflected in the fact that he is more likely to expect to be successful but is probably less likely to be dismayed at failure. While the egophobe appears to see his future as both bleak and threatening, the egophile sees his future as bright and friendly.

What the future holds in store for these youngsters is impossible to say. Yet if one speculates on their prospects, one can easily envision the possibility of a self-fulfilling prophecy. The young man who is confident of himself and not afraid of failure is likely to throw himself wholeheartedly into his work and to make full use of his creative potentialities. The insecure youngster, on the other hand, is likely to be inhibited by his fear that he will make mistakes, etc. Similarly, the former would probably enjoy competition with others, would willingly assume responsibility, and would seek out positions of leadership, whereas the latter would tend to avoid competition, responsibility, and leadership. Furthermore, it is possible that, broadly speaking, other people tend, more or less unconsciously, to accept the opinions we hold of ourselves. If we communicate, through our manner and action, the view that we are good, they are likely to think we are good; if we show that we consider ourselves unworthy, they may be disposed to agree that we are right. Finally, of course, the egophobe's anxiety, depression, interference with concentration, and interpersonal difficulties are in fact likely to interfere with his quest for occupational success. Ability aside, then, there are a number of powerful reasons for expecting the egophobe's dire predictions about his occupational future to be true. The very thing that makes him so strongly desire success, viz., his low self-esteem, also makes him anticipate failure and very likely helps to produce failure. This vicious circle is calculated to reduce his potential occupational contributions at the same time that it enhances his emotional distress.

PART VI
SELF-VALUES

CHAPTER 13

SOCIETY AND SELF-VALUES

RECENT empirical research in the area of the self-image has almost completely neglected the issue of self-values. For example, one common research procedure is to present a subject with a list of adjectives or descriptive phrases, obtain his self-assessment with regard to these qualities, and then compute a self-esteem score by totaling the self-ratings. Each quality is thus assigned equal weight. The point is, however, that each quality may not be equally important to the individual.[1] He may care a great deal about certain qualities but not care in the least about others. It is thus of utmost importance to know the individual's self-values.

This point was strongly emphasized by William James as far back as 1890. James expressed the matter with such felicity that it is worth quoting him at length.

"With most objects of desire, physical nature restricts our choice to but one of many represented goods, and even so it is here. I am often confronted by the necessity of standing by one of my empirical selves and relinquishing the rest. Not that I would not, if I could, be both handsome and fat and well-dressed, and a great athlete, and make a million a year, be a wit, a *bon-vivant*, and a ladykiller, as well as a philosopher; a philanthropist, statesman,

[1] In *The Self-Concept*, Wiley, summarizing her analysis of a large number of studies designed to measure self-esteem, notes: ". . . One final comment is in order concerning *all* the instruments which purport to tap self-regard directly. Each yields a global score which is obtained by summing across items. In no case has it been demonstrated, however, that the items within the instrument are comparable to one another with respect to their perceived salience for S's self-regard, or with respect to their psychological metrics." (P. 69.)

243

warrior, and African explorer, as well as a 'tone-poet' and saint. But the thing is simply impossible. . . . So the seeker of his truest, strongest, deepest self must review the list carefully, and pick out the one on which to stake his salvation. All other selves thereupon become unreal, but the fortunes of this self are real . . . Our thought . . . here chooses one of many possible selves or characters, and forthwith reckons it no shame to fail in any of those not expressly adopted as its own.

"I, who for the time have staked my all on being a psychologist, am mortified if others know much more psychology than I. But I am contented to wallow in the grossest ignorance of Greek. My deficiencies there give me no sense of personal humiliation at all. Had I 'pretensions' to be a linguist, it would have been just the reverse. So we have the paradox of a man shamed to death because he is only the second pugilist . . . in the world. . . .

"Yonder puny fellow, however, whom everyone can beat, suffers no chagrin about it, for he has long ago abandoned the attempt to 'carry that line,' as the merchants say, of self at all. With no attempt, there can be no failure; with no failure no humiliation. So our self-feeling in this world depends entirely on what we *back* ourselves to be or do." [2]

In a sense some attempt has been made to deal with the problem of values by those studies which have included the "ideal self." These studies characteristically calculate the discrepancy between the individual's self-estimate and his self-ideal, and then compute self-esteem on the basis of the totalled discrepancies. One might be disposed to consider the "ideal self" as the value attached to a trait. But this is not quite the case. As James has noted, ideally we would like to be all great things. Realistically, however, we must pick and choose. By their very nature, then, val-

[2] James, *op. cit.*, pp. 309–310.

ues are hierarchically organized. The issue, essentially, is: Among all these desirable things, which are most important, which are highly important but not in the first rank, which are important and desirable but of lesser concern, etc.? It is questionable whether the ideal self does reflect such a hierarchy of values. But it seems highly likely that this hierarchy of values is of central importance to self-esteem.

In the present study we have taken as our point of departure the notion that values are conceptions of the desirable which are hierarchically organized and are reflected in choices.[3] In order to study these self-values,[4] we presented the following instructions:

> Below is a list of qualities which may be used to describe people. We would like to know which of these are IMPORTANT or UNIMPORTANT to you. In other words, which of them do you CARE ABOUT a great deal and which do you CARE ABOUT very little or not at all.
>
> For example, the first item on the list is "ambitious." Regardless of whether you think you *are* or *are not* ambitious, how important is ambitiousness to you? We are not concerned with whether you do or do not possess this characteristic, but just whether you consider it *important* to you, PERSONALLY.

[3] Clyde Kluckhohn, *op. cit.*

[4] We have examined the content of self-values in terms of traits and skills. This is not the only relevant aspect of the self-image, but it is an important one. Gardner Murphy, *Personality,* p. 506 notes that at a fairly early age, children classify one another by good or bad names. "The vocabulary of the self . . . becomes a language of traits. These labels are generalized . . . and the child lives up to the terms employed. . . . appelations which become part of the self work more and more to produce behavior appropriate to them. The child forms general ideas of himself. In short, the self becomes less and less a pure perceptual object, and more and more a conceptual trait system."

How important is it to you, or how much do you care about, whether or not YOU are . . .

There then followed a list of 44 characteristics; the respondent was instructed to indicate how much he cared about each of them. Through a series of filtering questions, we obtained the nine qualities which were of outstanding importance, and from these nine, the top three.

Self-Values, Self-Estimates, and Self-Esteem

In the present discussion, we will use the term *self-estimate* to indicate how the individual actually rates himself with regard to a *particular* characteristic (e.g., whether he actually feels he is "very likeable," "fairly likeable," etc.) and the term *self-value* to indicate how much he cares about the quality (e.g., whether he cares "a great deal," "somewhat," "a little," or "not at all," whether or not he is likeable). Global *self-esteem* will refer to the individual's over-all level of self-acceptance or self-rejection which has been employed in previous chapters.

It follows from James' discussion that, if a person highly values a quality, then his self-estimate with regard to this quality will be closely related to his global self-esteem. If, on the other hand, he cares little about this quality, then whether he considers himself good or bad with regard to this quality will make less difference for his self-esteem.

With regard to the quality "likeable," let us first look at those who highly value this quality, i.e., who say they "care a great deal" about it. Table 1 indicates that among those who believe they actually are very likeable, 54 percent have high self-esteem, whereas among those who do not consider themselves likeable, only 17 percent have high self-esteem—a difference of 34 percent. On the other hand, among those who care little about this quality the corresponding figures are 46 percent and 31 percent—a difference of only 15 percent.

TABLE 1

Self-Estimate as "Likeable" and Global Self-Esteem,
by Value Attached to Being "Likeable"

	Care about being "likeable" (self-value)					
	* Care a great deal			Care somewhat, little, or not at all		
	Actually consider oneself likeable (self-estimate)					
Global self-esteem	Very	Fairly	Little or not at all	Very	Fairly	Little or not at all
High	54%	45%	17%	46%	49%	31%
Medium	39	42	33	39	43	50
Low	7	13	50	15	8	19
Total percent	100	100	100	100	100	100
(Number)	(345)	(569)	(52)	(41)	(133)	(34)

We thus see that, in the case of the quality "likeable," the relationship of self-evaluation on this quality to global self-esteem is greater among those who care about this quality than among those who do not.

But the most pertinent test of the importance of self-values would probably be among those who consider themselves poor with regard to a certain quality; if this quality is important to them, then the belief that they are poor at it should lower their self-esteem.

In order to examine this question, we have selected the sixteen qualities most often highly valued in our sample. Let us consider those who rated themselves as relatively poor in terms of these qualities. Table 2 indicates that, with regard to 15 of these 16 qualities, those who highly valued these qualities were more likely to have low self-esteem

TABLE 2

Valuation of Qualities and Low Self-Esteem, among Those Who Estimate Themselves as Equally Poor in Terms of These Qualities

Self-Estimate: Consider oneself as *poor* in terms of the following qualities . . .	Self-Values Care about quality . . .			
	A great deal		Somewhat, a little, or not at all	
	Percent	Total	Percent	Total
	(Proportion with *low* self-esteem)			
likeable	50	(52) *	19	(32)
dependable and reliable	36	(58)	23	(31)
intelligent, good mind	34	(68)	26	(100)
clear-thinking, clever	34	(111) *	22	(113)
hard-working, conscientious	28	(114)	17	(99)
easy to get along with	38	(45)	23	(52)
realistic, able to face facts	30	(82) *	17	(76)
friendly, sociable, pleasant	29	(55)	24	(49)
honest, law-abiding	42	(24) *	21	(72)
mature, not childish	29	(49)	31	(48)
good sense, sound judgment	33	(70)	26	(38)
kind and considerate	28	(53)	22	(65)
get along well	30	(46) *	21	(53)
well-liked by many different people	35	(80)	23	(70)
stand up for rights	27	(45)	26	(65)
moral and ethical	32	(31)	25	(76)

than those who cared little about these qualities. For example, 50 percent of those who thought they were not likeable, but who cared about it, had low self-esteem, compared with only 19 percent of those who thought they were not likeable, but did not care about it. To know that someone ranks himself low on a particular quality is thus an inadequate indication of what he thinks of himself. We must also know how much he values this quality.

Since self-values are of such importance to the individual, we are led to the broader question: What social and psychological factors influence the selection of self-values? Let us begin with certain psychological factors and then consider the significance of social statuses and group membership for self-values.

Psychological Factors

The range of motivations behind the selection of self-values is undoubtedly very wide. For example, a youth who strongly identifies with his father may value those qualities in which his father is outstanding or which his father emphasizes. If, on the other hand, he has a fundamental hatred of his father, he may raise to the fore of his self-value system precisely those qualities which his father lacks or disdains. The choice of self-values may thus be motivated by love or by hatred, by a desire for vengeance or a desire to spread happiness, etc.

Our survey data are obviously inadequate to probe the depth and range of unique experiences and unconscious processes involved in the selection of self-values. However, there is one general psychological motivation behind the selection of self-values which merits comment, namely, the desire to maintain or enhance one's self-esteem. How does this process operate?

One way to think well of oneself is to select a system of self-values which correspond to positive self-estimates. In other words, if a person thinks he is good at something, then he may decide that this quality is important to him; if he thinks he is poor at something, he may decide that he doesn't care about it anyway.

An example of this is the characteristic "good student in school." Table 3 shows that four-fifths of those who con-

TABLE 3

* Self-Estimate and Self-Value of "Good Student in School"

| Self-Value: Care about being "a good student" | Self-Estimate (Actually consider oneself "a good student in school") | | | |
	Very	Fairly	A little	Not at all
Care a great deal	79%	59%	33%	35%
Care somewhat, a little, or not at all	21	41	67	65
Total percent	100	100	100	100
(Number)	(245)	(659)	(195)	(43)

sidered themselves very good students said they cared a great deal about this quality, compared with only one-third of those who considered themselves relatively poor students. In this case, the self-estimate with regard to this quality enables us to make a good prediction about the self-value. At the same time, respondents who value "being a good student" are more likely to feel they actually are very good. Only 12 percent of those who cared a great deal about being a good student thought they actually were poor students compared with 33 percent of those who cared less.

In addition to academic success, we examined the relationship of self-estimates to self-values for the 16 most highly valued qualities. In every case, the results were the same; people who felt they excelled at a quality were more likely to value it and those who valued it were more likely to believe they excelled at it. Without exception, the relationships were clear and unequivocal.

In the long run, then, we would expect most people to value those things at which they are good and to try to become good at those things they value. They may still consider themselves poor at those things which, to them, are unimportant, but this is likely to have little effect on their global self-esteem.

If each person can choose his own values, we are led to an interesting paradox of social life, namely, that almost everyone can consider himself superior to almost everyone else, so long as he can use his own system of values. Take four boys. One is a good scholar, the second a good athlete, the third very handsome, and the fourth a good musician. So long as each focuses on the quality at which he excels, each is superior to the rest. At the same time each person may blithely acknowledge the superiority of the others with regard to qualities to which he himself is relatively indifferent.

The trouble is, however, that self-values are not infinitely malleable or subservient to the demands of psychological comfort. This point is illustrated in Tables 3 and 4. There

TABLE 4

Relationship Between Self-Value and Self-Estimate
in Regard to Being "A Good Student in School"

| | Care about being a good student | |
Consider oneself a good student	A great deal	Somewhat, a little, or not at all
Very	29% ⃰	11%
Fairly	59	56
A little or not at all	12	33
Total percent	100	100
(Number)	(660)	(482)

we noted that those who thought they were good students tended to value this quality and those who thought they

251

were not good students tended to disvalue it. But let us examine Table 3 again. It is interesting to note that even among those who considered themselves poor students, over one-third said that they cared a great deal about this quality. Still more striking results appear when we consider the quality "good sense and sound judgment." Among those who felt they did not possess this quality, nearly two-thirds (65 percent) said they cared a great deal about it. Similarly, among students who felt they actually were not "well-liked by many different people," over half (53 percent) said they valued this quality highly. Approximately the same results appear with regard to the qualities "friendly, sociable, and pleasant" and "hard-working and conscientious." These results are not unusual. With regard to many of these qualities, substantial proportions of those who actually consider themselves poor in these respects nevertheless say they care a great deal about them. And since almost without exception these youngsters have the lowest self-esteem, the results suggest that people do not completely select their self-values in the interests of psychological comfort.

There are several reasons why it is often difficult to gear one's self-values into one's self-estimates. For one thing, many self-values are acquired long before the opportunity to test them adequately is at hand. Thus, a child from a musical family may early learn to value musical skill, but only as time goes by does it become compellingly apparent that he has insufficient talent. Self-values, particularly if established early and reinforced by "significant others," may be quite difficult to change even if, at a later time, it is in the individual's interest to do so.

The second point is that in many cases traits are to goals as means are to ends. We cannot conveniently abandon the importance of a particular quality without at the same time abandoning the goal for which this quality is required. Take the son of a doctor who wants to follow in his father's footsteps. This young man will consider it very important whether or not he has the qualities necessary for academic success. It would be absurd to assume that he can dismiss this value and raise to priority the value of being a good dancer, a skill in which he excels. So long as he maintains the goal of becoming a doctor, he must be concerned with academic competence; dancing skill will hardly enable him to achieve this goal. Similarly, a girl who wishes to marry and have a family cannot dismiss the importance of physical or social attractiveness and simply place in the forefront the value of being "dependable and reliable." In other words, since certain traits are relevant means for the attainment of certain goals, their importance to the individual, so long as the goals are maintained, cannot easily be dismissed. Needless to say, many goals are not easily changed.

The third—and probably major—reason why self-values do not accord with self-estimates is that self-values often derive from social role definitions and social group norms. So long as men live in society they cannot completely evade the values stemming from these roles and groups. At an early age the child learns what is right or wrong, important or unimportant for him. As he grows up, he finds himself judged by these criteria. He finds that if he desires the approval of his group, he must seek to excel in terms of their values, not his own. True, he may enhance his self-esteem by abandoning their values, but this is likely to call down upon him the disapproval or contempt of significant others, which would probably diminish his self-esteem all the more.

Self-values thus cannot be casually manipulated to suit the individual's psychological convenience. That such self-values are not purely idiosyncratic becomes evident when we observe that people occupying different roles or enjoying membership in different groups also differ characteristically in their self-values. We therefore turn to the consideration of status and social group differences in self-values.

In the following discussion, we shall distinguish two orders of value emphasis: *Pre-eminent* self-values are those selected as one of the nine values considered of outstanding importance; *high* self-values are those about which the individual says he cares a great deal. Almost all pre-eminent selections are therefore also high, but not all high selections are pre-eminent. In the tables in this chapter, the symbol [P] signifies that the value is a pre-eminent choice; all others are high choices.

Self-Values of Boys and Girls

There is a good deal of similarity between the value systems of boys and girls. Both groups tend to consider it important to be intelligent, to be sociable and well-liked, to be dependable and reliable, to have "interpersonal courage" (i.e., to stand up for your rights), to be independent and self-reliant, and to be mature (i.e., not to behave childishly). There are, however, certain conspicuous differences in the self-value systems of boys and girls in our society.[5]

While boys and girls are both highly concerned with being well-liked by others, girls more consistently give this value top priority. They are more likely to stress values of interpersonal harmony and success (likeable; easy to get along with; friendly, sociable, and pleasant; a person who knows how to get along well with all kinds of people; well-liked by many different people). Girls are also significantly more likely than boys to stress the tender virtues (kindness and consideration, sympathy and understanding), the moral virtues (moral and ethical, deeply religious, honest and law abiding), and aesthetic appreciation (a refined person who shows good taste in things). (Table 5)

[5] In the tables which follow, we shall only present qualities in which the contrasting groups differ by at least 10 percent and in which the differences are significant at the .05 level. The data dealing with social class are based upon chi-square; all other comparisons are based upon significance of difference between percentages.

TABLE 5

Self-Values of Boys and Girls

A. Self-Values More Strongly Emphasized by Boys

How important is it to you, or how much do you care about, whether or not YOU are . . .	Boys	Girls
(Number)	(762)	(765)
good at working with your hands	32%	22%
a good athlete	31	12
good at fighting or wrestling	16	2
tough, not afraid of a fight	27	10
good at many different kinds of things	53	38
good at getting people to do what you want	21	10
a person who knows quite a bit about many different things	52	41
a person whom it is hard to fool or put one over on	34	19
[P] clear-thinking or clever	20	10

B. Self-Values More Strongly Emphasized by Girls

How important is it to you, or how much do you care about, whether or not YOU are . . .	Girls	Boys
(Number)	(765)	(762)
sympathetic and understanding	72%	45%
kind and considerate	85	63
likeable	87	74
easy to get along with	84	65
friendly, sociable and pleasant	87	71
a person who knows how to get along well with all kinds of people	84	68
[P] well-liked by many different people	38	27
a person with a good sense of humor	66	54
a moral and ethical person	76	60
a deeply religious person	32	21
honest and law-abiding	84	65
a well-respected person who is looked up to by others	67	55
a refined person who shows good taste in things	54	42
a logical, reasonable type of person	71	61

Boys, on the other hand, are more likely to stress motoric values and physical courage (good at fighting or wrestling; tough, not afraid of a fight; good at working with your hands; a good athlete). In addition, boys are more likely to value interpersonal control or dominance in their relationships with others (i.e., good at getting people to do what you want). Hardheadedness, or freedom from naïveté (i.e., a person whom it is hard to fool or put one over on), is also more of a male value. Finally, and somewhat more surprising, boys appear to place greater stress on being versatile. They are more likely to care about being "good at many different kinds of things" and about being "a person who knows quite a bit about many different things."

Social Class and Self-Values, among Boys

Since the self-values of boys and girls differ substantially, it seems best to consider the sexes separately in examining the relationship of social class to self-values. Among boys, the results indicate that the higher the social class, the more likely is the boy to be concerned with intellectual values. This is strikingly demonstrated with regard to intellectual success (a good student in school), but it also appears prominently with regard to certain other intellectual qualities (intelligent, a person with a good mind; a logical, reasonable type of person; and imaginative and original).

Higher class boys are also more likely to say that it is very important to be "well-respected, looked up to by others." This is particularly the case when we consider whether this quality is pre-eminently valued (i.e., whether it is one of the nine qualities selected out for special stress by the individual).

Of the 44 self-values considered, "well-respected, looked up to by others" is the single value most likely to be chosen as pre-eminent in the highest class (46 percent). This value

TABLE 6

Social Class and Self-Values, among Boys

Self-Values More Likely to be Stressed in Higher Classes

How important is it to you, or how much do you care about, whether or not YOU are . . .	Social Class			
	High 1–2	3–4	5	Low 6
(Number)	(31)	(295)	(164)	(54)
a good student in school	71%	56%	51%	39%
intelligent, good mind	79	73	65	55
logical, reasonable type	68	68	56	38
imaginative and original	31	35	29	19
[P] well-respected, looked up to by others	46	30	21	16

Self-Values More Likely to be Stressed in Lower Classes

How important is it to you, or how much do you care about, whether or not YOU are . . .				
tough, not afraid of a fight	15%	25%	28%	39%
good at fighting or wrestling	10	11	20	25
good at working with hands	17	28	32	53

is third most likely to be considered pre-eminent in the next highest class (30 percent), eleventh most likely to be chosen in the next highest class (21 percent), and seventeenth most likely to be selected in the lowest class (16 percent).

What does "well-respected, looked up to by others" mean? To some extent, it probably reflects a concern with status or reputation in the society. Max Weber has emphasized that status groups are characterized by different degrees of "status honor." [6] But there are two aspects of concern with social honor. The first is that, in American society, it is largely based on achievement. This means that the individual must usually exercise effort, maintain self-control, defer certain gratifications, and display other qualities which will enable him to rise in the world. Such striving inevitably involves strain and frustration.

The other aspect of social honor is the concern with behavior which will tarnish the reputation. It may be for this reason that the idea of scandal is greeted with such horror in the middle classes. One thoughtless act—one yielding to impulse—may make the individual an outcast and mar his life. To those less concerned with social honor, the social and psychological consequences of such behavior are less serious. In part, the differential concern with social honor may be behind the characterization of the lower classes as "id-oriented" and the middle classes as "superego-oriented."

The concern with social honor or reputation inevitably imposes a burden on those who value it. They must work hard to excel and they must ever be wary of needs, urges, and impulses which may besmirch their reputations. True, social honor has its compensations, but it is acquired at a price. Research has established that social mobility striving is greater in the higher classes, whereas delinquency, illegitimacy, and other forms of norm violation are greater in the lower classes. To some degree these differences probably stem from a differential concern with social honor or reputation in the broader society.

Now let us consider the self-values of the lower-class adolescent. Miller and Swanson,[7] in their work on "expres-

[6] H. H. Gerth and C. Wright Mills (trans. and eds.), *From Max Weber: Essays in Sociology*, New York: Oxford Univ. Press, 1946, pp. 186–187.

[7] Daniel R. Miller and Guy E. Swanson, *Inner Conflict and Defense*, New York: Holt-Dryden, 1960, Chap. 15.

sive styles," have suggested that middle-class children are more likely to manifest a "conceptual" style whereas the lower-class youngster is more disposed to manifest a "motoric" style. Our analysis of self-values shows a similar pattern. The lower the class, the more likely is the boy to consider important, or care about, whether or not he is good at working with his hands, good at fighting or wrestling, or tough, not afraid of a fight.

Two general points may be made regarding the relationship of social class to self-values among boys. The first is a phenomenon which might be described as an "upward drift" in value internalization. In other words, as a general pattern, the higher classes are less likely to accept the lower-class values than the lower classes are to accept the higher-class values.[8] For example, the higher classes tend to de-emphasize working with one's hands, fighting, toughness, etc., but the lower classes do not highly emphasize these values; they are simply less likely to reject these values. Conversely, the lower classes are less likely than the upper classes to emphasize intellectual values, but they are still quite likely to stress these values. Thus, even though, relatively speaking, the upper-class boys stress intellectual values and the lower-class boys stress motoric values, it is still true that the lower class itself is at least as likely to stress intellectual values as to stress motoric values. For example, among the lowest class boys, 55 percent highly emphasize being intelligent, 39 percent stress "good student," 65 percent stress "good sense and sound judgment," and 38 percent stress "logical and reasonable." Within this same class, however, 53 percent stress working with hands, 39 percent stress being tough, and 25 percent stress fighting or wrestling. Even within the lower class, then, intellectual values are as likely (if not more so) as motoric values to be

[8] It should be emphasized that this is among boys who have not dropped out of school.

259

frequently chosen. Values distinctive of the lower class are not necessarily common in this class.

The second point has to do with adjustment to the school system. From an examination of the data, it is crystal clear that the values of the higher classes and the values of the educational system are one and the same. A concern with school performance and, more generally, intellectual excellence; the improvement of taste or refinement; a concern with serious, profound, or important matters [9]—these are all aims of the educational system. What is not the aim of the educational system is to encourage fighting, toughness, or suspiciousness and cynicism [10]—self-values more likely to be held in the lower classes. The only acceptable working class value is "good at working with your hands," the importance of which is somewhat grudgingly acknowledged by the school system in the form of vocational training courses or schools, but which tends to be shifted to the periphery of educational concern. The values of the educational system are those distinctive of the higher classes and are antagonistic to many of the values distinctive of the lower classes.

Social Class and Self-Values among Girls

In contrast to the boys, the self-values of girls in the various social classes are strikingly similar. This conclusion is suggested by the following two facts:

1. Although the number and distribution of girls in the various social classes is very similar to that of the boys, the relationship of social class to self-values attains statistical

[9] The upper class is more likely than the lower class to stress the values "a refined person who shows good taste in things" and "serious and profound, concerned with important things," although the differences are not statistically significant.

[10] The lower class is more likely to value the quality, "a person whom it is hard to fool or put one over on," although the difference is not significant.

significance with regard to only one quality ("good student in school"), and even here the relationship is not completely linear.

2. Similarity of values was also assessed in the following way: Within each social class, the 44 self-values were rank-ordered from those most frequently chosen as highly important to those least frequently chosen. Since we were dealing with four social class groupings, an average inter-correlation of ranks [11] was computed. The average inter-correlation of ranks for girls was .93; for boys it was .85. This difference is sharpened when we consider contrasting class groups—the upper class and the lower class. Among girls, the Spearman rank order coefficient of correlation between these two classes is .91 whereas for boys it is .71. In terms of these values, upper- and lower-class girls are more similar to one another than upper- and lower-class boys.

It should be emphasized, of course, that these results are based upon the choice of these particular 44 qualities and that another set of qualities might yield different results. At the same time there is reason to think that the self-values of girls in the various social classes would be more similar. Let us consider the factor of occupational functions and goals. Whereas boys have radically different job expectations and values, this is less true of the girls. For one thing, the range of occupations effectively available to girls is narrower than that of the boys. Also, in the long run, girls overwhelmingly want and expect to become housewives and mothers. The tasks they will perform, the challenges they will face, and many of the qualities they will require are quite similar, irrespective of their social class positions.

The second point is that, as various studies of social de-

[11] The formula for the average intercorrelation of ranks is drawn from John H. Mueller and Karl F. Schuessler, *Statistical Reasoning in Sociology*, Boston: Houghton Mifflin, 1961, p. 276.

viance have shown, the lower-class girl is more likely to be a conformist to the dominant social value system than the lower-class boy. The lower-class boy is often frankly defiant toward the established institutions—the schools, the law, etc.—and, in fact, this defiance may represent an important part of his pride system. Lower-class girls, too, may not adhere strictly to the dominant norms, but we suspect that they are less likely to take pride in such norm violations. The dominant social norms are usually the values of the higher class, and it seems likely that lower-class girls may more often accept higher-class values. The frequent observation that women of all classes are more likely to support the established institutions of school, church, and state would tend to support this supposition.

We may, however, point to certain differences in the self-values of upper- and lower-class girls which, though not statistically significant, are nevertheless suggestive.[12]

As with the boys, the main differences appear to be with regard to intellectual values; upper-class girls tend to place greater stress on these qualities. Upper-class girls are also somewhat more likely to emphasize firmness of principle (a person who sticks to his principles) and tact.

The lower-class girls, on the other hand, show a somewhat greater tendency to emphasize the "tender virtues." They are more likely to rank "sympathetic and understanding" high and are more likely to rank "kind and considerate" as a pre-eminent value. Another difference appears in the value of "interpersonal appeal" (likeable; well-liked by many different people). Although girls in the various social classes are about equally likely to consider these values highly important, girls in the lower classes are more likely to rank them pre-eminent in importance. Lower-class girls are also somewhat more likely to highly value religiosity (a deeply religious person) and efficiency (efficient

[12] The qualities mentioned are those in which the highest and lowest class girls differ by 10 percent or more.

and practical). Since most of these differences are not large, however, they must at this point be considered as suggestive.

Religion and Self-Values, among Boys

On the whole, religion does not seem to exercise as distinctive an influence as class on the self-values of boys, but certain differences do appear. One general finding is that the greatest differences appear between the Jewish boys and the Catholic boys; in the large majority of the cases, the Protestants are between these groups. Unless otherwise noted, then, when we compare Jews and Catholics, we shall mean that Protestants are between these groups with regard to the trait under consideration.

In our sample, Jews are clearly more likely than Catholics to come from well-educated and occupationally well-situated families. We have therefore controlled on the class factor by means of standardization. In this section, we will describe those self-values by which Jews and Catholics differ by 10 percent or more, and which differ significantly at the .05 level, then indicate which of these appear to be attributable largely to the class factor and which are not.

Catholic boys are more likely than Jewish boys to stress motoric values (good at working with hands, fighting, tough, good athlete). They are also more concerned with being efficient and practical and with being a "deeply religious person." These differences would obtain even if both groups had equal proportions in each of the social class categories. (Table 7)

There is some tendency for Jewish boys to be more likely than Catholics to emphasize intellectual values, although the differences are not striking. Jewish boys are significantly more likely to stress being "clear-thinking and clever" and "logical and reasonable." They are also—at a level approaching, but not attaining, significance—more likely to stress being "imaginative and original" and having "good sense and sound judgment." On the whole, however, the differences are not very great and are in part accounted for by social class factors. Jewish boys are also more likely to stress being "tactful" and "well-respected."

Protestants are distinctive in the following respects: They are more likely than Catholics to emphasize being

TABLE 7

Religion and Self-Values among Boys

Traits which Catholics value more highly than Jews	A. Original figures			B. Figures standard-ized on social class		
	Cath.	Prot.	Jews	Cath.	Prot.	Jews
(Number)	(322)	(273)	(97)	(322)	(273)	(97)
work with hands	39%	31%	14%	38%	33%	12%
fighting, wrestling	20	15	6	21	16	6
tough	35	21	21	35	22	17
good athlete	37	31	25	38	31	25
efficient, practical	61	51	49	62	51	49
deeply religious	24	21	11	25	21	11

Traits which Jews value more highly than Catholics

	Cath.	Prot.	Jews	Cath.	Prot.	Jews
[P] clear-thinking and clever	17%	19%	31%	18%	19%	35%
logical and reasonable	63	57	74	65	55	70
tactful	41	44	55	42	43	56
[P] well-respected, looked up to	20	32	37	20	30	29

Traits which Protestants value more highly than Catholics

	Cath.	Prot.	Jews	Cath.	Prot.	Jews
[P] well-respected, looked up to	20%	32%	37%	20%	30%	29%

Traits which Jews value more highly than Protestants

	Cath.	Prot.	Jews	Cath.	Prot.	Jews
[P] a person who stands up for rights	38%	28%	47%	36%	29%	50%

"well-respected, looked up to by others." They are more likely than Catholics—but not significantly so—to emphasize being "dependable and reliable," "moral and ethical," and "honest and law-abiding." They tend, in other words, to emphasize qualities dealing with adherence to the dominant social norms.

In general, then, Jews are somewhat more likely than Catholics to emphasize intellectual values and community reputation; Catholics are somewhat more likely to stress motoric prowess and religiosity; and Protestants tend somewhat more to emphasize qualities reflecting adherence to dominant social norms.

One other point is worthy of mention, viz., that Protestant boys are less likely than Jewish and Catholic boys to value "a person who stands up for his rights." This result suggests that standing up for one's rights is more likely to be a salient consideration for those whose rights are challenged or violated, i.e., minority group members. This illustrates how specific situational factors may bring certain values to the fore.

In sum, while there are certain differential value emphases among religious groups, the differences are in general not very great. Among boys, social class appears to be a more powerful differentiator of self-values than religion.

Religion and Self-Values, among Girls

Among the boys, we have seen, the two groups most dissimilar in values are Jews and Catholics; among the girls, on the other hand, Jews are most strongly differentiated from Protestants.[13] Jewish girls are significantly more likely than Protestant girls to stress certain aspects of intellectual competence. In addition, Jewish girls are distinctly more likely to emphasize "culture," in the sense of *belles lettres*,

[13] As noted in Chapter 4, however, the self-values of Jews, as a total group, are more similar to those of Protestants than of Catholics.

etc. This is suggested by their unusual emphasis upon being "a refined person who shows good taste in things" and one who is "good at painting or writing." Jewish girls are also more likely to value highly being "good-looking, attractive in appearance," "ambitious," and "good at many different kinds of things." (Table 8)

This emphasis upon intellectual and "cultural" qualities suggests that Jewish girls are more disposed than Protestant girls to embrace an "upper class style of life." But this is not due to the fact that Jewish girls are more likely to be upper class, for even when these groups are equalized in terms of social class distribution, the value differences are generally maintained.

Now let us consider the self-values of the Protestant girls. It is difficult to find a capsule term or phrase which adequately reflects their value emphasis, although the traits do seem to have something of a psychological unity. Most of these values appear to refer to qualities of "character" in the popular, rather than the technical, sense of the term. They are largely sober virtues and firm principles, rather than conspicuous sources of distinction. Protestant girls are more likely to emphasize being hard-working and conscientious, efficient and practical, and dependable and reliable. They are also, though less substantially, more likely to emphasize being moral and ethical, honest and law-abiding, a person who sticks to his principles, and a person with good sense and sound judgment. Max Weber's classical description of the "Protestant Ethic" [14] today appears to be especially distinctive of Protestant girls.

Catholic girls are strikingly more likely than Jewish girls and somewhat more likely than Protestant girls, to emphasize the importance of being "a deeply religious person." [15]

[14] Max Weber, *The Protestant Ethic and the Spirit of Capitalism*, New York: Scribner's, 1930.

[15] Had parochial school youngsters been incorporated into our sample, this last difference might have been still more conspicuous.

TABLE 8

Religion and Self-Values among Girls

Traits which Jews value more highly than Protestants	A. Original figures			B. Figures standard-ized on social class		
	Cath.	Prot.	Jews	Cath.	Prot.	Jews
(Number)	(281)	(280)	(101)	(281)	(280)	(101)
clear-thinking, clever	70%	61%	76%	72%	61%	78%
imaginative, original	24	21	35	28	21	29
intelligent	68	61	72	71	63	74
[P] good student	15	13	24	16	13	30
knows many different things	44	30	45	43	29	49
refined, shows good taste	53	45	64	55	47	72
good at painting, writing	17	11	22	17	11	20
good-looking, attractive	53	41	56	54	42	61
[P] ambitious	17	10	22	17	11	24
good at different things	37	29	43	39	27	52

Traits which Protestants value more highly than Jews

efficient and practical	64%	64%	54%	62%	65%	56%
[P] dependable and reliable	36	44	29	38	44	25

Traits which Protestants value more highly than Catholics

[P] hard-working and conscientious	14%	28%	21%	13%	28%	22%

Traits which Catholics and Protestants value more highly than Jews

a deeply religious person	42%	35%	16%	44%	37%	18%

As an over-all description, the following pattern appears to emerge: Jewish girls are especially likely to emphasize intellectual and aesthetic values; Protestant girls tend to stress "character" traits or sober virtues; and Catholic girls are somewhat more likely than Protestant girls, and conspicuously more likely than Jewish girls, to emphasize religiosity.

In sum, these results suggest that while the individual's values are to some extent a matter of personal choice and convenience and may derive from any number of sources, such values do not just "happen." They are, on the contrary, largely the product of social learning; and such learning tends to differ among those who play different social roles or who are raised in different social groups.

Not that the values of these youngsters are radically dissimilar. They are all products of Western civilization; all residents of the United States; all living in New York State; all exposed to similar experiences in the schools, from the mass media, etc. In general, then, the similarities of their value systems are more striking than the differences. But differences do exist, and they illustrate the significance of social status and group membership for personality development.

PART VII
NEW DIRECTIONS

CHAPTER 14

AREAS FOR FURTHER RESEARCH

IN RECENT years literally hundreds of articles dealing with the self-image have appeared primarily in the professional literature.[1] On the whole, the major stimuli to self-image research by psychologists appear to be the Q-methodology of Stephenson,[2] the clinical work of Rogers,[3] and the phenomenological theory of Snygg and Combs.[4] Quantitative work in this area, however, does not appear to have begun in earnest until 1948, when Victor Raimy published his article "Self-Reference in Counseling Interviews."[5] From that time on, an ever-widening stream of self-image research has appeared in psychological journals which has threatened to become a deluge.

While clinical and theoretical psychiatry and psychology have not, on the whole, used the self-image as a central orienting concept, there have been a number of important exceptions. Karen Horney, in her later work, placed the idealized image in the center of her theoretical scheme,[6] and valuable contributions dealing with the self have been

[1] A bibliography of studies conducted between 1949 and 1958 (and part of 1959) appears in Wiley, *op. cit.*, pp. 325–348.

[2] William Stephenson, *The Study of Behavior: Q-Technique and Its Methodology,* Chicago: Univ. of Chicago Press, 1953.

[3] Carl Rogers, *Client-Centered Therapy,* Boston: Houghton Mifflin, 1951, and Carl Rogers and Rosalind Dymond, eds., *Psychotherapy and Personality Change,* Chicago: Univ. of Chicago Press, 1954.

[4] D. Snygg and A. W. Combs, *Individual Behavior: A New Frame of Reference for Psychology,* New York: Harper, 1949.

[5] *Jour. Consult. Psych.,* Vol. 12 (1948), pp. 153–163.

[6] The idealized image came to the fore of Horney's work in *Our Inner Conflicts,* New York: Norton, 1945, Chap. 6, but was most fully elaborated in *Neurosis and Human Growth.*

made by Erikson, Lecky, Murphy, Moustakas, Fromm, Maslow, G. Allport, White, Rogers, and others.[7]

Much, then, has been accomplished on the empirical and theoretical level. Yet as one considers the complexity of the task and the vast array of unsolved problems, one can hardly evade the conclusion that the surface has barely been scratched. Even to attempt a detailed discussion of the unsolved problems of the self-image would far exceed the purpose of this report. All we can do here is to point to a few selected areas wherein research might profitably be pursued, without thereby implying that these problems are more important than many others.

A word about methodology. Many problems of self-image research are technical and methodological. There is no generally accepted measure of self-esteem, the phenomenon is not easily amenable to experimental manipulation, and the problem of validating something so quintessentially phenomenological is difficult in the extreme. The methodological problems of self-image studies have been discussed admirably by Ruth Wiley in her book *The Self-Concept* and therefore will not detain us. Our concern in this chapter, then, will be with substantive questions.

[7] Erik H. Erikson, "The Problem of Ego Identity," *Jour. Amer. Psychoanal. Ass'n,* Vol. 4 (1956), pp. 56–121; Prescott Lecky, *Self-Consistency: A Theory of Personality,* New York: Island Press, 1945; Gardner Murphy, *Personality,* New York: Harper and Bros., 1947, Chaps. 20–25; Clark E. Moustakas, ed., *The Self: Explorations in Personal Growth,* New York: Harper, 1956; Erich Fromm, *Escape from Freedom,* New York: Rinehart, 1941, and *Man for Himself,* especially pp. 119–140; Abraham H. Maslow, *Motivation and Personality,* New York: Harper, 1954; Gordon Allport, *Becoming: Basic Considerations for a Psychology of Personality,* New Haven: Yale University Press, 1955; Robert White, *The Abnormal Personality,* New York: Ronald, 1956; Carl Rogers, *Client-Centered Therapy;* Theodore Newcomb, *Social Psychology,* New York: Dryden, 1950; Bartlett H. Stoodley, ed., *Society and Self,* Glencoe, Ill.: The Free Press, 1962; Ernest R. Hilgard, "Human Motives and the Concept of the Self," *Amer. Psychologist,* Vol. 4 (1949), pp. 374–382.

The Variety of Self-Images

The present self-image—how an individual now sees himself—is only one of a number of self-images which might be considered. A great deal of empirical work by psychologists has distinguished between two types of self-images—the (present) self and the ideal self. In addition, Horney has developed the concept of the "idealized image," [8] Hilgard has spoken of the "inferred self," [9] and Freud has given attention to the "ego ideal" or superego.[10]

The simplicity of several of these concepts is somewhat deceptive. The most important example—important because it has been used in so many studies—is that of the "ideal self." The connotation of the ideal self appears simple enough: it is what the individual would like to be. Many studies, particularly those using the Q-sort technique,[11] compute the self-ideal discrepancy score in order to obtain a measure of self-esteem. But what is an "ideal self"? If we were asked ideally whether we would like to be millionnaires, tennis champions, outstanding mathematicians, superb musicians, we would probably want these things in the abstract. But this does not mean that we perish from frustration at not being them. The more important consideration is, as James has noted, what the individual has staked himself on being.

Some people, then, see the ideal self as limited only by the bounds of imagination, whereas others think of it in more realistic terms. These are two different self-images. The one might be called the committed self—what the individual more or less realistically stakes himself on being, with a fairly confident expectation that he will become such a person. (This self may not be objectively realistic,

[8] *Neurosis and Human Growth.*

[9] "Human Motives and the Concept of the Self."

[10] Sigmund Freud, *A New Series of Introductory Lectures on Psychoanalysis,* New York: Norton, 1933, Chap. 3.

[11] See Stephenson, *The Study of Behavior.*

but it is felt to be realistic by the individual.) The other is a fantasy self—a self which is pleasurable to reflect on, dream about, or contemplate (*à la* Walter Mitty), in which there is perhaps a wistful yearning or intense longing to be such a person, but no confident belief that this self will ever become a reality.

The concept of the "idealized image" is also beset with problems. In Horney's terms, the idealized image consists of exalted attributes which the individual feels "he has, could have, or should have." [12] The common element is that it is a picture that the individual enjoys thinking of himself as. At the same time, Horney is directing our attention to three different self-pictures—the individual as he sees himself at present, the future (or possible) self-picture, and the picture of what one should be (corresponding, probably, to Freud's conception of the ego-ideal).

There are, then, a number of different self-pictures which may be psychologically important to the individual: his present self-image; his committed self-image (the type of person the individual has staked himself on being); the fantasy self-image (the type of person he would like to be if unencumbered by reality); the ego-ideal (the type of person he feels he should be); the future or possible self (the type of person he feels he may become); and the idealized image (the type of person he most enjoys thinking of himself as) [which may include components of his present self, his ego-ideal, his future self, etc.]. In addition, one would wish to learn about the "presenting self"—the picture of the self that the individual attempts to set forth to the world.

How does social experience influence each of these self-images? Which people have discrepant self-images and what are the consequences of such discrepancies? To what extent are each of these self-images internally contradic-

[12] *Neurosis and Human Growth,* p. 13.

tory and to what extent are they contradictory to one another? Which of these self-images are psychologically most prominent (one person's idealized image may be at the center of his attention whereas another is relatively unconcerned with it), and what are the consequences of this relative emphasis? To what extent is the individual able to keep these self-images separate? How are these various self-images related to Hilgard's "inferred self" (what the scientific investigator is able to learn about the individual), and how are they related to what might be called the "accorded self" (the picture other people hold of this person)? This is but a superficial sampling of the question on types of self-images awaiting future research.

Typological Analysis

One of the fundamental operations employed by the human mind to bring order to the world it observes is the construction of typologies. In the present study, we have classified people into two "types"—the egophobes and the egophiles—on the basis of their location along the single dimension or continuum of self-esteem. Further research, however, must also be concerned with multidimensional typological classification.[13]

The importance of multidimensional classification was brought home to us forcefully in interviews with egophobic and egophilic high school students. In the course of these interviews, we were struck by the fact that some egophiles were expansive, outgoing, spontaneous personalities whereas others were fairly subdued and showed little affect. Yet it was our strong impression that both types of adolescents accepted themselves for what they were. If we can classify people in terms of meaningful types, we will

[13] A discussion of typological construction appears in Allen H. Barton, "The Concept of Property-Space in Social Research," in P. F. Lazarsfeld and M. Rosenberg, eds., *The Language of Social Research*, Glencoe, Ill.: The Free Press, 1955, pp. 40–53.

be better able to understand why people with the same level of self-esteem so often behave differently. Prediction and control inevitably increase with the acquisition of such knowledge.

Stanley Coopersmith has made an important contribution to the construction of self-esteem typologies. He has classified his subjects both by self-esteem and by "self-esteem behavior," i.e., behavior described by outsiders which is differentially associated with high or low self-esteem. Thus he classified his subjects as high in self-esteem but low in self-esteem behavior, low in self-esteem but high in behavior, etc. His detailed clinical and experimental studies of these various types undoubtedly represent one of the most impressive bodies of research in the self-image literature.[14]

Another meaningful two-dimensional typology would be based upon attitudes toward oneself and attitudes toward others. In Chapter 9, we saw that people who had favorable attitudes toward themselves tended to have favorable attitudes toward others, and vice-versa; this finding is supported by other research.[15] Yet what about the person who has great contempt and hatred for others and at the same time considers himself the last word in perfection, or the person who despises himself but admires others inordinately? Are these people expressing attitudes which are actually at variance with their unconscious feelings? Do

[14] Stanley Coopersmith, "Self-Esteem and Need Achievement as Determinants of Selective Recall and Repetition," *Jour. Abn. and Soc. Psych.*, Vol. 60 (1960), pp. 310–317; "A Method for Determining Types of Self-Esteem," *Jour. Abn. and Soc. Psych.*, Vol. 59 (1959), pp. 87–94; "Self-Esteem as a Determinant of Conformity Behaviors," paper delivered at Western Psychological Association, San Jose, California, Apr. 22, 1960; "Clinical Explorations of Self-Esteem," paper delivered at Fourteenth International Congress of Applied Psychology, Copenhagen, Aug. 15, 1961.

[15] William F. Fey, "Acceptance of Self and Others, and Its Relation to Therapy-Readiness," *Jour. Clin. Psych.*, 10 (1954), pp. 266–269.

these constitute distinctive syndromes? What behavioral consequences issue from such combinations of attitudes? Behavior which appears to be at variance with self-esteem may be clarified by analysis of these more complex types.

What about the socially or academically successful ego-phobe and the unsuccessful egophile? Who are the people with stable, unchanging low self-esteem and those with unstable high self-esteem? Among what groups would we find the calm, relaxed, anxiety-free egophobe? What kind of person is the egophile who is ridden with psychosomatic symptoms and other indicators of anxiety?

Some typologies may involve the classification of individuals along more than two dimensions. Typically, location along these dimensions is empirically interrelated, but the relationships are imperfect. This is typically the case with social stereotypes which are internalized by individuals. Thus, someone who thinks of himself as an "intellectual" may not be simply a person who values intelligence. He may also see himself as concerned with profound matters; he may adopt a sober mien; he may be scornful of the concrete, the trivial, and the frivolous; he may admire art, literature, history, science; he may exercise appropriate emotional control. In other words, an extensive variety of attitudes and behavior may issue from the self-concept of "intellectual."

Or we may consider a person who thinks of himself as a "beatnik." He has not simply rebelled against middle-class conventions. He affects a certain style of dress, sports a beard, takes pleasure in a certain type of poetry, adopts appropriate attitudes of disenchantment and detachment, interests himself in certain Eastern philosophy, has distinctive attitudes toward people, toward the mind, toward the world.

At the opposite end is the person who sees himself as a "hail-fellow-well-met." He likes to see himself as cheerful, extroverted, well-liked, the life of the party, optimistic, gregarious, good-humored, etc. To say that he sees himself as "popular" or "well-liked," as he might describe himself on adjective check lists, would be to reflect inadequately the distinctive nature of his self-image.

Society recognizes a number of these types.[16] These are largely social stereotypes, but the individual may well apply them to himself, either in his present image, his committed image, his idealized image, his ego-ideal, etc. Thus, an individual may see himself as a dreamer, an adventurer, a rugged individualist, a live wire, a sophisticated type, a middle-of-the-roader, a down-to-earth type, an average man, etc. Each of these types reflects a complex combination of traits, skills, statuses, interests, attitudes, etc., each of which is not necessarily distinctive of that type exclusively but which produces a socially recognized combination of qualities. To clarify the nature of these types, to uncover their social sources, and to trace out their emotional and behavioral consequences remain tasks for future research.

The Intervening Variable

While sociologists are generally agreed on the importance of examining the relationships between the individual's social characteristics and his attitudes or behavior, there is varying concern with specifying those factors which are consequences of the independent variable and causes of the dependent variable, i.e., intervening variables. Yet even those researchers dedicated to conforming their analyses strictly to the social level often implicitly introduce psychological factors as intervening variables.

For example, in conducting his various studies of social integration, Durkheim contended that social phenomena

[16] Samuel M. Strong's study of empirical types among Negroes is a good case in point. See his "Social Types in a Minority Group. Formulation of a Method," *Amer. Jour. Soc.*, Vol. 48 (1942–43), pp. 563–573.

could be examined without reference to the psychological structure of the individual.[17] An outstanding illustration of this approach is his examination of the relationship of certain social statuses and group memberships to rates of suicide.[18] Yet it is abundantly clear at many points that Durkheim takes account of psychological states which are presumed consequences of social experiences and uses these psychological states to explain the differential suicide rates. It should not be inferred from this that Durkheim has "reduced" social conditions to psychological conditions; rather, he has treated psychological conditions as intervening variables in attempting to account for the association between group memberships or social statuses, on the one hand, and social behavior, on the other.

We suggest that an important, but neglected, intervening variable between social characteristics and attitudes or behavior is the self-image, including the present image, committed image, idealized image, ego-ideal, or future image. In using the self-image as an intervening variable, however, it will be necessary to specify what aspect of the group affiliation is presumed to influence the image. Does the self-image derive from a set of group norms for behavior which the individual internalizes and which becomes a part of his ego-ideal? (Example: the middle class is more likely to internalize the value of intellectual competence; this results in certain exposure to mass communications.) Do certain group norms have unanticipated consequences for the self-image? (Example: group norms vary with regard to the physical punishment of, or expression of affection toward, children. These norms may ultimately have a bearing upon self-esteem.) In what way may characteristic "conditions of existence" influence the self-image?

[17] Emile Durkheim, *The Rules of the Sociological Method,* Chicago: Univ. of Chicago Press, 1938.

[18] Emile Durkheim, *Suicide* (trans. J. G. Spaulding and G. Simpson), Glencoe, Ill.: The Free Press, 1951.

(Example: a civilian drafted into the army may come to think of himself as brave, good at marksmanship, well-disciplined, etc.—qualities which probably would not have entered into any of his self-images had he not been drafted; this self-image may have a bearing upon his occupational plans, interpersonal relationships, etc.)

To trace the path leading from a social characteristic to a self-image and from a self-image to social behavior is a complex task. Operationally, it would have to be shown that if groups did not differ in their self-images, then they would differ less in their other attitudes and behavior. We would hypothesize that the self-image is a major variable intervening between social position and individual action.

A related problem is the specification of variables intervening between social factors and self-esteem. Studies dealing with group differences in the distribution of pathology are typically referred to as "epidemiological." [19] By noting group differences in the incidence or prevalence of a disease, the scientist is alerted to certain other conditions of life by which the groups are differentiated. Further investigation of such differences may eventually lead to the isolation of the causative agent. An outstanding case in the history of medical science was Goldberger's discovery of the cause and cure of pellagra.

In the present study, we noted the following kind of "epidemiological" finding: that students of Russian Jewish origin appear more likely to have high self-esteem than students of Polish Catholic origin. Assuming this result were supported by other research, we would still want to know in what ways the characteristic experiences of members of these groups varied. Is it a consequence of contrasting family structures, child-rearing practices, "styles of life,"

[19] A recent treatment of this subject appears in August B. Hollingshead, "The Epidemiology of Schizophrenia," *Amer. Soc. Rev.*, Vol. 26 (February 1961), pp. 5–13.

AREAS FOR FURTHER RESEARCH

values, or what? Further research designed to specify the decisive intervening factors is required.

Social Values

It is a curious paradox of social life that society, which so importantly determines what men want out of life, often works to frustrate the desires it has generated. Men are urged to pursue certain goals with all the resources at their command, but such goals necessarily remain beyond the reach of many. This is true of the value of success in American society. Americans are urged to advance as far as possible in the occupational realm, but it is inherent in the competitive nature of the system that some must fall by the wayside.

The relevance of competitiveness to self-esteem, however, is not confined to occupational or social success; it can refer to any value which is strongly emphasized by the group and which can be achieved by only a limited number of its members. Religious distinction would illustrate this point. In Puritan New England, as Samuel Morison points out, only a small proportion of the people were certified church members.[20] Membership required, as a minimum, having a "religious experience." A board of examiners carefully checked the authenticity of this experience. Those who failed to achieve membership, therefore, were likely to feel that they lacked God's grace and hence to consider themselves unworthy.

The general point is that whenever a value is set forth which can only be attained by a few, the conditions are ripe for widespread feelings of personal inadequacy. An outstanding example in American society is the fierce competitiveness of the school system. No educational system in the world has so many examinations, or so emphasizes

[20] Samuel E. Morison, *The Builders of the Bay Colony,* New York: Houghton-Mifflin, 1930.

281

grades, as the American school system. Children are constantly being ranked and evaluated. The superior achievement of one child tends to debase the achievement of another.

A thorough investigation of the relationship of competitiveness to self-esteem is yet to be done. What is the effect of the high rate of business failure in American society? How many millions of men fail to reach the positions to which they aspire? How much bitterness and self-contempt is engendered among those who are not able to maintain the style of life to which they aspire or by which they are surrounded? What is the effect upon children in school who obtain poor grades? upon college students who fail to be accepted into professional schools? upon graduate students who do not obtain advanced degrees? What is the effect upon actors who fail to achieve stardom, scientists who fail to make discoveries, athletes who do not achieve outstanding distinction?

As one views modern society, one is forcefully struck by the enormous amount of "failure," i.e., the gap between aspirations and achievements, which exists. It is readily apparent that such failure takes an important psychic and emotional toll and that the effect of failure on the self-image is a major mediating mechanism. And yet it seems equally apparent that the psychological effect is considerably less than one would expect. Most people do not drown in a sea of self-contempt, most are not bitter, sullen, frustrated, etc. This suggests that the value of success tends to be ambiguous, that society provides certain "cushioning mechanisms" for softening the blow of failure, and that the individual develops certain "coping mechanisms" which interrupt the direct translation of objective failure into a sense of personal inadequacy. Research into these coping mechanisms appears to merit high priority.

What these coping mechanisms are; by whom they are used; how successful they are for maintaining self-esteem;

how much the self-image is dependent upon relative performance in competitive situations; how useful the threat to self-esteem is as a functional device for motivating men to do what has to be done in order to keep the society going—these important questions await further analysis and research.

One further aspect of self-values has been neglected; one might call it the issue of "self-taboos." The definition of values as conceptions of the desirable also implies conceptions of the undesirable. A person may not only stake himself on possessing certain qualities but also on not possessing others. He may take special pride in not being a striver or a "grind" or a Rotarian or an optimist or a cold calculator, etc. A youth rebelling against his father may not clearly know what he wants to be like but may be very clear that he wants to be as different from his father as possible. One may wonder whether the delinquent is more concerned with becoming a certain kind of person than he is with being different from the middle-class conformists. The degree to which the individual's pride system is invested in such "self-taboos" appears to represent an important area for self-image research.

Changes of the Self-Image

If we simply confine our attention to the present self-image, leaving aside the other self-images, we are confronted by a large array of questions of change. One question is: Are there perceptible stages in the development of the self-image characteristically associated with certain age or experience levels? For example, Piaget has traced the development of children's thought processes with reference to the use of language and process of communication, judgment and reasoning, the origin and development of rules and moral precepts, etc.[21] What is

[21] Jean Piaget, *The Language and Thought of the Child,* London: Routledge and Kegan Paul, 1926; *Judgment and Reasoning in the*

clearly needed are similar studies of the origin and development of the self-image: the emergence of self-awareness, the development of self-evaluation, the differentiation of global self-conceptions into component elements or the synthesis of elemental self-attitudes into global self-judgments; the differentiation between "me" and "mine"; the changes in the focus of the pride system over time; etc. While the most interesting time to study the intellectual processes discussed by Piaget is generally middle childhood and pre-adolescence, the topic of the self-image may be investigated profitably well into middle adulthood or even old age, for the self-image continues to change throughout life. The work of Havighurst and Macdonald,[22] dealing with changes in types of role models over time, appears to be highly promising, but no large-scale developments along these lines have emerged.

In addition to the investigation of stages of development, naturalistic studies of change are required. In particular, it is important to learn how the self-images of individuals (not groups or age-grades) change as a result of their life experiences. This would require clinical investigations of individuals over time as well as the panel analysis of large samples. The great question is: What kinds of stimuli, influences, or experiences, under what kinds of conditions, acting upon what kinds of people, produce what kinds of change in what parts of the self-image? A large body of specific studies dealing with each of these questions is obviously needed.

One interesting area of investigation might be situations involving a decline in fortunes. A good example of this

---

Child, London: Routledge and Kegan Paul, 1928; *The Moral Judgment of the Child,* Glencoe, Ill.: The Free Press, 1948.

[22] R. J. Havighurst and D. V. Macdonald, "Development of the Ideal Self in New Zealand and American Children," *Jour. Educ. Res.,* Vol. 49 (December 1955), pp. 263–275.

phenomenon has been presented by Robert White in his description of Joseph Kidd in *Lives in Progress*.[23] Raised in a favorable family environment, Joseph Kidd was an assertive, outgoing, happy child. He was also somewhat brighter than other children in school, completing his work with less effort and in a shorter time than the other children. His parents were very pleased with his performance and he was well-respected by the other children. Through an accident of circumstance, combined with his mother's high aspirations for her children, he had an opportunity to advance rapidly in school. At about the age of 10, he was suddenly given a double promotion. From this point until the completion of high school, he was fully two years younger than the other pupils in his classes. Although he could keep up with his school work, he was, of course, no longer so outstanding. Nor could his athletic prowess match that of the other boys. Similarly, when the others became interested in girls, he was no match for them. He then started to play the baby, the child, the clown, in order to gain attention and approval. As time went on his self-esteem was undermined, and he showed most of the reactions which are typical of the low self-esteem respondents we have studied.

In a sense, the case of Joseph Kidd is symbolized in the dictum that "pride goeth before a fall." It is characterized by an initial sense of worthiness, self-acceptance, and elation, followed by a subsequent feeling of worthlessness, self-rejection, and depression.

In some societies, this phenomenon may be socially patterned. For example, there are primitive societies in which it is customary to give the child abundant love, affection, and praise until he is five or six. Then he is suddenly let loose on his own and these external evidences of his worth

[23] R. W. White, *Lives in Progress: A Study of the Natural Growth of Personality,* New York: Dryden, 1952, Chap. V.

are withdrawn. We would expect low self-esteem to be quite common in this society.

Such changes in self-conceptions may be a frequent consequence of shifts in age-grades. We judge a young child by certain standards, an older child by other standards, an early adolescent by still other criteria, etc. This means that a child who, by the standards of early childhood, elicits extravagant praise may call forth scorn when he exhibits the same characteristics at a later time. The long blond curls of the young boy, which produce so much parental cooing and affection, calls forth the taunting of his playmates a few years later. As Benedict points out, traits of dependency and irresponsibility, which are fostered in the child, are abjured in the adult.[24] In other words, various traits which are appropriate and laudable at one stage may be quite inappropriate at a later stage. Such shifts from an initial level of acceptance to one of rejection might be especially likely to induce feelings of unworthiness. Of course, the opposite situation may also occur. The gawky young girl who blossoms into an attractive young lady may experience a sharp and gratifying elevation in the level of her self-esteem.

Just as one can shift from age-grade to age-grade, with changing standards of evaluation, so can one shift from subculture to subculture, with similar consequences. An adolescent youth who has achieved status on the basis of his intellectual achievements in his own subculture may develop feelings of inadequacy when he finds himself in a college stressing athletic prowess. A working-class child who has attained the respect of his peers for his toughness may feel at a loss when he moves to a middle-class area which does not prize this talent. An individual's self-esteem depends importantly on what others think of him,

[24] Ruth Benedict, "Continuities and Discontinuities in Cultural Conditioning," *Psychiatry*, Vol. 1 (1938), pp. 161–167.

but the criteria by which others judge him are based on social factors—the values of a societal subculture or the prescriptions and proscriptions of an age status.

Rapid shifts from a state of social praise to one of dispraise may occur in later years as well. A well-known example is the "skidder"—the person who has experienced a decline in occupational fortunes.[25] Men make and lose fortunes, theatrical stars shine brightly and grow dim, talented scientists and artists never live up to their promise; and so on. In these cases a success which has been achieved elevates the individual's level of self-esteem; the failure which follows is thus all the more devastating.

Such a sudden decline is not a matter of pure "accident." It may be related to a variety of social influences and developments. One might, for example, speculate on the self-esteem implications of the depression following 1929. In the '20s, success was largely equated with the acquisition of money. The economic prosperity of this period might have produced widespread feelings of pride and personal worth. The economic blows of the '30s might thus have been all the more keenly felt. Economic failure could easily have been interpreted as personal inadequacy, just as economic success had been interpreted as evidence of personal worth. Even if many people could have salvaged their battered self-esteem by attributing their failures to external "social conditions," it was difficult for them to evade the conclusion that their previous economic success might equally well have been due less to their personal merit than to external "social conditions."

Another problem has to do with social or cultural change. We have pointed out that the individual is not judged in the abstract, but rather in terms of the system of values of his social groups (class, religious group, gang, etc.)

[25] See Harold Wilensky, "The Skidder: Ideological Adjustments of Downward Mobile Workers," *Amer. Soc. Rev.*, Vol. 24 (1959), pp. 215–231.

and of his statuses (sex, age, occupation, etc.). An additional set of standards of judgment are those enveloping the entire society. The point is, however, that a society can change its values. Thus, the traits which are applauded in one era may be treated with indifference, or even ridicule, during another. This would be true, for example, of a skilled craftsman whose pride in his work was originally confirmed by social evaluation but whose prestige declined as mass production methods surpassed his efforts. It could occur in the transition from war to peace. A man whose military skills and exploits gain him general respect during wartime may find, upon his return to civilian life, that these skills are no longer prized and that the abilities which are valued in civilian life are either inadequately developed in him because of lack of training or are nonexistent because of lack of native ability.

Then there are those people who are simply "passed by" in the forward sweep of social change. A person who built his esteem system upon piety and moral rectitude in his earlier years, and who received outside confirmation of his worth, may find these qualities looked at askance in an era of more lax moral standards. A person who has been acclaimed for his political vision in an era of political upheaval may be viewed as strange, in espousing these ideas, at a later period of stable political conservatism. We still have much to learn about the influence of such social experiences upon the individual's self-conception.

From the therapeutic viewpoint, of course, the main question is: Can techniques be developed which will enable us consciously and systematically to produce change in the individual's self-image? Psychotherapeutic techniques are, in fact, largely oriented toward this end. The question is whether additional techniques specifically focused on certain aspects of the self-image may profitably be utilized.

For example, to listen to oneself on tape or see oneself

in a film may often catch one by surprise. Can such procedures help the individual to start seeing himself differently? Can role-playing be focused more directly upon self-image problems? One virtue of the psychodrama is that it enables the individual to see himself in action and to reflect upon the self he sees. Can this technique be usefully employed in clarifying and modifying specific aspects of the self-picture? Can "public commitment" have the effect of changing behavior which in turn may modify self-attitudes? For example, if one proclaims before a group that one plans to behave in a certain way, then it appears more difficult to withdraw from this decision later.[26] Under certain circumstances, the group therapist might deem it advisable to induce patients to make such "public commitments" before the group. Another mode of approach is to ask whether some characteristic sequence of self-attitude change might be adopted. For example, social psychological research has suggested that it is easiest to change people's minds about new facts, less easy to change opinions, still harder to change attitudes, and hardest of all to change "motivation." [27] Might such a sequence, proceeding from the easiest to the hardest, be employed in changing the individual's self-image, i.e., might one start by clarifying facts, then challenging opinions, then attempting to modify attitudes and values? For it may be that if one begins by attempting to change values, the resistance will be so great that one's efforts will be fruitless.

The difficulties of changing self-attitudes, as every psychiatrist will ruefully agree, are enormous. At the same time, it must be recognized that the careful, systematic investigation of methods of changing self-attitudes has

[26] Kurt Lewin, "Group Decision and Social Change," in E. E. Maccoby, T. M. Newcomb, and E. L. Hartley, eds., *Readings in Social Psychology,* third edition, New York: Holt, 1958, p. 203.

[27] Carl Hovland, Arthur Lumsdaine, Fred Sheffield, *Experiments on Mass Communication,* Princeton: Princeton Univ., 1949, Chaps. 2–3.

barely begun. If the full range of possible techniques is considered, if the problem is stated clearly, and if the various techniques are tested systematically, we may have real confidence that progress will be made.

Family Influences

While no one has adequately spelled out the various family conditions which are likely to generate low self-esteem, a number of suggestive ideas are available in the literature. Angyal has maintained that a fundamental feeling of unworthiness is characteristic of neurosis, and he has attempted to specify certain conditions of early childhood which foster this condition of worthlessness.[28]

One of the conditions mentioned by Angyal is the "overprotective attitude of an insecure, anxious parent." He reasons that this attitude conveys to the child a feeling that the world is full of dangers and that he is inadequate to cope with them. Thus the child is likely to develop feelings of helplessness, fright, insignificance. The result is a fundamental feeling of weakness and worthlessness.

Second, Angyal points out: "When the parent is too eager for the child to do well and is excessively critical of him, he is likely to instill in the child the feeling that 'something must be wrong with me; I can't do anything right.' "

Third: "When parents distort and exaggerate the child's achievement, have great expectations of him, they plant the seed of self-derogation in him, since deep down he knows he is not that good."

Other factors mentioned by Angyal are: restrictiveness —too many "don'ts" make the child feel that what he wants is evil, which makes him an evil person; and treating the child without understanding or respect, which makes him feel worthless.

"Summing up . . . , we have assumed that certain trau-

[28] Angyal, *op. cit.*, pp. 138–141.

matizing experiences create in the child a derogatory picture, a feeling of the worthlessness of his self. This feeling of worthlessness has two components: first, the feeling that one is inadequate, too weak to cope with the environment; and second, the feeling that one is unloved and unworthy of love."

Robert White feels that self-esteem is associated with the expression of one's "competence," deriving from the active exercise of one's potentialities.[29]

In Fromm's terms, the idea is expressed as "spending oneself" or "using one's potentialities."[30] The overprotective mother, for example, might generate low self-esteem in her child, since the child cannot develop the self-confidence which can only come from the actual mastery of problems. Fromm has argued that the child's feeling of weakness and worthlessness is likely to derive from the authority structure of the family. In the authoritarian family, irrational authority is the rule. Rules are followed and orders are obeyed, not because they are inherently sound or correct, but because they are transmitted from a superior to an inferior. The child is treated as lacking in dignity and value; his spirit is broken and he is forced to go along with the will of others. His independence and spontaneity thus tend to be smothered. The result is weakness, helplessness, an absence of dignity—in sum, a feeling of weakness and worthlessness.

The hypothesis may also be advanced that frustration in childhood tends to generate low self-esteem. It may be suggested that if the individual gets what he wants, he has no strong need to think of himself. It is only when he does not get what he wants that he is likely to turn his attention to himself and to ask what there is in him which prevents him from fulfilling his desires. The frustration of

[29] Robert White, *The Abnormal Personality*, Chap. 4.
[30] Erich Fromm, *Escape From Freedom*, New York: Rinehart, 1941.

important needs at an early time, then, is likely to lead to a heightened awareness of self. This heightened awareness, however, tends to be focused on those self-characteristics which have failed to fulfill the needs of the individual, which might lower the self-estimate.

It is also possible that conditions fostering extreme self-consciousness may have implications for self-esteem. Parents may make their children self-conscious in a number of ways. They may ask them to perform in public or they may constantly sit in judgment over their every act. Parents who ask their children to "show off" in front of company—to sing, dance, recite; who, in the child's presence, talk to one another or to other adults about his virtues or defects; who are constantly judging his performance and evaluating his traits, and who tell him their reactions—these parents are likely to induce in their children a high level of self-awareness. This in itself need not result in low self-esteem. However, a child exposed to this influence can no longer simply accept himself for what he is; he must constantly sit in judgment upon himself and his performance. Such judgment inevitably turns up flaws or inadequacies which, in a less self-conscious person, would simply make no impression. No one is ever as good as he might be. The unself-conscious person, giving little thought to the matter, accepts himself for what he is. The self-conscious person, on the other hand, is keenly aware of himself, becomes conscious of his flaws and deficiences, and thus certainly develops doubts about himself. It seems highly likely that this would lead to shaky, and probably low, self-esteem.

These are but a few of the possible ways in which family factors may contribute to the child's self-estimate. Unfortunately, it is far easier to speculate on the influence of these factors than to conduct research on them. How to obtain samples of behavior which adequately reflect the whole; how to avoid misinterpreting behavior in a family because of ignorance of "private meanings" of acts and words which are known only to the participants; how to overcome dependence upon verbal responses of subjects who are often motivated to conceal certain facts from themselves as well as others; and how to deal with the time problem; i.e., the fact that we are interested in the connection between early parental behavior and self-images many years later—these are problems which can severely strain the ingenuity and the persistence of investigators for years to come.

These, then, are but a few of the directions which research on the self-image may take—the study of various self-images, the development of typologies, the utilization of the self-image as an intervening variable, the investigation of the role of social values, the study of change, and the study of family influences. That the student of human behavior must take account of the self-image seems obvious. It is equally obvious that the problems in this field are sufficiently abundant and exciting to challenge the energy, imagination, and skill of research investigators for years to come.

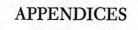

APPENDICES

APPENDICES

APPENDIX A

---◄◆►---

SELECTION OF THE SAMPLE

THE study plan involved the selection of a random sample of eleven public day high schools in New York State, stratified by size of community, in order to obtain a sample of approximately 4,600 students. Working from the U.S. Office of Education's Biennial Survey of Education in the United States—1954–1956,[1] we calculated that 61.5 percent of the secondary school students were located in communities of 100,000 or more; 27.0 percent were in communities of 10,000–100,000; and 11.5 percent were in communities of 2,500–10,000. The data show, however, that schools in larger communities are considerably larger than schools in smaller communities. Taking account of the size of the school, we calculated that six schools should be located in communities of 100,000 or more, three schools in communities of 10,000–100,000, and two schools in communities of 2,500–10,000. Since this sampling procedure would involve an underrepresentation of the rural population, it was decided to select one of the last two schools from a community of 2,500 or less.

A list of public high schools in New York State was obtained; the community in which the school was located was identified;[2] and the size of each community was obtained from census data for New York State.[3] All schools

[1] *Statistics of Local School Systems—Staffs, Pupils, and Finances: 1955–1956. Cities.* U.S. Government Printing Office, Washington, D.C., 1959.

[2] The University of the State of New York. The State Education Department. *Handbook 24. Organization and Institutions,* 1957–1958, pp. 68–132.

[3] U.S. Department of Commerce, Bureau of the Census, *Census of Population: 1950, Vol. II, Characteristics of the Population, Part 32, New York,* Washington, D.C.: U.S. Government Printing Office, 1952, Table 7.

in cities of 100,000 or more were assigned separate numbers. The same procedure was followed for communities of 10,000–100,000, and 2,500–10,000. Finally, using a Table of Random Numbers, we selected six schools from communities of over 100,000 population, three schools from communities of 10,000–100,000, one school from communities of 2,500–10,000, and one school from communities of 2,500 or less.

Stratification of communities in terms of other characteristics, such as socio-economic status, religion, and nationality, was considered. Unfortunately, it was not possible to obtain such information, particularly for smaller communities.

A letter was sent to each principal and each superintendent of schools informing him briefly of the nature and purpose of the study and advising him that I would phone him within a few days to arrange an appointment. It proved possible to arrange appointments with the officials of ten of the eleven schools selected. An appointment was refused by the acting superintendent of schools of a high school in a medium-sized community. This man expressed sympathy with the purposes of the study but indicated that the request had come at a peculiarly unfortunate time and that it was not possible to discuss the matter.

I was fortunate in being able to schedule my meetings with the principals and superintendents or their representatives on consecutive days. I met with these school officials, explained the purposes of the study, showed them the questionnaires, and answered their questions. In every case, cooperation was obtained.

We had planned, in case of refusals, to make substitutions on a random basis. Unfortunately, the spring semester was rapidly nearing completion when the appointments were arranged and it proved too late to substitute an eleventh school without conflicting with preparations for final examinations and Regents examinations.

Questionnaires were mailed to each of the cooperating schools. In class, each teacher read instructions to his students and then distributed the questionnaires. The questionnaires, which were anonymous, were so ordered that each of the three questionnaire forms was alternately distributed.

In total, 5,077 questionnaires were returned to us. Each questionnaire was carefully edited to filter out "jokers." Blatantly ridiculous responses, frivolous comments, gross carelessness, obvious contradictions, etc., were sought. Fifty-three questionnaires—about 1 percent of the total— were eliminated. The remaining 5,024 questionnaires were retained. The general consistency of the responses, the favorable reactions to the questionnaires, and, most important, the fact that reliable Guttman scales appeared, suggested that these questionnaires had been answered seriously. For about one-half of the questionnaires, a 100 percent verification of the coding was performed; a 50 percent verification of the remainder of the questionnaires was performed. All punching, of course, was verified.

Although the schools were selected on a strictly random basis, their representativeness of the population of New York State high school juniors and seniors cannot be determined. Certain characteristics of the sample should be noted, however. For one thing, parochial and private secondary schools are excluded. Second, students who have dropped out of school before their junior and senior years are omitted. Third, students who were not present in school on the day of the questionnaire administration were not followed up. The sample, then, refers only to juniors and seniors in public day high schools present on the day of questionnaire administration.

APPENDIX B

THE SOCIO-ECONOMIC STATUS INDEX

THREE items of information are included in this index: median income of father's occupation (obtained from the 1950 Census), father's education, and father's primary source of income. Father's occupation was classified according to the three-column Census Code. A score of 3 was assigned to occupations whose median incomes exceeded $5,000; a score of 2 was assigned to occupations with incomes between $3,400–5,000; and a score of 1 to occupations with incomes under $3,400. Father's education was rated 4 for postgraduate work, 3 for some college or college graduate, 2 for some high school or high school graduate, and 1 for some grade school or grade school graduate. Primary source of income was rated 2 for profits, fees, savings, investments, or pensions, and 1 for salary or wages.

Scores assigned to father's occupation and education were weighted by 2; source of income was weighted by 1. The scores which appeared ranged from a low of 5 (median occupational income under $3,400, grade school, salary or wages) to a score of 16 (median occupational income over $5,000, postgraduate training, income from profits, fees, investments, etc.). The weighted scores of the various social class groups appear below.

SES Group	Weighted Score
I	15–16
II	13–14
III	10–12
IV	8–9
V	7
VI	5–6

In the discussion in the text, "upper class" indicates SES groups I and II; "middle class" indicates SES groups III–V; and "lower class" indicates SES group VI.

It was not possible to learn about the father's actual income, since pre-tests indicated that many high school students simply did not know how much their fathers earned. In addition, the danger existed that this question might arouse resentment among some parents, particularly since the sponsoring organization was a branch of the Federal Government. The Hollingshead Index could not be used because this score requires information on the size of businesses, organizations, or firms; we lacked this information. Nor was it feasible to use the Warner Index of Status Characteristics, since we could not obtain adequate information about the neighborhood or the condition of the house from an anonymous questionnaire. Status indicators requiring observation, such as the Sewell or Chapin scales, were ruled out by the use of a self-administered questionnaire. Finally, an attempt to use the North-Hatt scale of occupational prestige failed because this scale encompassed so few occupations.

Some students failed to give sufficiently precise information concerning father's occupation or source of income and a number of students did not know the educational levels of their fathers. The social class background of these respondents was classified as "unknown" and they were omitted from the social class calculations.

APPENDIX C

NOTE ON SELECTED ETHNIC GROUPS

IN CONSIDERING the significance of ethnic group status for self-esteem, two results were so unexpected that they raised the suspicion that sampling accident might have been responsible for distorted results.

The first group are the youngsters of English or Welsh descent. Here we have what is certainly the heart of the "Old Yankee" stock. As a group, these people have long held the highest prestige position in the society and this pride is buttressed by a long tradition and a historical location in an established position. If any national group is completely accepted in the society, feels unquestionably integrated in the society, this is it. And yet this group has a self-esteem level which is actually slightly lower than that of other groups. To be sure, the level is not very much lower; the surprising thing is that it is not much higher than average. We therefore wondered whether we had, by accident, chanced upon an unusual pocket of Old Yankees—people of low socio-economic status and poor education or a group which was backward in its studies, deficient in its aspirations, and so on.

The answer is: apparently not. For one thing, they are, relatively speaking, "Old" Yankees. Nearly two-thirds of them had both maternal grandparents born in the United States, compared, for example, with none of the adolescents of Russian descent and one-thirteenth of the youngsters of Italian descent. Second, the English-Welsh group tend to possess other status characteristics which are more likely to be associated with high self-esteem. (Table C-1) They are considerably less likely to come from families of low socio-economic status; they are less likely to have poorly educated fathers and mothers; and they are more

302

likely to be taking academic course work (which is positively related to self-esteem). They are slightly more likely to come from smaller communities (which is generally true of the English or Welsh in New York State), but size of community is unrelated to self-esteem. They are thus not a group whose associated status characteristics would tend to depress their self-esteem. In any event, there is certainly nothing in these results to suggest that the self-esteem of the students of English or Welsh descent is lower than what one might expect if one drew another sample from the same population.

TABLE C-1

Comparison of Students of English or Welsh Origin and Students of Other National Origins

Proportions who . . .	English-Welsh	All others
Are from the two lowest social classes	23%	42%
(Number)	(107)	(3259)
Have fathers who have not completed high school	21	37
(Number)	(150)	(4718)
Have mothers who have not completed high school	17	34
(Number)	(149)	(4750)
Are not taking academic courses	31	50
(Number)	(149)	(4773)
Live in communities of 25,000 or less	30	24
(Number)	(151)	(4819)

The second group are the Negroes. The self-esteem of these youngsters is slightly below that of whites—39 percent of the Negroes and 45 percent of the whites had high self-esteem—but it is not nearly as low as one might expect if general societal status were an important determinant of self-esteem. Has a small pocket of well-to-do, successful, and educated Negroes chanced to fall in our sample? Our data suggest that this is not so. Table C-2 shows that

TABLE C-2

Comparison of Negro and White Students

Proportions who . . .	Negro	White
Are from the two lowest social classes	78%	41%
(Number)	(37)	(3329)
Have fathers who have not completed high school	55	39
(Number)	(73)	(4431)
Have mothers who have not completed high school	49	35
(Number)	(80)	(4565)
Are not taking academic courses	69	49
(Number)	(97)	(4725)
Live in communities of 25,000 or less	11	25
(Number)	(99)	(4817)

Negroes in our sample are considerably more likely to come from the lowest classes and to have poorly educated parents, and are less likely to be taking academic course programs and to come from small towns. The social characteristics of these Negroes are thus generally in accord with expectations. Of course, we know nothing about the Negroes who have dropped out of school before the junior year. There is nothing in these data, however, to suggest that these Negroes are socially atypical of those who have remained in school at least until near the end of the junior year.

———————— ◄◆► ————————

SCALES AND SCORES

TABLES D-1 through D-6 are Guttman scales; D-7 through D-11 are scores. The Guttman scale items are here presented in order from the strongest to the weakest responses. In the questionnaires, of course, the items were presented in a different order. In the Self-Esteem Scale, positive and negative statements were presented alternately in order to reduce the danger of respondent set. In all other scales, the items were intentionally scattered at different points throughout the questionnaire.

In all of the scales and scores presented, "positive" responses are indicated by asterisks. Where contrived items have been used, the basis for scoring the contrived items is indicated. Reproducibility and Scalability Coefficients appear at the foot of the Guttman scales. All other indices are based upon unweighted scores.

D-1: Self-Esteem Scale

"Positive" responses indicate low self-esteem.

Scale Item I was contrived from the combined responses to the three questions listed below. If a respondent answered 2 out of 3 or 3 out of 3 positively, he received a positive score for Scale Item I. If he answered 1 out of 3 or 0 out of 3 positively, he received a negative score for Scale Item I.

I feel that I'm a person of worth, at least on an equal plane with others.

       1   Strongly agree
       2   Agree
     *3   Disagree
     *4   Strongly disagree

I feel that I have a number of good qualities.

    1_____Strongly agree
    2_____Agree
  *3_____Disagree
  *4_____Strongly disagree

All in all, I am inclined to feel that I am a failure.

  *1_____Strongly agree
  *2_____Agree
    3_____Disagree
    4_____Strongly disagree

Scale Item II was contrived from the combined responses to two self-esteem questions. One out of 2 or 2 out of 2 positive responses were considered positive for Scale Item II.

I am able to do things as well as most other people.

    1_____Strongly agree
    2_____Agree
  *3_____Disagree
  *4_____Strongly disagree

I feel I do not have much to be proud of.

  *1_____Strongly agree
  *2_____Agree
    3_____Disagree
    4_____Strongly disagree

Scale Item III

I take a positive attitude toward myself.

    1_____Strongly agree
    2_____Agree
  *3_____Disagree
  *4_____Strongly disagree

Scale Item IV

On the whole, I am satisfied with myself.

    1_____Strongly agree
    2_____Agree
  *3_____Disagree
  *4_____Strongly disagree

Scale Item V

I wish I coud have more respect for myself.

  *1_____Strongly agree
  *2_____Agree
    3_____Disagree
    4_____Strongly disagree

Scale Item VI was contrived from the combined responses to two self-esteem questions. One out of 2 or 2 out of 2 positive responses were considered positive.

I certainly feel useless at times.

  *1_____Strongly agree
  *2_____Agree
    3_____Disagree
    4_____Strongly disagree

At times I think I am no good at all.

  *1_____Strongly agree
  *2_____Agree
    3_____Disagree
    4_____Strongly disagree

Reproducibility and Scalability

Reproducibility: 93%
Scalability (items): 73%
Scalability (individuals): 72%

D-2: *Stability of Self Scale*

"Positive" responses indicate instability.

Scale Item I

Does your opinion of yourself tend to change a good deal, or does it always continue to remain the same?

　*1＿＿Changes a great deal
　2＿＿Changes somewhat
　3＿＿Changes very little
　4＿＿Does not change at all

Scale Item II

Do you ever find that on one day you have one opinion of yourself and on another day you have a different opinion?

　*1＿＿Yes, this happens often
　2＿＿Yes, this happens sometimes
　3＿＿Yes, this rarely happens
　4＿＿No, this never happens

Scale Item III

I have noticed that my ideas about myself seem to change very quickly.

　*1＿＿Agree
　2＿＿Disagree

Scale Item IV

Some days I have a very good opinion of myself; other days I have a very poor opinion of myself.

　*1＿＿Agree
　2＿＿Disagree

Scale Item V

I feel that nothing, or almost nothing, can change the opinion I currently hold of myself.

    1____Agree
  *2____Disagree

Reproducibility and Scalability

    Reproducibility: 94%
    Scalability (items): 77%
    Scalability (individuals): 77%

D-3: Faith in People Scale

"Positive" responses indicate low faith in people.

Scale Item I

No one is going to care much what happens to you, when you get right down to it.

  *1____Agree
    2____Disagree

Scale Item II

Human nature is really cooperative.

    1____Agree
  *2____Disagree

Scale Item III

Some people say that most people can be trusted. Others say you can't be too careful in your dealings with people. How do you feel about it?

    1____Most people can be trusted
  *2____You can't be too careful

Scale Item IV

If you don't watch yourself, people will take advantage of you.

    *1____Agree
    2____Disagree

Scale Item V

Would you say that most people are more inclined to help others or more inclined to look out for themselves?

    1____To help others
    *2____To look out for themselves

Reproducibility and Scalability

    Reproducibility: 90.1%
    Scalability (items): 68.2%
    Scalability (individuals): 60.9%

D-4: Sensitivity to Criticism Scale

"Positive" responses indicate high sensitivity.

Scale Item I

How sensitive are you to criticism?

    *1____Extremely sensitive
    2____Quite sensitive
    3____Somewhat sensitive
    4____Not sensitive

Scale Item II

Criticism or scolding hurts me terribly.

    *1____Agree
    2____Disagree

Scale Item III

How disturbed do you feel when anyone laughs at you or blames you for something you have done wrong?

*1_____Deeply disturbed
*2_____Fairly disturbed
3_____Not disturbed

Reproducibility and Scalability

Reproducibility: 98.8%
Scalability (items): 94.6%
Scalability (individuals): 95.7%

D-5: Depressive Affect
"Positive" responses indicate high depression.

Scale Item I

On the whole, how happy would you say you are?

1_____Very happy
2_____Fairly happy
*3_____Not very happy
*4_____Very unhappy

Scale Item II

On the whole, I think I am quite a happy person.

1_____Agree
*2_____Disagree

Scale Item III

In general, how would you say you feel most of the time —in good spirits or in low spirits?

1_____Very good spirits
2_____Fairly good spirits

*3_____Neither good nor low spirits
*4_____Fairly low spirits
*5_____Very low spirits

Scale Item IV

I get a lot of fun out of life.

1_____Agree
*2_____Disagree

Scale Item V

I wish I could be as happy as others seem to be.

*1_____Agree
2_____Disagree

Scale Item VI

How often do you feel downcast and dejected?

*1_____Very often
*2_____Fairly often
*3_____Occasionally
4_____Rarely
5_____Never

Reproducibility and Scalability

Reproducibility: 95.3%
Scalability (items): 76.5%
Scalability (individuals): 75.2%

D-6: Daydreaming Scale

"Positive" responses indicate high daydreaming.

Scale Item I

Most of the time I would rather sit and daydream than to do anything else.

*1_____Agree
2_____Disagree

Scale Item II

I guess you could call me a "dreamer."

*1_____Agree
2_____Disagree

Scale Item III

I daydream a good deal of the time.

*1_____Agree
2_____Disagree

Scale Item IV

Do you often find yourself daydreaming about the type of person you expect to be in the future?

*1_____Very often
*2_____Sometimes
3_____Rarely or never

Reproducibility and Scalability

Reproducibility: 96.3%
Scalability (items): 85.9%
Scalability (individuals): 85.3%

D-7: Psychosomatic Sympton Score II

"Positive" responses indicate many symptoms.

Do you ever have trouble getting to sleep or staying asleep?

*1_____Often
*2_____Sometimes

3——Almost never
4——Never

Do your hands ever tremble enough to bother you?

*1——Often
*2——Sometimes
3——Almost never
4——Never

Are you bothered by nervousness?

*1——Often
*2——Sometimes
3——Almost never
4——Never

Are you ever bothered by your heart beating hard?

*1——Often
*2——Sometimes
3——Almost never
4——Never

Are you ever bothered by pressures or pains in the head?

*1——Often
*2——Sometimes
3——Almost never
4——Never

Do you ever bite your fingernails now?

*1——Often
*2——Sometimes
3——Almost never
4——Never

Are you ever bothered by shortness of breath when not exercising or not working hard?

    *1____Often
    *2____Sometimes
    3____Almost never
    4____Never

Are you ever troubled by your hands sweating so that they feel damp and clammy?

    *1____Often
    *2____Sometimes
    3____Almost never
    4____Never

Are you ever troubled with sick headaches?

    *1____Often
    *2____Sometimes
    3____Almost never
    4____Never

Are you ever bothered by nightmares?

    *1____Often
    *2____Sometimes
    3____Almost never
    4____Never

D-8: Interpersonal Threat Score

"Positive" responses indicate high interpersonal threat.

If you were to offer your opinion on some subject of national or international importance, and someone were to laugh at you for it, how would this make you feel?

    *1____Deeply hurt and disturbed
    *2____Somewhat hurt and disturbed
    3____Wouldn't bother me very much

When national or international questions are discussed, I often prefer to say nothing at all than to say something that will make a bad impression.

    *1_____Agree
    2_____Disagree

In discussions of public affairs, I think I would prefer to say nothing at all than to say something that will make people angry with me.

    *1_____Agree
    2_____Disagree

D-9: Intensity of Discussion Index

Would you say you discuss international matters:

    *1_____A great deal
    *2_____A fair amount
    3_____Very little
    4_____Not at all

When you and your friends discuss international questions, what part do you usually take?

    1_____Just listen
    2_____Express an opinion once in a while
    *3_____Take an equal share in the conversation
    *4_____Try to convince others

D-10: Parental Interest Index

"Positive" responses indicate lack of parental interest.

When you were about 10–11 years old, did mother know most of your friends?

    1_____Knew who all were
    2_____Knew who most were

*3____Knew who some were
*4____Knew none, almost none

During this period, did your father know who your friends were?

1____Knew who all were
2____Knew who most were
*3____Knew who some were
*4____Knew none, almost none

When you were in the 5th/6th grades, mother usually paid no attention when you brought home report card with high grades:

*1____Item checked
2____Item blank

When you were in the 5th/6th grades, father usually paid no attention when you brought home report card with high grades:

*1____Item checked
2____Item blank

When you were in the 5th/6th grades, mother usually paid no attention when you brought home report card with low grades:

*1____Item checked
2____Item blank

When you were in the 5th/6th grades, father usually paid no attention when you brought home report card with low grades:

*1____Item checked
2____Item blank

As far as you can tell, how interested were other family members in what you had to say?

    1____Very interested
    2____Fairly interested
   *3____Not interested

D-11: Relationship with Father Score

"Positive" responses indicate good relationship with father.

When you were growing up, who appeared to be your father's favorite child?

   *1____I did
    2____Older brother
    3____Older sister
    4____Younger brother
    5____Younger sister
    6____Had no favorite as far as I know
    7____Different children at different times

During this period, did your father know who most of your friends were?

   *1____Knew who all were
   *2____Knew who most were
    3____Knew who some were
    4____Knew none, almost none

Which parent is it easier for you to talk to?

   *1____Father much more
   *2____Father somewhat more
   *3____Both about same
    4____Mother somewhat more
    5____Mother much more

Which parent is more likely to praise you?

    *1____Father much more
    *2____Father somewhat more
    *3____Both about same
    4____Mother somewhat more
    5____Mother much more

Which parent shows you more affection?

    *1____Father much more
    *2____Father somewhat more
    *3____Both about same
    4____Mother somewhat more
    5____Mother much more

When your parents disagree, whose side are you usually on?

    *1____Father much more
    *2____Father somewhat more
    *3____Both about same
    4____Mother somewhat more
    5____Mother much more

INDEX

321

self-esteem scale, 305–07; coefficient of reproducibility, 17, 307; coefficient of scalability, 17, 307; items, 17–18, 305–07; practical and theoretical measurement considerations, 16–30; reliability, 30; validity, 18–30
self-estimates, 246–49
self-image: changes in, 283–90; defined, 5; difference from other attitudes, 8-12; as intervening variable, 278–81; similarity to other attitudes, 6–8; social experience and, 12–14; types of, 273–75
self-taboos, 283
self-values, 14–15, 36, 243–68; psychological determinants of, 249–54; by religion, 263–68; self-esteem, and relevance for, 246–49; by sex, 254–56; by social class, 256–63
sensitivity to criticism, 157–60; Guttman scale, 310–11
Sewell, W., 301
Sheffield, F., 289n
Sherif, M., 11n, 153
Shils, E. A., 75n
sibling rivalry, 118
siblings, sex distribution of: and self-esteem, 112–25. See also only child and younger-minority boy
significance tests, 19n, 20n
Silber, E., 30n
"skidder," 287
Snygg, D., 271
social class: and self-esteem, 39–48; and self-values, 256–63
social mobility, 237–39
socio-economic status: and father's closeness to sons and daughters, 42–46; index of,

39–40, 300–01; and parental values, 41–45; and self-esteem, 39–48
sociometric data, 25–26, 28, 198–99
stability of self-image: Guttman scale, 308–09; and psychosomatic symptoms, 153–54; and self-esteem, 150–54. See also instability of self-image
standardization, 33–35
Star, S. A., 22n
Stein, M. R., 149n
Stephenson, W., 271, 273n
Stoodley, B. H., 272n
Stouffer, S. A., 17n, 22n
stratification hypothesis, 60; vs. sub-cultural hypothesis, 60–63
Strong, S. M., 278n
sub-cultural hypothesis, 60–63
Suchman, E. A., 17
Swanson, G. E., 258

tests of significance, see significance tests
Thielens, W., 65n
threat, interpersonal: score, 315–16; and self-esteem, 213–14
Tippett, J. S., 30n
traits, interpersonal, 176–78
typological analysis, 275–78

unconditional self-acceptance, 119–27
U.S. Department of Commerce, 297n
U.S. Office of Education, 297
University of the State of New York, 297n
"upward drift," 259

values, 75–77; social, 281–83. See also self-values

Other Titles of Related Interest
Available in Princeton and
Princeton/Bollingen Paperbacks

AMOR AND PSYCHE: *The Psychic Development of the Feminine*, by Erich Neumann (P/B #239), $2.95

ART AND THE CREATIVE UNCONSCIOUS, by Erich Neumann (P/B #240), $3.45

COMPLEX, ARCHETYPE, SYMBOL IN THE PSYCHOLOGY OF C. G. JUNG, by Jolande Jacobi (P/B #241), $3.45

ESSAYS ON A SCIENCE OF MYTHOLOGY: *The Myth of the Divine Child and the Mysteries of Eleusis*, by C. G. Jung and C. Kerényi (P/B #180), $2.95

FOUR ARCHETYPES: MOTHER/REBIRTH/SPIRIT/TRICK-STER, by C. G. Jung, translated by R.F.C. Hull, Extracted from *The Archetypes and the Collective Unconscious*, Vol. 9, part I, Collected Works (P/B #215), $1.95

FROM CALIGARI TO HITLER: *A Psychological History of the German Film*, by Siegfried Kracauer (#45), $2.95

JOSEPH CONRAD: *A Psychoanalytic Biography*, by Bernard C. Meyer, M.D. (#188), $2.95

ON THE NATURE OF THE PSYCHE, by C. G. Jung, translated by R.F.C. Hull, Extracted from *The Structure and Dynamics of the Psyche*, Vol. 8, Collected Works (P/B #157), $2.95

THE ORIGINS AND HISTORY OF CONSCIOUSNESS, by Erich Neumann (P/B #204), $3.95

PSYCHOLOGY AND EDUCATION, by C. G. Jung, translated by R.F.C. Hull, Extracted from *The Development of Personality*, Vol. 17, Collected Works (P/B #159), $2.95

THE PSYCHOLOGY OF THE TRANSFERENCE, by C. G. Jung, translated by R.F.C. Hull, Extracted from *The Practice of Psychotherapy*, Vol. 16, Collected Works, (P/B #158), $2.95

THE SOCIAL MEANINGS OF SUICIDE, by Jack D. Douglas (#186), $2.95

SOCIETY AND THE ADOLESCENT SELF-IMAGE, by Morris Rosenberg (#111), $2.95

THE SOCIETY OF CAPTIVES: *A Study of a Maximum Security Prison*, by Gresham M. Sykes (#227), $1.95

THE SPIRIT IN MAN, ART, AND LITERATURE, by C. G. Jung, translated by R.F.C. Hull, Vol. 15, Collected Works (P/B #252), $1.95

WHY MEN REBEL, by Ted Robert Gurr (#233), $2.95

Order from your bookstore, or from

Princeton University Press, Princeton, N.J. 08540